# RA

*The Story of British India*

'a valuable contribution to knowledge of Britain's colonial history'

*Manchester Evening News*

'a well-written panorama of Indian history, full of insights for all who are interested in imperial history'

*British Book News*

'his ideas are beautifully clear for expert and non-expert alike'

*The Economist*

'of immense value to students and all those interested in the political, economic, cultural and social aspects of British rule in India'

*History Today*

'fascinating in its detail and stamped with authority ... highly commended'

*The Glasgow Herald*

'spiced with interesting reflections on the two-way traffic in art, literature and thought between Britain and India'

*Royal Central Asian Society*

'one commends this book for its lively style, its agreeable evocation of aspects of the past, and its urbane observations'

*Asian Review*

'sharply written and pleasantly illustrated'

*The Guardian*

The front cover illustration shows a detail of the painting 'Government House from the Eastward' from J. B. Fraser *Views of Calcutta* 1824–1826 and is reproduced by courtesy of the India Office Library, London

# RAJ

*The Story of British India*

MICHAEL EDWARDES

PAN BOOKS LTD : LONDON

First published 1967 as *BRITISH INDIA 1772–1947*
by Sidgwick & Jackson Ltd
This edition published 1969 by Pan Books Ltd,
33 Tothill Street, London, S.W.1

330 02322 5



Made and printed in Great Britain by
Cox & Wyman Ltd,
London, Reading and Fakenham

# Contents

## PART TWO
## *The Indian Empire*
## *1858–1947*



## PART THREE
## *India and the West*

# *Preface*

THE THEME of this book is the meeting of two civilizations and its consequences in the fields of human and state activity. It is not an orthodox history of British India but a survey of aspects of British rule which are seldom dealt with in any detail in the more usual histories, where political events are given the largest space. For the purposes of this work, the words 'British India' refer only to those parts of the country directly ruled, over the years, by the British. The princely states, which remained virtually untouched by the impact of British rule, are not discussed. Neither is Burma, which, as it was gradually conquered, was administered as part of India until its separation in 1937. I have given fairly detailed treatment to the political ideas of the British, both the men involved in the administration in India and those in Britain – political philosophers and legislators – who had considerable influence on Indian affairs. Without some knowledge of these ideas and of the continuing debate about the best means of ruling India, it is impossible to understand the real nature of British rule. I have also given some space to the attitudes and extra-official activities of the British community in India.

In writing a work about an empire which has been dead for less than a quarter of a century, it would be difficult to keep out references to what has happened since India became independent in 1947. In cases where India's experience since independence throws light on some aspect of British India, I have made no attempt to exclude such references. Elsewhere, I have tried to treat the consequences of British rule in contemporary terms.

This work is by no means exhaustive. It could hardly be so in one volume. I have therefore included a bibliography of works for further reading.

# *List of Illustrations*

# INDIA IN 1772

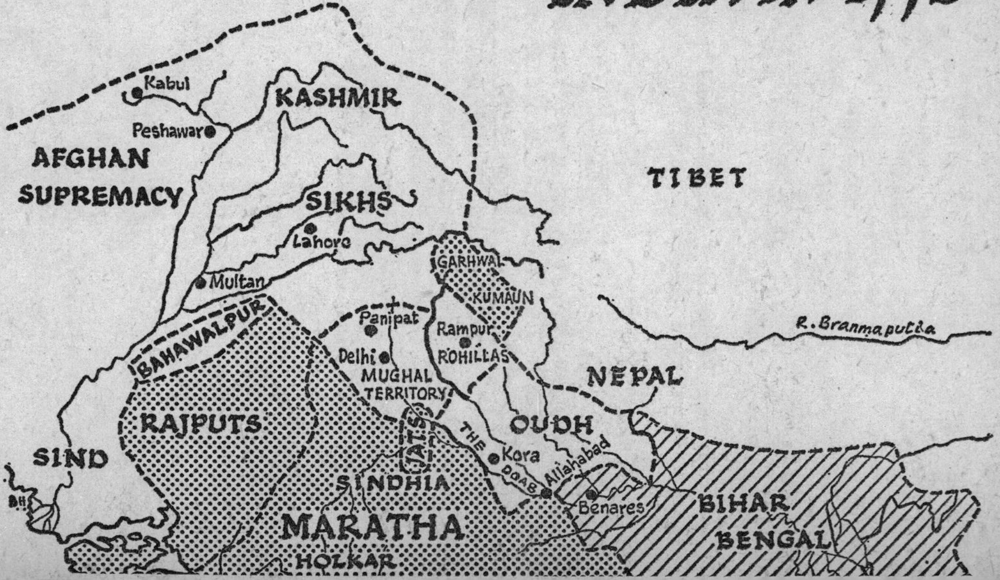

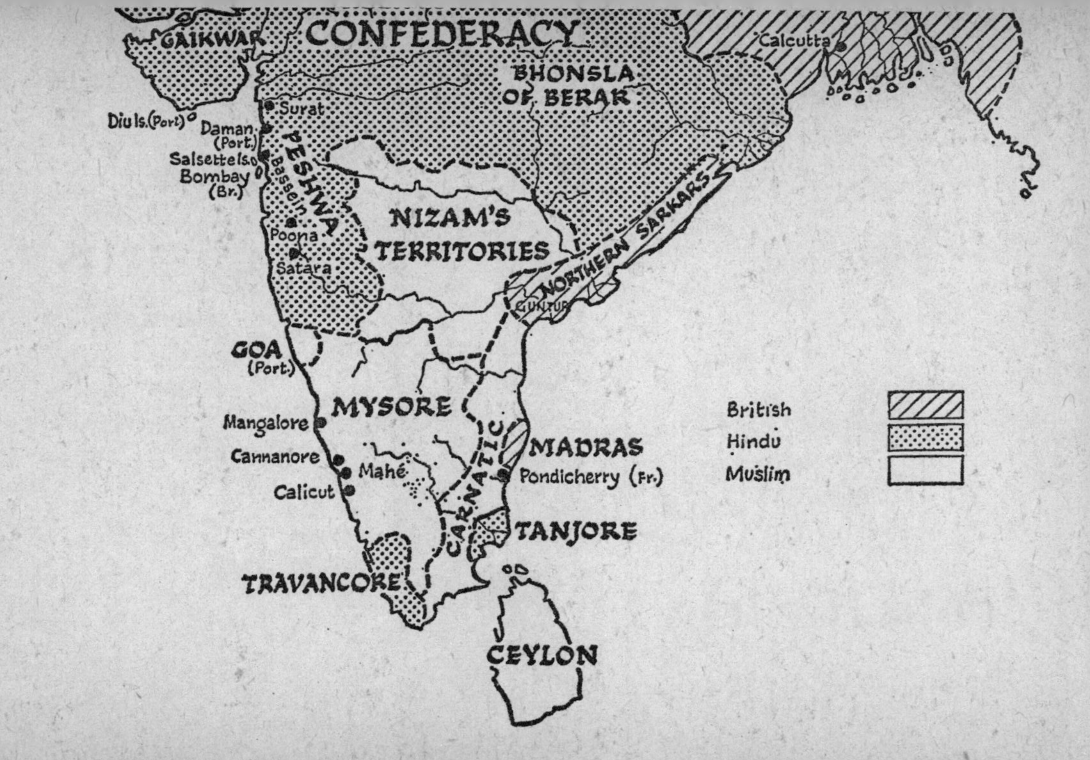

CONFEDERACY
GAIKWAR
BHONSLA OF BERAR
Calcutta
Surat
Diu Is. (Port.)
Daman (Port.)
Salsette Is.
Bombay (Br.)
Bassein
PESHWA
Poona
Satara
NIZAM'S TERRITORIES
NORTHERN SARKARS
GUNTUR
GOA (Port.)
MYSORE
Mangalore
Cannanore
Mahé
Calicut
CARNATIC
MADRAS
Pondicherry (Fr.)
TANJORE
TRAVANCORE
CEYLON
British
Hindu
Muslim

# INDIA IN 1947

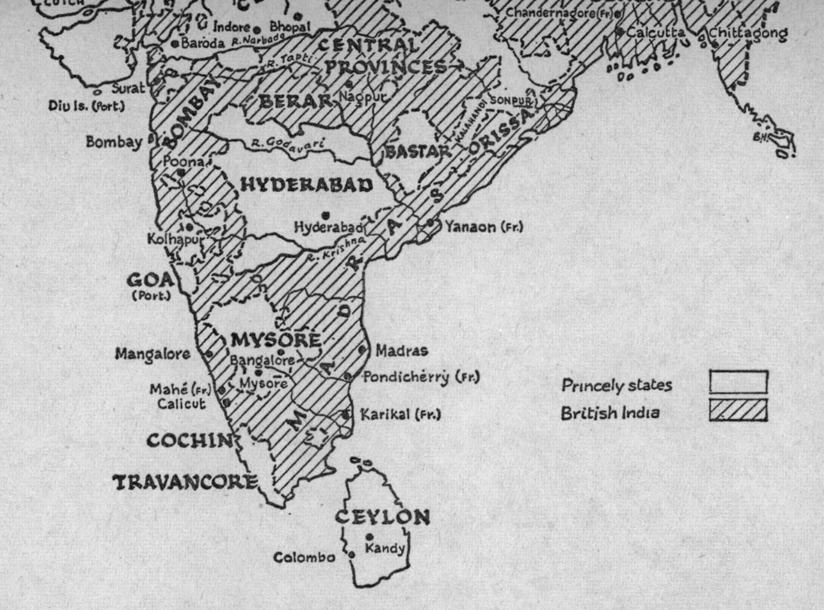
CUTCH
Indore
Bhopal
Baroda
R. Narbada
CENTRAL PROVINCES
R. Tapti
Surat
Diu Is. (Port.)
BOMBAY
BERAR
Nagpur
KALAHANDI
SONPUR
Bombay
R. Godavari
BASTAR
ORISSA
Poona
HYDERABAD
Hyderabad
Yanaon (Fr.)
Kolhapur
R. Krishna
GOA
(Port.)
MADRAS
MYSORE
Mangalore
Bangalore
Madras
Pondicherry (Fr.)
Mahé (Fr.)
Mysore
Calicut
Karikal (Fr.)
COCHIN
TRAVANCORE
CEYLON
Kandy
Colombo
Chandernagore (Fr.)
Calcutta
Chittagong
Princely states
British India

# INTRODUCTION

## *India before the imposition of British rule*

'LET US strike at the trunk of the withering tree and the branches will fall by themselves.' With these words – uttered by a Hindu leader in 1723 – northern and central India entered a period of chaos and anarchy which was to last for almost a hundred years. The 'withering tree' was the Mughal empire founded in 1526 by Babur, a direct descendant of the Mongol conquerors Timur and Jinghiz Khan, and the Mughals themselves were the last of the great Muslim invaders who had established their presence in northern India since the beginning of the eleventh century. Babur's successors spread Mughal rule over much of India, but the Mughals were Muslims, followers of Muhammad, and the majority of their subjects were Hindus. The Mughals – like the British who were to follow them – were foreigners, and, though many Hindus had been converted over the years to their religion, both the rulers and the converted remained a minority in India, encapsulated by an alien faith and alien social institutions.

A conquering minority, especially in a country the size of India, could not hope to rule without the assistance of the majority. The Mughals were not colonists; immigration from their central Asian homeland was on much too small a scale for that. Their role, and that of the Indians who identified themselves with them by changing their religion, was as rulers, administrators and merchants. The Mughal civil administration rested upon the work of Hindu clerks. Its advanced industrial undertakings depended upon Hindu labour. Trade was carried on through Hindu middlemen acting on behalf of Muslim entrepreneurs. In effect, Mughal rule existed in terms of an undefined contract between the rulers and the ruled. In some parts of the empire, the contract was explicit. There were areas in which Hindu rulers continued to administer their states as feudatories of the emperor in return for a circumscribed independence, supplying troops for the imperial armies and acting as collectors of revenue for the central authority. Other parts of India, mainly in the south, remained totally outside Muslim rule for some centuries. In the areas which were subjected to direct Muslim rule, however, opposition to the Mughals was to crystallize into rebellion.

At the epicentres of Muslim power, large-scale conversions to Islam took place. This was hardly surprising. Some Hindus became Muslim out of fear for their lives or their possessions. Others did so to escape discriminatory taxes. Most of the converted came – as did those who turned to Christianity during the British period – from the underprivileged sectors of the Hindu social order; they hoped, by accepting the religion of the conquerors, to participate in some way in the advantages of religious identification. The extent of conversion in India, however, was small in comparison with other countries conquered by Muslim armies. The reason for this lies in the gulf between Islam and Hinduism.

Essentially, the difference between the two faiths is one of quantity, the difference between one god and many. But it is also one of texture. Islam is austere, and its temples contain no image of god. Hinduism, on the other hand, is rich, highly-coloured. Its deities are known, identifiable, and the object of separate and particular devotion.

In itself, the division between Islam and Hinduism might not have meant very much had it not been for the fact that the most distinctive feature of Hinduism was that religion permeated the social order. It was the dynamo of society, the ideology of everyday life. Its ordinances were socially binding. Art and literature were essentially religious. Institutions were accepted as divinely inspired. The whole structure of Hindu life – the joint family, the village community, the caste system

– had the sanction of the gods. Because of all this, social activity was largely unaffected by political matters. The history of India might be a record of invasions, of the rise and fall of dynasties, of the instability of the state, but social conditions remained unaffected by changes of ruler because their divine origin placed them, generally speaking, outside political control. Indeed, the stability of the Hindu social order was reinforced by the instability of the political system. The divide between politics and the mechanics of living was precise. A man's loyalty was to the group, to family, village and caste rather than to the community as a whole; and to the state, not at all. His relationship with the state was always subordinate to that with the group. Even military service was the group concern of a professional caste. The majority of the people – the cultivators of the land – took no part in wars or political upheavals. Their real interest was not in who governed, but in how they governed; in, essentially, the incidence of taxation, and the absence of interference in religion and customs.

The Muslims were cut off from this social system by the fact that they were the rulers *and* by their religion. They remained a people apart. Although their own social institutions were influenced by Hinduism – for minorities cannot resist absorbing some of the characteristics of the majority – this brought them no closer, socially, to the Hindus. Muslim religious ideas, in turn, had their effect on Hinduism, and attempts were made to produce a synthesis between the two faiths; the religion of the Sikhs is a continuing example. Over the centuries, even, a certain community of thought and culture grew up between Muslims and Hindus; the Muslims looked outwards to the great area of Muslim civilization beyond India, and there was a considerable influx of ideas. The partnership of Hindus and Muslims in the administration produced a common language, Urdu, which is Hindi in grammar and Persian in alphabet. Urdu became the equivalent of Latin in medieval Europe, the *lingua franca* of the educated. But the cross-fertilization of cultures, however significant, was a minority concern. The majority of the people were unaffected by it, and fundamentally indifferent to it. Their preoccupation was with the pressure of taxation, for on the extent of taxation depended the economic condition of the rural population.

Revenue from the land was the principal source of state finance. Following Hindu tradition, the land itself was assumed to be the property of the king, who was entitled to the 'king's share' either in kind or cash. The traditional proportion, according to Hindu law, was one-sixth, but under the Mughal emperor, Akbar (1556–1605) – the most enlightened of Mughal rulers – it had been fixed at one-third, a not unreasonable proportion in a time of prosperity. His successors raised the figure to one-half, reducing the peasantry to bare subsistence and giving them no opportunity to save against bad harvests. The result was that, when famine broke out, there were no stocks to fall back on and starvation became widespread. Throughout the seventeenth century, the pressure of taxation and the recurrence of famines produced wide civil disorders, shifts in population, and a general disruption of the rural economy. The Mughal administration had become a machine for squeezing the masses in the interests of the rulers – a state of affairs which, it must be added, was not confined to Mughal territories. But there was wide scope for exploitation. Merchants and shopkeepers, mainly Hindus, were often prosecuted on trumped-up charges and their property was confiscated. Craftsmen were virtually shanghaied and forced to work for some great official. Trade and industry were crushed by taxation. Local governors operated local monopolies and, generally speaking, ignored the central authority until actually forced to accept it.

None of this, however, would materially have affected the political situation in India if it had not been accompanied by a progressive deterioration in relations between the Hindu princes and the Mughal emperors. In the time of Akbar, there had been considerable toleration towards Hinduism on all levels. Akbar had associated Hindus closely with his administration and many of them occupied high offices of state, both military and civil. The poll-tax on non-believers had been abandoned, and Akbar had made the slaughter of cows – a particular crime in the eyes of Hindus – an offence punishable by death. His successors, Jahangir and Shah Jahan, at first continued the policy of toleration, and although in 1632 Shah Jahan forbade the building of new Hindu temples and ordered the demolition of any under construction he did not actively discriminate against Hinduism. This was left to his successor, Aurangzeb (1659-1707).

Perhaps the ablest of the Mughal emperors, Aurangzeb was determined to restore the Islamic character of the state, which he believed had been lost in Akbar's attempt to create a working partnership between Muslims and Hindus. Aurangzeb began with a number of inoffensive reforms, including the appointment of a censor of morals to supervise and punish heretical tendencies amongst Muslims. A number of court ceremonies adopted from Hindu practice – such as weighing the emperor in gold – were abandoned. A few Hindu temples were torn down. But in 1669 an order was issued that all temples and schools 'of the infidels' (i.e. the Hindus) should be demolished. A number of shrines of great sanctity were destroyed. In 1679, the poll-tax on Hindus was revived, and other discriminatory taxes were imposed. The administration which had to put the emperor's orders into practice was staffed almost entirely by Hindus, and Aurangzeb ordered their dismissal. The chaos that followed, however, led to a compromise by which some Hindus remained in the service, though under continuous pressure to be converted to Islam. As if determined to antagonize every level of Hindu society, the emperor even prohibited the great religious fairs which were simultaneously acts of faith and popular entertainments.

Under this persecution, there grew up a climate favourable to rebellion. Many historians, both European and Indian, have seen the reaction of the Hindu princes in terms of a revival of Hinduism, a sort of national awakening. But the princes' resistance to Aurangzeb was not undertaken in defence of Hinduism; it was designed to protect their own positions. They would have resisted – as their predecessors had resisted the first Muslim invaders – even if there had been no ideological content to the conflict. They had been quite willing to participate in the profits of partnership with the Mughal emperors as long as it was possible to do so. When the situation changed, some of the heroes of this so-called Hindu revival did not scruple to ally themselves with Muslim princes in revolt against the Mughal emperor. Nor did they behave towards the Hindu peasantry any differently from Muslim governors and nobles. The truth is that, though Aurangzeb moved against the princes because they were Hindus, the princes fought to protect their material rather than their religious interests. Undoubtedly, there were orthodox Hindus who tried to inspire the princes with a sense of religious fervour and poets and minstrels to compose and sing the *chansons de geste* of Hindu India. But if indeed there had been a Hindu revival – rather than a revival of militancy amongst the Hindu princes threatened with expropriation – then the Hindus should have been able to work together to establish a united Hindu dominion on the ruins of the Mughal empire. They were not able to do so because of the divide between the Hindu social system and the concept of the state.

After the death of Aurangzeb, whose military expertise and administrative ability had kept the empire together in face of rising rebellion, the Mughal dominion began to fall apart. The main reason for this lay in the nature of the Mughal administration, which was at once highly centralized and loosely organized, a personal empire too vast to be personally controlled. While the centre was dominated by an active and intelligent ruler, the provincial governors and officials remained loyal and obedient under threat of vigorous retaliation if they should be otherwise. But Aurangzeb was the last of the strong emperors and, as the central authority weakened under his successors, the parts of the empire began to assert their independence. Governors became independent princes. Landholders, petty rulers, and adventurers carved out kingdoms for themselves.

Aurangzeb's immediate successor, Bahadur Shah I, managed to preserve an uneasy peace with his principal Hindu enemies, the Rajputs and the Marathas, but after his death the process of decay accelerated. All that was now needed to bring down the central authority was a sharp push. This was given in 1739, not by the Hindu princes but by the Persian ruler, Nadir Shah. Nadir Shah was out more for loot than for conquest. Entering India, he met little resistance, none of the Mughal governors being prepared to aid their emperor. But some Persian soldiers were murdered and, in retaliation, Nadir Shah's forces sacked Delhi, the imperial capital – an operation which lasted for nine hours. Afterwards, according to an eye-witness, 'the streets were strewn with corpses like a garden with weeds. The city was reduced to ashes and looked like a burnt plain.' Though Nadir Shah (laden with the Kohinoor diamond and the Peacock Throne) retired to Persia, the sack of Delhi had struck the death blow at Mughal sovereignty.

Between 1748 and 1762, north-west India was repeatedly invaded by the Afghans, while central and northern India were laid waste by the Marathas, making a conscious bid for succession to the Mughal empire. Though Hindus, the Marathas destroyed temples, slaughtered cows, and murdered Hindu priests and holy men. Wherever they went, they left destruction and death behind them.

The general breakdown of the central authority soon had its effect on the tiny European trading settlements scattered along the coasts of India. These trading centres had, to some extent at least, been protected by guarantees from the central government, but, with the collapse of the empire, officials intent upon creating and preserving their own independence now disregarded the immunities and privileges for Europeans which had been extracted – often with much difficulty – from the Mughal emperor. In self-defence, the Europeans began to fortify their settlements. But defence was to bring a measure of involvement, for there is an interior logic essential to the maintenance of simple security; it is always necessary to occupy a little more territory than one actually needs in order to defend the area one actually holds. Expansion always produces conflict and participation in the intricacies of local politics. The French entered the vortices of Indian politics consciously, the British reluctantly, but once the step had been taken a continually increasing involvement proved irresistible as it became obvious that no indigenous power was capable of restoring the political equilibrium shattered by the collapse of Mughal authority. The Mughals had destroyed all authority but their own. The native system of chiefs exercising power at various layers between the rulers and the ruled had been eliminated from the structure of government. When the Mughals fell, there was no organized system to take their place. Forms of government did survive, but they became the tools of force and oppression. The scaffolding of law was distorted or destroyed. Society disintegrated into elements unaffected by politics – the joint family and the caste system – which continued to regulate inter-group relations within the surviving and essentially self-supporting village community.

As British dominion spread slowly over India – the major areas were not absorbed until 1856 – it met anarchy and political chaos. But it also found a functioning society whose institutions had become petrified by the effects of a collapsed civil polity. Force was the sole arbiter, and it was superior force backed by purpose which gained India for the British. From the beginning, their primary task was to reconstruct some system of government and bring about civil peace.

When, after the battle of Plassey in 1757, the British first began to exercise power in Bengal, they were forced to improvise an administration. In Bengal, as elsewhere, any man strong enough to bully others did so until someone stronger took his place. Initially, the British were no better than their predecessors, allowing chaos and oppression to continue – and profiting from it. But this changed with the assumption of direct rule in 1772, and by 1788 a Muslim historian was able to say that the English were 'unrivalled in their laws for the administration of justice, for the safety of their subjects, for the extermination of tyranny and for the protection of the weak'. They were also praised for not interfering in matters of religion.

No settled government, however reluctantly established, can afford to tolerate on its perimeter areas of civil disorder and political instability. Even in those parts of India where native rulers had been able to keep strong and tolerant control, their deaths were inevitably followed by a return to chaos. In the south, where the British expanded their dominion from 1766 onwards, the general situation was one of uncontrolled oppression by robbers, mutinous troops and local rulers. The population was thinly spread, for there were few large towns. The peasants lived in fortified villages, cultivating only the land nearest to the village. The surrounding countryside was allowed to go to waste. In territories ceded to the British in 1800 by the Nizam – a descendant of the Mughal viceroy of the Deccan, who had declared himself independent – a constant state of war had made the peasantry unwilling to tolerate any attempt at control. Feuds between neighbouring villages were common and often led to bloodshed and arson. Everyone carried arms, but travellers were frequently murdered by the robbers who infested the countryside. The inhabitants were harassed by some eighty chiefs with about thirty thousand men, as well as by the rapacity of the Nizam and his troops. There were no courts of justice and, generally speaking, village headmen and caste leaders settled disputes without the aid of any outside authority.

All this had produced 'such a universal state of savage independence and opposition to all regular government that it was every year necessary to besiege a number of villages before their rents could be collected'.

Central and northern India, at the beginning of the nineteenth century, were still under the control of a loose confederacy of Maratha princes owing purely nominal allegiance to a minister known as the Peshwa. In their territories, the administration was designed only to raise revenue and their armies were no more than robber bands. The revenue was derived from direct taxation – protection money squeezed from neighbouring states – and from war. By such methods, the Marathas had not only reduced their own territories to exhaustion, but much of the surrounding country as well. The princes borrowed money from bankers and mortgaged their revenues for years to come. Offices great and small were auctioned to the highest bidders. The peasantry could raise enough only to pay the 'king's share' and keep their families at subsistence level. The incidence of famine was high, and it was not uncommon for quite large towns to lose three-quarters of their population in times of scarcity. Villages fell to ruin. The land remained uncultivated. The only activity was that of the tax-gatherer and robber, who continued their work even in famine conditions.

The one surviving judicial institution left unscathed by the Maratha rulers was the *panchayat*, a representative body regulating village affairs and pronouncing judgement on matters of real and personal property. On other levels, justice was capricious and punishments varied according to caste status – higher castes were seldom severely punished – or bribery. Village communities managed somehow to survive in the absence of civil government, but the cities and towns suffered badly. They were easier to plunder, and – to begin with, at least – had more worth plundering. Cities which had once been important centres of commerce, industry and culture, fell into decay, and their citizens and craftsmen emigrated, when they could, to the security of the European settlements. The public buildings, palaces, tombs and mosques of the Mughals were allowed to crumble, and the Taj Mahal – the tomb of one of the wives of Emperor Shah Jahan – was used as a private residence by a Maratha chief.

In the Punjab, where a powerful Sikh ruler, Ranjit Singh, had imposed discipline at the end of the eighteenth century, a system of controlled expropriation operated until he died in 1839, when wars of succession returned the country to the same uncontrolled anarchy as had preceded his reign. Village communities began to collapse under the pressure of civil war, and the country was finally annexed by the British in 1849.

The last major area to be annexed to British dominion was the state of Oudh. Here, the Mughal emperor's former chief minister had set himself up as an independent ruler on the collapse of the imperial authority. Oudh had been left isolated by the tide of British expansion. Indeed, its ruler was frequently squeezed to pay for British campaigns. As a reward, he had been given the title of 'king' in 1819. On occasion, over the years, the king was threatened with annexation and told to clean up his administration, but improvements were no more than superficial and temporary. In 1850, the situation in Oudh differed very little from that in the Maratha territories before 1818. The landholders, wrote Sir William Sleeman after a journey through Oudh in the years 1849 and 1850, 'keep the country in a perpetual state of disturbance and render life, property and industry everywhere insecure. Whenever they quarrel with each other or with the local authorities of the Government, from whatever cause, they take to indiscriminate plunder and murder over all lands not held by men of the same class; no road, town, village or hamlet is secure from their merciless attacks; robbery and murder become their diversion – their sport; and they think no more of taking the lives of men, women and children who never offended them than those of deer and wild hog. They not only rob and murder but seize, confine, and torture all whom they seize and suppose to have money or credit till they ransom themselves with all they have or can beg or borrow.'

Within the general chaos of life in India before the imposition of British rule, there were certain continuities. That of the Hindu social system has already been emphasized. Unless a village was totally destroyed, the communal institutions of village life survived, though often distorted by an inter-group violence which was a reflection of the larger violence of the world outside the village. The agrarian system was shaken, but not destroyed. Peasants often returned to their lands when peace came, and reasserted their rights. Economic life was, obviously, disrupted, but the movement of produce and the manufacture of goods continued at a level high enough to justify the interest and profit of European merchants. Centres of learning still flourished. Poets and painters continued their work, preserving traditional culture in the same way as the monasteries of Europe did in the tenth century, after the collapse of the Carolingian empire. When India emerged from the twilight of anarchy, both institutions and traditional cultures were to be confronted with the most subversive of ideas – about justice, administration, philosophy, politics – and were to be transformed, in some cases superficially, in others fundamentally, by the impact of the West.

# PART ONE

# *Under Company Rule*
# *1772–1857*

# Historical Framework

UNTIL 1858, British India was ruled by a chartered commercial corporation, the East India Company, operating under ever-increasing interference from the British Crown. But there had been no thought of dominion in the minds of the eighty hard-headed businessmen who, in 1599, met in the City of London to found the Company. Their concern was with trade – in spices, silks, gems, camphor and indigo – and the first voyages were fitted out not for India at all, but for Sumatra. In 1608, however, the Company's agents in Bantam and the Moluccas reported that the people there were good customers for Indian calicoes and suggested that a trading post should be set up in India to buy them. The Mughal emperor, Jahangir, gave permission for such a post to be established, and finally – in face of strong opposition from the Portuguese, who had been the first Europeans to arrive in the East – the Company established warehouses at Surat, the chief port in western India, in 1612. After Surat, further 'factories' (as the trading posts were called) were set up at Ahmedabad, Burhanpur, Ajmer and Agra.

By 1622 the Company had nothing more to fear from the Portuguese, who had suffered a series of defeats at the hands of the English and the Dutch. But the English themselves had been soundly defeated by the Dutch in the Spice Islands between 1618 and 1620, in spite of the fact that England and Holland were nominally allies in Europe. When, in 1623, the Dutch in Amboyna seized ten Englishmen and nine Japanese, tortured them into confessing to a conspiracy to assassinate the Dutch governor, and executed them, the Company turned its face away from the East Indies and towards India.

By 1647, the Company operated twenty-three Indian establishments, but the civil war between king and parliament in England almost proved disastrous. The Company's pepper cargoes were seized by the king and guns meant for Company ships were requisitioned by parliament. For a while, the abandonment of Eastern trade was considered. Even when, in 1655, arbitration produced £85,000 from the Dutch in reparation for the Company's losses at Amboyna in 1623, the Company saw less than half the sum. Cromwell, in urgent need of money, borrowed £46,000 of it 'for twelve months' and never repaid it.

With the restoration of Charles II, better times came. The Company received a new charter, and the right to coin money and exercise jurisdiction over English subjects in the East. In 1668, in exchange for a substantial loan, the king transferred Bombay – part of the dowry his wife, Catherine of Braganza, had brought to him six years earlier – to the Company.

Within the Mughal empire, there was anarchy and unrest. Hindu merchants, under the pressure of Aurangzeb's anti-Hindu policies, began to look for some place of safety. They suggested that, if they were offered adequate protection, they would move to Bombay with their families, and presumably, their businesses. This was a tempting proposition, for the Dutch were trying to take over the Portuguese stations on the Malabar coast of India, the French (whose own Company had been formed in 1668) were beginning to establish factories on the same coast, and commercial competition showed signs of becoming intense. Furthermore, the power of the warlike Marathas was increasing and they had already, in 1664, attacked Surat. In 1669, therefore, the chief merchant of Surat began to fortify Bombay as the new headquarters of the Company's interests in India. It was the beginning of a new phase for the East India Company. The 'quiet trade' so dear to the Directors in London was to be defended by the Company's servants in India, and in that defence lay the origins of the British Empire.

In 1674 the Maratha, Sivaji, enthroned himself as an independent king, and an Englishman, Henry Oxinden, was officially present at the coronation. He returned with a peace treaty which he believed would prove of 'no small benefit' to the Company's affairs. Sivaji had realized that British naval expertise might make the Company a valuable ally in his wars against the Mughals, particularly since a Mughal fleet – sheltering near Bombay during the monsoon – occupied its energies by raiding the Maratha coast. Unfortunately, the combined depredations of Sivaji and the Mughal admiral had an almost ruinous effect on the trade of Bombay. Even Sivaji's death in 1680 brought no relief. His son attacked the Portuguese and plotted to take Bombay. Pirates infested the coast and the interior was in continuing disorder.

Bombay had grown fast, its military strength and religious tolerance making it a haven, not only for Hindus escaping the Mughal terror, but for Christians fleeing from the Inquisition in Portuguese Goa. When it was taken over by the English, Bombay had had a population of ten thousand; by 1674 it was a city of sixty thousand inhabitants. But the Company's employees were badly paid and subjected to salary cuts and petty economies at the slightest excuse. When Aurangzeb, for example, re-imposed a poll-tax on non-Muslims, the Company protested, whereupon the emperor increased customs dues from two per cent to three and a half per cent. The resultant miserliness on the Company's part brought protests from the garrison – never happy under its merchant bosses – and further discrimination against the armed forces led to rebellion. The garrison commander, one Richard Keigwin, in 1683 assumed authority in Bombay in the name of the king. He tightened up the city's defences and, when the Mughal admiral arrived in 1684 for his usual wintering in the harbour, he was ordered to leave – and went. Ultimately, in exchange for a complete pardon, Keigwin surrendered to a fleet sent from England.

On the other side of India, in Bengal, the Company's agent, Job Charnock, blithely declared war on the entire Mughal empire in 1686 over a quarrel about customs dues. The Company's ten ships and six hundred men – all that were available in the area – proved inadequate for the task, and the English were forced to abandon their conquests and their factories and flee to Madras. In the end, a treaty was signed, and in 1690 the Company's ships were moored once again in the Hugli river, near a spot where Charnock founded what was to become the capital of British India. In 1696, the English were given leave to fortify Calcutta, and a fort – named in 1699 Fort William, in honour of the Dutch king of England – was erected. In the same year, the three villages of Chutanuti, Govindpur and Calcutta were rented from the Nawab of Bengal. The Company had become an Indian landowner.

The Company's possessions, as distinct from agencies or trading stations, were now four in number – Fort St George, Madras; Bombay; Calcutta; and, acquired at almost the same time as Calcutta, Fort St David opposite the town of Cuddalore on the Coromandel coast. The Marathas, who had acquired the latter town in the course of their free-booting activities, sold the site and all the land within 'ye randome shott of a piece of ordnance' – a method of property dealing which so appealed to the English that they sent to Madras for the gun with the longest range and the most expert gunner. This demarcation by artillery was carried out in September 1690, and the villages within the radius are known to this day as 'cannonball villages'. Of the Company's four possessions, Madras was by far the most efficient and vigorous; Elihu Yale, whose name is perpetuated in Yale University, was governor from 1687 to 1692 and applied anti-piracy laws with great severity against Indians and English alike.

Matters were not running smoothly for the Company in England. Sir Josiah Child – who saw it as the Company's duty to lay the foundations of British dominion in India – had purchased for £80,000 from Charles II a prohibition against British subjects competing with the Company in India. But in 1694, the English parliament passed a resolution against the Company's monopoly and expressed the opinion that all English subjects had an equal right to trade in the East Indies. In 1697, Spitalfields silk-weavers demonstrated against cheap imports of Indian textiles. In 1698, Child's commercial rivals – offering the government a loan of £2,000,000 at eight per cent – were granted a charter for a rival company, and the New English Company was founded. It fared badly, however, having first lent almost all its capital to the Crown, and then employed men who had been dismissed by the old Company. In 1702, the two companies agreed to an armistice, and six years later they amalgamated.

In 1707, the last great Mughal emperor, Aurangzeb, died. The anarchy that followed was to give both Britain and France the opportunity – and the incentive – for empire. Just as they began to feel their strength, the great central land power began to fall apart and an enveloping chaos threatened.

The English were tolerably ready to keep afloat in the troubles to come. Their settlements had been fortified, and a degree of friendship existed between them and the men who seized power in the provinces of the empire. The English had come as traders; then they became armed traders; soon they needed soldiers to defend their settlements; and, as the Mughal empire disintegrated, 'spheres of influence' became necessary if the Company was to survive. Slowly, the rhythm of empire-building had imposed itself on the simplicities of trade.

The French East India Company, however, was not a trading corporation in the same manner as the English. It was primarily an instrument of French foreign policy, strictly subordinate to its home government, and lacking the gambling instinct of the profit-seeker.

To it, in 1742, came a man of genius determined on creating an empire. Surrounding himself with great magnificence, he lived orientally and was recognized by Indian rulers as one of themselves. The quasi-independent princes aspiring to full independence were often equally matched in strength and resources, and Dupleix realized that, by throwing even the meagre weight at his disposal on one side or the other, he could prove the decisive factor. He also discovered that native troops trained and led by European officers could defeat vastly superior numbers of the irregular cavalry of the Indian princes. This discovery was to be invaluable for both the French and the English.

Unfortunately for Dupleix, he was bedevilled by the plans of the French government, and by the great French sailor, La Bourdonnais, who had been sent to harass English ships in the

Indian Ocean. In 1746, La Bourdonnais captured Madras, only to see it returned in 1749 under the Treaty of Aix-la-Chapelle which ended the War of the Austrian Succession in Europe. The war might be over in Europe, but Dupleix continued to intrigue with the princes in India in an endeavour to encircle the British. His own government, however, failed to appreciate the extent of his plans. To the home authorities at that moment in time, India was a minor theatre of operations in danger of prejudicing affairs in Europe. Dupleix was replaced in 1754.

In 1751, one of Dupleix's intrigues had been ruined by the military talents of a young English civilian turned soldier, Robert Clive, who had captured Arcot and held it against a besieging force for a crucial fifty-three days. In 1755, when Clive returned to India after two years in England, he found the French and English at peace. But events in Bengal were soon to shatter the deceptive calm of the Indian scene.

In Bengal the English had become arrogant and lordly – presumably because of the Company's successes in the south – and acted as if they were an independent and sovereign power. In 1756, Siraj-ud-daula became Nawab of Bengal. He was a weak youth, with a violent temperament and an unsavoury reputation. Already prejudiced against the British, whom he suspected of intriguing in favour of one of his rivals to the throne, he was further incensed when he heard that they were extending the fortifications of Calcutta. This was true enough though the works were trifling in extent and had in fact been put in hand because of the rumour that war between England and France was again imminent. It was reported that the French were engaged on similar works. The Nawab was aware of what had happened in the south, and he ordered both the English and the French to cease fortifying their settlements immediately. The French were conciliatory, the English offensive. The Nawab's answer was to march on Calcutta.

Siraj-ud-daula took the fort after it had been deserted by the governor and many of the inhabitants. The English had been so confident that they had neglected their defences and had not even troubled to organize a regular militia. When the

Nawab entered the town, he found Josiah Holwell, the magistrate of Calcutta, in charge. Holwell and 54 other prisoners were confined for the night in the Black Hole, which was to become part of the martyrology of British India. The 'black hole' was the name officially given by the British to any garrison lock-up normally used for confining drunken soldiers (and the name was not, in fact, abandoned in the army until 1868). There is no reason to assume that the Nawab knew this place of confinement to be only eighteen feet long and fourteen wide, or that intentional cruelty rather than ignorance and negligence was responsible for the death by suffocation of 43 of the prisoners.

When news of the loss of Fort William reached Madras, an expedition was fitted out under the joint command of Clive and Admiral Watson, who recaptured Calcutta without any great difficulty in January 1757. There then followed a period of conspiracy and intrigue out of which few of the principal characters emerge unsullied.

The Nawab was surrounded by a web of deceit and treachery and at the heart of it were the English. They finally decided to replace the Nawab with his general, Mir Jafar, and, after the French had been neutralized by the capture of their settlement at Chandernagore, fought the untidy but fateful skirmish at Plassey on June 23rd, 1757. This 'battle' consisted of two parts, an artillery display in the morning followed by severe monsoon rain which put most of the Nawab's ammunition out of commission; then a foolhardy but successful attack by Major Kilpatrick in the afternoon. Clive's forces consisted of eight hundred Europeans and two thousand native troops, the Nawab's of some fifty thousand men. The English suffered twenty-three killed, the Nawab's forces about five hundred.

The political results were immense. The East India Company became landlords (*zamindars*) of the 'Twenty-four Parganas' – nearly nine hundred square miles of territory south of Calcutta yielding substantial rents. Clive himself received gifts of £234,000, and others lesser sums. Mir Jafar became a puppet Nawab, and Siraj-ud-daula was murdered in his prison at Murshidabad. The Dutch made an attempt to back their claims to trade, but the expedition they sent from Batavia was defeated. The French tried again in the south to contest the onward march of the English. Under the generalship of Lally, a brave attempt was made to seize the initiative, but after his defeat at Wandiwash the French finally dropped from the race, though intrigue and conspiracy continued through agents and mercenaries at the courts of Indian princes.

The position of the English in Bengal was now supreme, and conditions remained fairly stable until Clive departed for England in 1760. His successor as acting governor was Josiah Holwell, who had survived the Black Hole of Calcutta. Holwell wanted to take over the direct administration of the country, since the death of Mir Jafar's son had raised problems of succession. Neither the Calcutta Council nor the permanent governor, Vansittart, would agree to this, and it was decided to give British support to the Nawab's son-in-law, Mir Kasim. The Nawab, however, would not consent to having Mir Kasim as his deputy. The Nawab was thereupon deposed, and Mir Kasim assumed the throne.

The new Nawab had no intention of being a puppet as his father-in-law had been, and began to interfere in the Company's trade. There was every reason for this. He could see the essential revenue of the state disappearing in the monopoly of duty-free trade demanded by the English as a right. They based their claim on a *firman* from the Mughal emperor which, in fact, related only to trade at seaports and not to the transit of goods inland. Because of this assumption of duty-free trading, the English – both as a Company and as individuals – could under-sell the native merchants, and soon built up dangerous monopolies which brought no revenue to the state but immense profits to their operators. When the Nawab found his protests unavailing, he declared *all* trade duty free. In response, the English sent troops against him, and Mir Kasim and his ally, the Nawab of Oudh, were defeated at the battle of Buxar in October 1764.

Buxar was the real foundation battle of British dominion in India. It was a bloody and determined engagement. Opposed to the British were not only the Nawabs of Bengal and Oudh, but the Mughal emperor, Shah Alam, and his prime minister. As a result of the battle, the Company ceased to be a company of merchants and became a formidable political force.

Robert Clive returned to India once more, for a second period of administration in Bengal, in 1765-67. During this period, the first sovereign act of the Company took place. It took on the office of *diwan*, i.e. collector and administrator of the revenues of the province. This was an appointment granted by the Mughal emperor, now practically a pensioner of the Company, and it meant that the entire civil administration of the province was the responsibility of the English East India Company.

While the Company was expanding its power in Bengal, the south was once more in a state of ferment. By the terms of the Treaty of Paris (1763), England and France had recognized the Nizam of Hyderabad as ruler of the Deccan (of which Hyderabad formed a part), and Muhammad Ali – the 'Nabob of Arcot', whose debts were to become something of a byword in the latter part of the eighteenth century – as ruler of the Carnatic. Muhammad Ali kept the Carnatic in a state of anarchy and corruption, demanding and receiving military aid from the Company's forces in various attempts to further his own personal ambitions.

Muhammad Ali planned to succeed to the thrones of the Nizam of Hyderabad *and* the Sultan of Mysore. They, in turn, thought the world would be a better place without him. The Nizam was a reluctant ally of the British, but the Sultan's son, Tipu, was engaged in ravaging the suburbs of Madras. To add to the confusion, the Marathas were recovering from a defeat by the Afghans and Mughals at Panipat, and were becoming active in south India. In these circumstances, no one was quite sure who was fighting whom. The uncertainty reached a climax when a British force – whose commander thought he was supporting the Nizam – found itself actually fighting the Nizam and the Sultan together. The fact that the British won could hardly have been said to clarify matters.

The Nizam, after some wavering, was guaranteed the

continuance of his dynasty by the Treaty of Masulipatam in 1768, but the Sultan of Mysore (Haidar Ali) and his son, Tipu, were able to dictate their own terms to the British at Madras.

The Company, entangled in a web of conflicting commitments, offered Haidar its support against attack. When it came, however – from the Marathas in 1771 – the British were in no position to fulfil their promise, and made for themselves implacable enemies in Haidar and his son.

To Madras in 1769, as second in authority, had come Warren Hastings. Three years later, he was appointed governor of Bengal with instructions to 'stand forth as *diwan*' – that is to say, take over the administration directly and publicly instead of hiding behind the fiction that the Nawab of Bengal still ruled. His first act was to cut down the expenses of administration. The allowance paid to the Mughal emperor in return for the *diwani* was stopped. Shah Alam had fallen prisoner to the Marathas, and Hastings did not see why he should subsidize a powerful potential enemy. The revenues of the Nawab of Bengal were also cut, and the districts of Kora and Allahabad were sold to the Nawab of Oudh.

By 1772, the financial state of the East India Company was such that, failing to extract a loan from the Bank of England, it approached the government with a request for a million pounds. Parliament appointed a committee of investigation, and its startling disclosures of the 'presents' received by the Company's servants between 1757 and 1766 led to the Regulating Act of 1773. This marked the beginning of the decline of the Company as a trading power. The Act, as well as reorganizing the constitution of the Company, called for the appointment of a royal governor-general and established the supremacy of parliament over the Company. A Supreme Court, consisting of a Chief Justice and three judges, was to be set up. In England, the Directors were to supply parliament with copies of all their correspondence and half-yearly accounts. A second Act authorized a loan to the Company.

Warren Hastings was appointed the first Governor-General in Bengal, with authority over Bombay and Madras – though how this was to be exercised remained obscure. Under his administration the outlines of British India were formed. He attempted for the first time to establish the concept of a central authority, to introduce a system based not upon the exigencies of the moment but upon considered policy and organization. Above all, he was the first to suggest that the Company's territories in India were not just a place of investment for shareholders, but a responsibility, an obligation requiring sympathy, understanding and good government. Hastings' relations with his council, where he was in a minority, were difficult. His administrative reforms were carried through like a battle at sea, in a continuous running fight, until the death of a member of the council put him in a majority of one.

Nor was Hastings free from military problems. In western India the Company had seized Salsette – an island long coveted by the English in Bombay – and found itself at war with the Marathas, in whose territories it lay. A weak force from Bombay marched against the Maratha capital of Poona, but was forced to come to terms – terms which were then repudiated by Hastings, who sent an army marching right across India through the Maratha territories, from the river Jumna to Bombay. The force occupied Ahmedabad and Gujarat, but was severely mauled in the course of a dash for Poona. In 1781, however, another British force defeated Sindia – who had long been aiming at leadership of the Marathas – and in the following year a treaty was agreed between the British, Sindia, and the Maratha chief, Nana Farnavis, which brought nearly twenty years of peace before the next phase of the struggle.

In southern India, a French fleet under the command of de Suffren had fought several engagements with the British, and France had found an ally in Haidar Ali, the Sultan of Mysore. In 1778, Madras drifted into war against Haidar, and in 1780 he descended upon it with ninety thousand men and a hundred guns, burning and pillaging as far as the very gates of Fort St George. The council at Madras appealed to Hastings for help and Hastings responded with men, money, and the services of Sir Eyre Coote. Coote defeated Haidar Ali (one of the finest exponents of guerrilla warfare) at Porto Novo. When Haidar died in 1782, he was succeeded by his son, Tipu Sultan – later to be dignified by the revolutionary leaders of France with the title of 'Citizen Tipu' – who signed a treaty with the British. But it was a treaty that did not last.

In 1785, Hastings resigned his appointment and sailed for England, where he was ultimately to be impeached before the House of Lords for his medieval treatment of India's medieval rulers. He was acquitted on every charge.

So the Indian empire began. Unformed, casual, but hardly accidental, it was constructed with mixed motives and powered by personal and commercial profit. Life was lived at speed. It was a race between man and circumstances. It was a period, not 'respectable', but infinitely rich and vigorous. It was ruthless and self-seeking, and – from the point of view of the Indian people – it was no better than what had gone before, and no worse than what came after. Times were soon to change. The old days of individual enterprise were going and a new India was in the making.

The first hint of the new India came with Pitt's India Bill of 1784. This set up a Board of Control consisting of allegedly impartial notabilities. The royal governor-general was to have the right to overrule his council as well as the governors of Madras and Bombay. The Directors of the Company were left with only one powerful tool, that of patronage.

Hastings was succeeded as governor-general, after a twenty-month interregnum under Sir John Macpherson – whose rule was charitably described by his successor as a 'system of the dirtiest jobbery' – by Lord Cornwallis, whose reputation had apparently not suffered by his surrender to George Washington at Yorktown. Quick to smell corruption, he was decisive in suppressing it at every level. Under his rule, the civil service was divided into executive and judicial branches, salaries were increased, and a revenue settlement (well-meaning but misguided) was imposed. In external matters, Cornwallis was forced – in defiance of the spirit of Pitt's India Act – to go to war in an attempt to counteract the anarchy of the surrounding native states. He himself besieged the capital of Tipu Sultan in 1791. The situation in the Carnatic was a constant threat. The Maratha chief, Sindia, continued consolidating his position and employed French officers to train his troops on European lines.

Cornwallis was succeeded in 1795 by Sir John Shore, a self-contained, timid man, whose period of office was the calm before the storm. In 1798, there arrived in India a new governor-general, Richard Wellesley. He brought with him his brother, Arthur, later to become Duke of Wellington. The empire-builders were on the march again.

Wellesley was ambitious and determined on building an empire. The Napoleonic wars were in progress and French agents were active in the native courts of India. Wellesley first turned his attention to Tipu Sultan in Mysore. Tipu had entered into an alliance with the French, and had to be crushed. The governor-general invoked the terms of the British treaties with the Marathas and the Nizam of Hyderabad, and forced them to countenance an attack on 'Citizen Tipu'. His capital, Seringapatam, fell, and Tipu himself – a progressive and enlightened ruler in eighteenth-century terms – was killed. The British then annexed the coasts of Kanara and Malabar and, in 1799, Tanjore. When the 'Nabob of Arcot' died, Wellesley annexed the Carnatic too. The Marathas were offered, and refused, a share in the conquered territories. In 1794, Sindia had died, to be succeeded by his nephew, Daulat Rao, who by 1802 was at war with Jaswant Rao Holkar, ruler of the native state of Indore. The Marathas were first defeated by Holkar, and then by the British, who entered Delhi victorious, there to find the ageing, sightless Mughal emperor, Shah Alam. The British had no intention of re-establishing the Mughal empire, though Wellesley was happy to indulge in a charade of courtesies. He spoke of delivering the unfortunate and aged Shah Alam from bondage, and the emperor, in return, was graciously pleased to confer on General Lake the title of 'Sword of the State'. In 1804, Holkar was in turn defeated, and India's native rulers appeared to be in eclipse.

Wellesley had achieved his purpose. Within six years, from holding a few pockets of territory, the Company had expanded into a major power holding Bengal and southern India, its troops in occupation at Poona and Hyderabad, its political Residents, or agents, at every native court. Only Rajputana, Sind and the Punjab remained outside the net.

Wellesley's success proved his own undoing. The Directors of the East India Company found this dazzling activity too much for their ledgers, and the British government saw it as merely vexatious. Britain was engaged on a life-and-death struggle with France in Europe, and interruptions to tranquillity elsewhere were distracting and undesirable. Wellesley was recalled, and Cornwallis was sent out to India for a second term, only to die two months after his arrival.

Under the governor-generalship of Lord Minto (1807-13) a significant change came over the administration. He found the Company's possessions ruled by a militarized, authoritarian government, and left them with the beginnings of a civilized system. An unpretentious personality, he was able to look with wry amusement at the pomp and splendour with which he was inescapably surrounded. During Minto's term of office, the British began to view with apprehension the countries bordering the western frontiers of their territories – Persia, Afghanistan, and the Central Asian Khanates. But on the very doorstep of British territory was the only powerful independent state left in India, the kingdom of the Punjab. Its ruler, Ranjit Singh, had converted the religious militancy of the Sikhs into a formidable military power, commanded partly by European officers. Diplomacy won a treaty between Ranjit and the British which was observed by both sides until Ranjit's death thirty years later.

Minto had restricted his military activity to a number of 'little wars', but under his successor, Lord Hastings – who arrived in India in 1813 – an expansionist policy was revived. There was war with Nepal – whose result was to enrich the Indian Army with Gurkha fighting men. There was a massive campaign against the marauding Pindaris, the robber bands of central India. Seeing the forces gathered to crush the Pindaris, the Marathas could not believe that such numbers were intended merely to suppress bandits. The resulting Maratha war lasted from 1816 to 1818, after which the whole of central India came under British control.

In the meantime, in London, the East India Company's charter had come up for renewal in 1813. The Company was permitted to remain the ruler of India for another twenty years, when the charter would again have to be reviewed, but its trading monopoly with India was abolished. It retained, however, the trading monopoly with China.

Under Lord Hastings' administration, there flourished some of the most remarkable men Britain ever exported to India – among them Mountstuart Elphinstone in the Deccan, Colonel Tod in the Rajputana, and Thomas Munro in Madras. They were men who knew India as a reality, not as an administrative or geographical fiction, and they felt a genuine responsibility for the people they governed. Hastings himself, though an expansionist in territorial terms, was a liberal and tolerant governor-general who set in train many of the reforms that have come to be associated with other and later names.

Each new governor-general who came to India in the first half of the nineteenth century brought with him his own preconceptions, instructions from London, and an ability either to galvanize or paralyse the Company's servants. Some periods of office were notable for military activity – as in the case of Lord Hastings, and of Lord Amherst who followed him in 1823. During Amherst's administration, the first war against Burma took place; Lord Combermere stormed the great Indian fortress of Bharatpur; and the 47th Bengal Native Infantry mutinied at Barrackpore over what they believed to be a threat to their caste. Other governors-general were more concerned with administrative and social reform. Among these was Lord William Bentinck, who held office from 1828 until 1835.

Bentinck's administration coincided with, and to a certain extent reflected, the climate of evangelical thought then prevailing in England. It was a climate which had resulted in the abolition of slavery, among other things. The evangelicals were determined to press the benefits of Christianity and civilization upon the heathen, and the fact that the heathen did not desire these benefits appeared only to be further proof of the outer darkness in which they existed. Under Bentinck, certain of the less humane practices of Hinduism were suppressed. But the attitude of mind which coloured these reforms also encouraged feelings of superiority among the younger servants of the Company, and made them view with horror the older type of administrator who had, it seemed to them, condoned terrible crimes in the attempt to be 'pro-Indian'. This, in fact, was the period which saw the beginning of belief in the 'white man's burden' and his divinely ordained civilizing mission.

Politically, Bentinck's administration completed the outline of the modern relationship between the Indian princes and the paramount power, an outline which was to be maintained until 1947. In Mysore, a peasant revolt against maladministration was suppressed by the Company's forces in 1831, and the state was taken over – although not actually annexed. The state of Coorg was annexed in response to 'the unanimous will' of the people. This period, too, saw the foundations of that fear of Russia which was to dominate the century. Russia was expanding its frontiers in Central Asia, and the Indian government sought to surround itself with buffer states. The 'Great Game' had begun, and agents of the government – sometimes publicly, sometimes secretly – explored Ladakh, Kashmir, Afghanistan, Balkh and Bokhara in pursuit of military and topographical information. The Indus river was surveyed and found to be navigable. The Amirs of Sind were instructed to permit commerce upon it. The surveying party had been inadequately disguised as a mission conveying gifts to Ranjit Singh in the Punjab, and the Amirs had viewed it suspiciously, as the van of an English conquest. In a way, they were right, but it was to be some years before the conquest came about.

Bentinck was followed in office for a short period by Sir Charles Metcalfe, one of the most distinguished members of the Company's civil service. But it was a rule that no servant of the Company should hold the highest office in India, and

Lord Auckland came out from England to take over in 1836.

Auckland's instructions from Palmerston, then prime minister, encouraged him to believe that a Russian attack on India was feasible – which it was not. They also authorized him to embark on the irresponsible and disastrous first Afghan war. Fear of Russia dominated Auckland's private world. It was the theme of all the apparently insane policy decisions of that nightmare period. It replaced sound judgement with hasty instinct, infecting even the most rational of men with irrational fancies. The historical figures who played the Great Game ignored facts, so tormented were they by rumours. Russia appeared to them to be on the very doorstep of British India – although Orenburg, the nearest Russian base, was over two thousand miles distant from the most advanced British post (at Ludhiana), and the whole of the Punjab and Afghanistan lay between.

The war against Afghanistan was the result of Auckland's ill-advised attempts at king-making, and it began with catastrophe. Out of a force of sixteen thousand British and Indian troops, most were killed or taken prisoner. It took bitter fighting for Britain to gain the final victory, and the Afghan war was followed – as if through some chain reaction – by an indefensible excursion against the Amirs of Sind, and then, at the end of 1845, by the first Sikh war. Ranjit Singh had died at Lahore in 1839, and his death had been followed by six years of assassinations, palace revolutions, and civil war in the Punjab. Finally, a Sikh army crossed the frontier into India. In less than three months, four major battles were fought by the British at tremendous cost. Although led by a general whose bravery was equalled only by his stupidity, Britain finally defeated the Sikhs, and a short-lived peace was signed. Henry Lawrence was appointed to Lahore to act as regent for the boy king.

Meanwhile, Auckland had gone home to be replaced in 1842 by Lord Ellenborough – who treated the Directors in London with such contempt that his appointment was revoked two years later. During his brief period in office, however, Britain occupied – though it did not annex – the state of

Gwalior. Ellenborough's successor, Hardinge, held office until 1848, during which time the predominantly Muslim state of Kashmir was annexed and sold to the Hindu Gulab Singh, a transaction which was to result a century later in the modern 'Kashmir problem'.

When Dalhousie arrived in India in 1848 to replace Hardinge, he was met with another revolt in the Punjab. It began with the murder of the British agent at Multan. Again, bloody battles were fought; again, Sir Hugh Gough commanded his troops on the principles he had learned in the Peninsular war almost forty years before; again, at Chilianwala, he was almost defeated. He managed, however, to win an overwhelming victory at Gujrat in 1849, and the Punjab was finally annexed.

Dalhousie's period as governor-general was one of the most decisive in the history of British India. It was a period of intense activity, and of consolidation, a period full of tremors foreshadowing the earthquake of the Indian Mutiny. Dalhousie rushed through reforms, and developed the 'doctrine of lapse' which denied rulers their immemorial right to adopt an heir in the absence of a natural one. By this method, the Company's dominions were greatly increased. The first state to fall to the British under this doctrine was Satara, which was followed by Jhansi and Nagpur. In 1851, the last Peshwa of the Marathas died. For thirty-three years, he had been a pensioner of the Company, but Dalhousie refused to continue paying the pension to his son, the Nana Sahib. In 1852, a war was fought with Burma, and Lower Burma was annexed. In 1853, the first railway was opened and the electric telegraph was introduced. In 1856, the kingdom of Oudh was annexed. Nearly two-thirds of the sepoys in the Company's Bengal army came from Oudh; annexation not only deprived the king of Oudh of his right to rule, it deprived the sepoys of Oudh of many of the privileges they had enjoyed in their native state by reason of their Company employment.

Dalhousie left India in 1856, and his successor, Lord Canning, inherited the products of his rule – unease among the princes, unrest among the sepoys. And the Indian Mutiny.

# 1

# *The British in India*

## ATTITUDES

FOR THE first fifty years of their rule in India, the British never felt wholly secure or even convinced of the permanence of their dominion. They were often critical of what they saw around them, but they were careful not to allow their feelings to influence their actions in case it aroused opposition which they might not be in a position to resist. At the same time, they had some respect for Indian culture or at least certain aspects of it. In the eighteenth century there was considerable social intercourse between the British and the Muslim aristocracy. Many British officials spoke and read Persian, the literary language. Some of them regarded themselves as Indian rulers. On one level, those British in India who had no intellectual interests enjoyed the superficial luxuries of Indian aristocratic life. English women, because they were few in a masculine society, generally accepted the men's opinions. They, too, enjoyed the luxuries. They were not in the least worried at attending balls and dinners given by Indians, even though Indian women were not present.

Towards the end of the century, however, the British were becoming conscious of a sense of racial superiority. The easy social relations they had had with Indians began to decline, though at first only in Calcutta. In other parts of India, where English society was numerically small and fashionable attitudes slow to arrive, the old relations with Indians continued.

The change in the social atmosphere began with the arrival of Lord Cornwallis in 1786. His purpose was to reform the administration, to clean up corruption and nepotism among the British. He succeeded. But in his desire to create a body of honest officials, he also excluded Indians from the higher posts of government. Cornwallis was convinced that every 'native of Hindustan' was corrupt. Unlike his predecessor, Warren Hastings, he had no intellectual interests to bridge the gap between himself and the Indian aristocracy. He replaced native judges with English judges. He abandoned, almost entirely, the traditional etiquette of diplomatic relations. Cornwallis succeeded in forcing the old Indian governing classes into isolation, leaving behind them only the Indian servant, the clerk, the merchant and the banker as representatives of India and Indian culture.

Not unnaturally, the remainder of the British community took its lead from senior officials and, in particular, the governor-general. As they withdrew from contact, so too did lesser beings. By 1810 a visitor to Calcutta was able to report that 'every Briton appears to pride himself on being outrageously a John Bull'.

The government's attitude was strengthened and expanded by Lord Wellesley who, arriving in India in 1798, brought with him a profound sense of racial arrogance. He had come to enlarge Britain's dominions – against the wishes of his nominal masters, the Directors of the East India Company – and imperialism needs the backing of pride, the consciousness of superiority. Wellesley had nothing but contempt for Indians.

There were other factors which contributed to the growing estrangement between Indians and the British. One of these was the growing number of women in the British settlements. They tended to bring with them the English prejudices of their time. Their attitude, generally speaking, was Christian, and narrowly so. They brought, too, a new sense of family life, and their arrival resulted in the expulsion of native mistresses who had at least injected something of India into the world of the British. The women had little to occupy their minds. Their life was a tedious social round. But they did have gossip. In a novel describing life in the 1840s, one character is made to remark: ' "In other parts of the world they talk about things, here they talk about people . . ."

' "But what," asked Peregrine, "do the people find to say about one another?"

' "Oh!" returned Miss Poggleton; "the veriest trifles in the world. Nothing is so insignificant as the staple of Calcutta conversation. What Mr This said to Miss That, and what Miss That did to Mr This; and then all the interminable gossip about marriages and no-marriages, and will-be marriages and ought-to-be marriages, and gentlemen's attention and ladies' flirtings, dress, reunions, and the last *burra-Khana*—"

' "Pictures, taste, Shakespeare, and the musical glasses," suggested Peregrine, with a smile.

' "Oh! dear no, nothing half as good as that," returned Julia Poggleton; "the only Shakespeare known in Calcutta is a high civilian of that name." '

The women were not interested in Indians, only in the inefficiencies of their servants. They wanted to create for themselves and their menfolk an island in the vast sea of India – and to a large extent they were successful.

Another factor in the estrangement was the influence of Christian missionaries who, though they mixed freely with Indians, had nothing but horror for their religion and frequently said so in the most violent terms. Their criticisms had great effect on the British in India, convincing them that it would hardly be worth while to make an attempt at any close relationship with such a barbarous people.

But the principal contribution to racial attitudes came from the expansion of British society in India. Gradually, it became large enough to take on a life and a character of its own. It was no longer necessary for a small number of Englishmen to accept what India had to offer for their pleasure. The English society in the principal towns and stations was now able to supply all that was needed, the support and understanding of fellow-countrymen, and a simulated England in which English life might be enjoyed. As the number of British men and women increased, they were able to construct a fortress into which to retire after the unavoidable engagements with the natives – in business, in the law, or in government. It also gave them something to defend and to justify.

Breaches were occasionally made in the barriers that were being erected between the British and Indians, but their effect was largely nullified by that feeling of superiority which was at once self-defence and an inspiration for social reform. The 'revelations' concerning widow-burning, female infanticide, and the Thugs, which led to the major reforms of Lord William Bentinck, intensified the British community's distaste for Indians and their way of life. After 1820, the evangelical Christianity of many of the Company's officers led them to see evil in almost everything.

This attitude was not shared by everyone in India, though – even in the case of those who showed most respect for Indians and their institutions – there was a basic element of contempt. But the individuals who did manage to bridge the gulf between themselves and Indians were the exceptions. As British rule spread across India and Englishmen came out from Britain in increasing numbers to administer the new territories, such attempts were regarded as more and more eccentric, un-English, and generally to be condemned. There were undertones of condescension even among those officials who advocated reform, although they believed they were doing the right thing for India as well as for Britain.

As they acquired a sense of purpose, the British in India began to acquire a sense of duty. They had always felt themselves to be exiles, a feeling reinforced by the rigours of the Indian climate. The author of the novel quoted above said: 'The great world is full of changes, but the Calcutta world is far more changeable than any of the lesser ones it contains in its vast cycle. Society, in these parts, is a sort of ever-moving procession, and the same characters are seldom to be seen upon the stage many months together.' What he meant was that the threat of an early grave hung over everyone. The British in India were mostly young. 'Among the Europeans in India', wrote a lady in 1827, 'there are scarcely any old persons as almost everybody is a temporary resident. Here, if you search the well-tenanted burying grounds of the large cities, you will discover few besides the graves of the youthful, who have been cut off by some violent disease amid the buoyancy of health, or the tombs of those of middle age arrested by death when just about to reap the fruit of long toil and privation by retiring to their native land. It is this which renders our Indian cemeteries so peculiarly melancholy: for though we bow to the decree which summons away the aged and the infirm, yet, humanly speaking, and in our blindness we are apt to pronounce the death of the young to be premature, and a fit subject of aggravated regret.'

The atmosphere in which the land itself was an enemy certainly affected the judgement of many. It reinforced their dislike of India, and explained, too, the occasional outbursts of hysteria among the British population.

By the 1850s, the British in India had virtually institutionalized their contempt for things Indian. Their sense of duty was fully supported by a militant Christianity which can be seen at its most aggressive in the careers of those men who have been called the Titans of the Punjab – John Lawrence, Herbert Edwardes, and John Nicholson. They admired the wild peoples – 'The wild barbarians, indifferent to human life . . . yet free, simple as children, brave, faithful to their master, sincere towards their God' – but were none the less convinced that they stood in need of Christ's teaching. These muscular Christians had a strong conviction of being engaged in God's work and spent a great deal of time in anguished fear that they might have failed Him.

By 1857 it was generally felt by British officials in India that Indians were a pretty evil lot and that it was Britain's duty to civilize and Christianize them. The non-official community was indifferent – to Indians, and to Britain's duty to 'improve' them. For its part, it was more concerned over the growth of an educated Indian middle class, which was already beginning to make demands. The non-official community was anxious to safeguard its own interests against attack from any direction, including the government in London. British residents in India had always resented the dictatorial authority of the governor-general. They believed that *they* should have a representative assembly, and asked for it. They did not suggest any such representation for Indians, whom they did not believe to be in need of it.

The British sometimes successfully resisted reforms which

they believed would lower their standing 'in the eyes of the natives'. They were able to resist, successfully, the government's attempt to equalize the application of the law. In 1837, the government passed what was known as the 'Black Act', designed to make British residents outside Calcutta subject to the jurisdiction of the Company's courts, in which Indian judges might preside. British residents sent a petition to parliament, and the Act was not enforced.

There was constant conflict between the non-official British community in India and the administration, a conflict in which the former were usually concerned with safeguarding their superior position. But all the British in India, official and non-official alike, used the same standards of judgement – those of their own country and their own culture. They discovered that practically everything Indian fell short of those standards, in business, in government, and in religion. A minority continued to suggest that something valuable could be learned from Indian experience, something that might help decide how best to run the country. But it was always a minority. After about 1830, though changes developed in the standards of judgement, both the changes and the standards were always British.

## CURIOSITY

Among that minority who felt that more should be found out about Indian institutions were a number of men who contributed to the discovery of India's past. In the late eighteenth century, Sir William Jones and others began to reveal something of the richness of Sanskrit literature. The Asiatic Society of Bengal, founded by Jones in 1785 with the support of Warren Hastings, became the centre for the Englishman's curiosity about the country he lived in and ruled. The first volume of the Society's publication, *Asiatick Researches*, contained transcripts of ancient inscriptions, and notes on the sculpture of the caves at Elephanta near Bombay. In the late eighteenth century, the journal carried descriptions of the antiquities of Delhi. Communications came from both civil and military officers in the Company's service. Captain Hoare sent a book of drawings and inscriptions from Delhi and Allahabad in 1801, Lieutenant Price a Sanskrit stone inscription in 1813. This amateur tradition was to continue until the end of British rule.

Early in the nineteenth century, the British showed great interest in a part of India not then under their control. In the independent Sikh kingdom of the Punjab, European adventurers in the employ of the ruler supplied valuable scientific information. One of the mercenaries, General Ventura, was inspired by stories of the treasures found in Egyptian pyramids to dig into some of the ruined towers which dotted the Punjab plains. Ventura found a large number of coins. Other men discovered more coins, some Greek, some Roman, some – at the time – unidentified. They also found sculpture that looked vaguely Greek.

Most of the discoveries ended up in Calcutta, and there an official of the Mint, James Prinsep, turned his attention to the new material. Prinsep might be called the founder of Indian archaeology. He had served under H. H. Wilson, the Sanskrit scholar, who had been head of the Mint before him. Not unreasonably, Prinsep was interested in coinage. From coins bearing bi-lingual inscriptions in Greek and Kharoshthi characters – in which certain names had already been identified – he was able to construct an alphabet. Later he turned to rock inscriptions of the period of the Mauryan emperor, Asoka, and by discovering on them the names of Greek kings (including Alexander) was able to deduce the date of the inscriptions.

Prinsep died in 1840 and his work was carried on by Alexander Cunningham, who had arrived in India as an army engineer in 1833. Cunningham remained in the army until 1860 and most of his discoveries until that date were more or less side products of geographical missions. In 1842, he discovered the important site of Sankissa, and nine years later he was responsible for opening the great Buddhist Dhamek *stupa* at Sanchi. After his discovery of Sankissa, Cunningham wrote to a friend in London. He gave him the news and suggested that an archaeological survey would be 'an undertaking of vast importance to the Indian Government politically, and to the British public religiously. To the first body it would show that India had generally been divided into numerous petty chiefships, which had invariably been the case upon every successful invasion; while, whenever she had been under one ruler, she had always repelled foreign conquest with determined resolution. To the other body it would show that Brahmanism, instead of being an unchanged and unchangeable religion which had subsisted for ages, was of comparatively modern origin, and had been *constantly* receiving additions and alterations; facts which prove that the establishment of the Christian religion in India must ultimately succeed.'

The idea of a survey was not new. In 1800, one Dr Buchanan had been instructed to make an agricultural survey of territories in Mysore. This had been so successful that he was ordered to make a statistical survey of Bengal in 1811. In both surveys he had marked archaeological remains. The beginning of scientific map-making in India also had an important bearing on discoveries, for geographical surveys were interpreted in the very widest sense by the men who carried them out. The first strictly archaeological tours were made by a Scottish indigo planter, James Fergusson, between 1835 and 1842. These resulted in the publication of the first systematic account of cave temples.

In the years before 1858, many military and civil officers contributed a great deal to the rediscovery of India's past. Such men as Colonel Tod, the Resident in Rajputana, not only compiled annals but collected antiquities and paintings. The work of oriental scholars in Europe had great influence on men in India who were interested in such subjects. When, for example, the Frenchman Abel Rémusat translated Fahsien's *Travels in India* (AD 405–441), it gave clues to the sites of forgotten cities which were followed up in India.

During the period of Company rule, the investigation of Indian antiquities, Indian literature, and Indian culture in general was the work of a few interested soldiers and officials. In one sense, it bore no relation to contemporary reality. Part of the interest was in throwing light on the legacy of Greece, that perennial interest of European intellectuals. Most of the men who made discoveries of great importance to Indian history did so without relating it to the Indian present. Yet their discoveries contributed to a new sense of India's greatness – not in the eyes of Europeans, but in the eyes of Indians. To the Indian nationalists who followed, they supplied the revelation of a past of great vitality and worth, which could be set against the arrogant assumption of their British rulers that Western civilization was superior to all.

## LITERATURE

The British connexion with India produced writers of prose and poetry, some of lasting interest, most of justly forgotten mediocrity. Robert Orme, in his still highly readable *History of the Military Transactions of the British Nation in Indostan* (of which the first volume was published in 1763), wrote of the period of Clive. One of Thackeray's characters (Clive Newcome) called it 'the best book in the world'. A number of the Company's servants produced historical works. Sir John Malcolm's *Political History of India* appeared in 1826, and he wrote other works of value. Mountstuart Elphinstone's *History of India* was published in 1841. James Grant Duff wrote his useful but virtually unreadable *History of the Mahrattas* in 1826. Malcolm's work was partly a justification of British rule. 'The great empire which England has established in the East', he wrote at the beginning of one of his books, 'will be the theme of wonder to succeeding ages.' Elphinstone accepted the fact that India had once had some institutions of value, but was now in need of what the West – and specifically Britain – had to offer. Grant Duff was really writing a justification of the British campaign against the Marathas.

T. B. Macaulay, on his return from India, wrote essays on Clive and Hastings (1840–41) which were highly critical and were designed, at least in part, to show how much the British administration had improved since the eighteenth century. The historians all had some axe to grind. J. D. Cunningham, whose

*History of the Sikhs* was published in 1849 just after the annexation of the Punjab, was concerned with convincing the British that they must continue with their 'civilizing' mission in India. 'The well-being of India's industrious millions', he said, 'is now linked with the foremost nation of the West, and the representatives of Judean faith and Roman polity will long wage a war of principles with the speculative Brahman, the authoritative Mulla, and the hardy believing Sikh.' J. W. Kaye, who became the chronicler of British administrators in India, wrote his *History of the War in Afghanistan* (1851) to remind the British that expansion for the sake of expansion could often lead to disaster.

Soldiers, civilians and their wives, wrote of their travels to and in India. From their works it is possible to gain a fairly clear picture of the life of the British. Many contain descriptions of 'picturesque' antiquities which provide a parallel in words of the aquatints of such artists as the Daniells (see page 60). James Forbes, who was in India between 1765 and 1784, disclosed in his *Oriental Memoirs* (1813) that he was driven by loneliness 'to investigate the manners and customs of the inhabitants, to study natural history, and to delineate the principal places and picturesque scenery'.

Later, it is possible to relate the reactions of the writers to their type of employment. Soldiers such as Herbert Edwardes (*A Year on the Punjab Frontier*, 1851) wrote of new frontiers and of wild places, newly conquered. Missionaries and deeply-involved Christian officers were determined to take the lid off pagan India (Charles Acland, *A Popular Account of the Manners and Customs of India*, 1843). Old-fashioned officials with paternalist leanings painted pictures of an India untouched by the West or sadly damaged by contact with it (William Sleeman, *Rambles and Recollections of an Indian Official*, 1844).

All these writers – the travellers and the historians – were critical, in most cases, of India and the Indians. All of what they wrote was primarily designed to influence opinion in Britain. It was from these works that the legislators, and that narrow section of the British people which made up 'public opinion', acquired their image of India. They preferred the evidence for India's depravity and backwardness to the apologetics of such men as Sleeman. One sector of 'Anglo-Indian' literary activity thus helped to create a climate *in Britain* favourable to the consolidation and advance of Western ideas of government and economics in India.

There was also a great deal of fiction written, much of which represented a growing racial consciousness amongst the British and was without literary merit. There were, however, one or two exceptions. Mrs Sherwood's children's books – *Little Henry and his Bearer* and *The Fairchild Family* (1818) – reveal a great deal about English society in India in the early years of the nineteenth century. J. W. Kaye's anonymous novel, *Peregrine Pultuney*, has already been quoted (see pp. 48–9). W. B. Hockley wrote *Pandarung Hari* (1826), a picturesque novel set in the times of the Maratha wars, and *The English in India* (1828). Meadows Taylor's *Confessions of a Thug* (1837) is a sort of non-fiction novel based upon the author's experiences in the suppression of Thuggee. Taylor's novel contributed – though it was probably not designed to do so – to the general impression in Britain that the moral standard of the Indians was low.

One of the most interesting of 'Anglo-Indian' novels was written (under the pseudonym 'Punjabee') by the poet Matthew Arnold's brother, William Delafield Arnold. This work, *Oakfield or Fellowship in the East* (1853), is more of a tract than a novel, primarily an exposure of the pettiness and – to Arnold – downright evil of most of the British in India. If there were no improvement in the moral standard of the British, India could hope for very little benefit from British rule. Arnold's idea of the Englishman's duty in India was that he should 'help in the work, or try to set it going, of raising the *European Society*, the great influence of Asia, first from the depths of immorality, gradually to a state of comparative Christian earnestness. I am quite certain that nothing less than Christianity, in the Cromwell or some other shape, will have any effect on the awful *vis inertiae* of Asiaticism. The protection of life and property, of which we hear so much, is of course a clear good; hardly, though, a very disinterested boon of ours to this country, for if life and property were insecure, whose throats or purses would go first? But for any purpose beyond protection to life and property (I, for one, will not believe that God gave England the Indian Empire for police purposes only) an eating and drinking, money-getting community is inefficient.'

As many of the British were amateur artists, so too they were amateur poets. Much of what they wrote was extremely bad, some reached a fairly high standard of mediocrity. There was a certain amount of humorous verse, but this form was to reach its apogee after the Mutiny. 'Anglo-Indian' poetry reflected the changing attitude of the British both to India and things Indian and towards their own situation. Sir William Jones, as well as making translations, wrote original poems on various Hindu gods which show a real attempt at understanding.

Wrapt in eternal solitary shade,
Th' impenetrable gloom of light intense,
Impervious, inaccessible, immense,
Ere spirits were infus'd or forms display'd,
  BREHM his own Mind survey'd,
As mortal eyes (thus finite we compare
  With infinite) in smoothest mirrors gaze:
Swift, at his look, a shape supremely fair
  Leap'd into being with a boundless blaze,
  That fifty suns might daze.

*Hymn to Brahma*

Later work on similar subjects is empty and facile, like the *Hymn to India* by William Waterfield.

God of the varied bow,
  God of the thousand eyes,
From all the winds that blow
  Thy praises rise;
Forth through the world they go
  Hymning to all below
Thee, whom the blest shall know
  Lord of the skies.

The beginnings of a poetry of exile, of the British spending long years among savage and barbarous peoples, can be found in the melancholy poems of Bishop Heber and John Leyden, who died of fever in 1811 and whose *Ode to an Indian Gold Coin* first stated the theme which was to be taken up by others later in the century. Heber, who also died in India – in 1826, after only three years' residence – expressed his longing for 'Home' in his poem, *An Evening Walk in Bengal*:

So rich a shade, so green a sod
Our English fairies never trod!
Yet who in India's bow'r has stood,
But thought on England's 'good green wood'?
And bless'd, beneath the palmy shade,
Her hazel and her hawthorn glade,
And breath'd a pray'r (how oft in vain!)
To gaze upon her oaks again?

## ART AND ARCHITECTURE

The art of the British in India divides conveniently into the amateur and the professional. After Tilly Kettle arrived in Madras in 1769, he was followed by a number of painters who stayed for varying periods of time. Tilly Kettle (in India 1769–76), John Zoffany (1783–89) and Arthur Devis (1785–95), painted in oils, but their works were ravaged by the climate, and were expensive to ship back to England because of their size. Under the circumstances, miniature painters had an obvious advantage. John Smart (in India 1785–95) and Ozias Humphry (1785–87) were the most important but they were followed by others almost as competent. In the early nineteenth century, George Chinnery (in India 1802–25) had the greatest reputation among the British.

Some Indian rulers had their portraits painted by European artists. The court of the rulers of Oudh at Lucknow early attracted European painters. Tilly Kettle, Zoffany, and Ozias Humphry all visited Lucknow and stayed for some time. During the reign of Ghazi-ud-din (1814–27), Robert Home was to all intents and purposes Court Painter.

All these artists painted in oils, but the most characteristic medium was water-colour. Most of the water-colour drawings were intended as studies for engravings, aquatints and, later, for lithographs. The vogue in Britain for the 'picturesque' – for Nature in the raw – was so widespread and profitable that it was only natural that artists should visit India. William Hodges began his tours in India in 1780 and produced his *Select Views* (London, 1786). Thomas Daniell and his nephew, William, stayed in India for eight years (1786–94) and produced their first work in Calcutta (*Views of Calcutta*, 1786–88), following it up with four volumes of *Oriental Scenery* (London, 1795–1808). The Daniells were followed by others who, with them, helped to create for people in Britain an idealized and picturesque India which must have seemed oddly at variance with the descriptions of travellers and, later, of missionaries.

One of the results of the cult of the picturesque in Britain had been the social acceptance of amateur sketching. The scenery of India, wild and romantic, intrigued the British. Their enthusiasm resulted in vast numbers of sketches and water-colours, some of them of quite high quality. Captain Williamson's *Oriental Field Sports* was published in 1807, Captain Grindlay's *Scenery, Costumes and Architecture* in 1826. Travellers did sketches to illustrate their books. Perhaps the most important of these amateur artists was Sir Charles D'Oyly, who lived at Patna. D'Oyly, who had taken lessons from Chinnery, produced a number of books of illustrations on his own lithographic press.

In the last twenty years of Company rule, the changes that were taking place in the general attitudes of the British in India affected their interest in art. They were no longer so concerned with recording the life of the natives, for curiosity had been replaced by indifference. Art suffered from the British withdrawal from active involvement. This withdrawal, of course, was not unanimous, and there were still people excited at the Indian scene. But they were rapidly decreasing in number.

*

As the British settled into the role of rulers, they began to assemble some of the outward show of the governing classes back in Britain. Their houses, even if they were only of one storey, had a classical portico. Calcutta, 'the city of palaces', had a large number of elegant public buildings in the classical manner. On the whole, classical architecture transplanted well, being an exotic product itself. But some adaptation had to be made to suit an intemperate climate. Lofty classical 'piazzas' – as they were called at the time – with their pillars rising to the full height of the house, let in the harsh sun of the early afternoon. They were therefore filled in with immense Venetian blinds. Churches designed by military engineers followed English patterns, and some were extremely elegant. In the early nineteenth century, indigo planters built themselves great mansions on their estates.

The high peak of British Indian architecture coincided with the greatest interest in the picturesque. It was an architecture demonstrative not so much of national pride as of a desire for social status. The classical villas which grew up around the early settlements were not constructed to impress Indians but to convince the British themselves of their wealth and standing by using the architectural vocabulary of the rich and powerful in Britain.

For roughly the first fifty years of British rule, the architecture of public buildings remained classical in inspiration. Outside Calcutta and the other large settlements, houses were usually simple, consisting of one storey surrounded by a veranda, and having a thatched roof. The British even took this style of building up into the hills with them when it became fashionable to desert the plains in the hot weather. 'The walls', wrote Richard Burton in *Goa and the Blue Mountains,* published in 1857 but relating experiences of ten years earlier, 'are made of coarse bad bricks – the roof of thatch or wretched tiles, which act admirably as filters, and occasionally cause the downfall of part, or the whole of the erection. The foundation usually selected is a kind of platform, a gigantic step, cut out of some hill-side, and levelled by manual labour. . . . As regards architecture, the style bungalow – a modification of the cow-house – is preferred: few tenements have upper storeys, whilst almost all are surrounded by a long low verandah, perfectly useless in such a climate, and only calculated to render the interior of the domiciles as dim and gloomy as can be conceived.'

## 2

# *The Nature of British Rule*

### GOVERNMENT: PRINCIPLES AND PRACTICE

WHEN THE British came to exercise power in Bengal, they were faced with a series of dilemmas. The first was – how to rule without revealing that the British had neither the capacity nor the manpower to operate an administration? Robert Clive's notorious system of 'dual government' was the first solution to be tried. The native administration and its officials continued to function, while the British remained in the background. This was primarily a matter of expediency, but what was, in essence, a puppet system also appealed to the British because their main interest was in profit. They considered themselves not as innovators, but as inheritors, and they hoped to make their inheritance work for them. They thought of themselves, not as colonists, but as transients, making their fortune before climate and disease prevented them from enjoying it back home in Britain. They were content to adapt themselves to Indian circumstances and to manipulate the traditional forms of government. Nevertheless, the very presence of the British in the Indian countryside, as well as their use of traditional forms to their own advantage, influenced the system of administration. And as the numbers of British increased, so did the influence. It was to curtail their predatory activities that the Crown first decided to interfere in the administration of British India.

When dual government was abandoned in 1772, the British were faced with their second dilemma. To what extent should the government be anglicized? Were existing institutions to be preserved, or swept aside? Warren Hastings felt that Indian institutions should be retained wherever possible. During his administration, Hindu and Muslim personal law received protection, Muslim criminal law was maintained, and Indians were employed in the administration. In effect, the principle of duality was continued, except that now it was operated directly by the British – who were themselves subject to English law, as exercised by the new Supreme Court set up by the Regulating Act of 1773 (see page 90).

It was hardly to be expected that the introduction of direct rule would completely eradicate abuse and corruption, and when Hastings' successor, Lord Cornwallis, arrived in India in 1786, he soon became convinced that there was not enough control exercised over the Company's servants.

The Supreme Court had been established with the intention of making individuals subject to English law; Cornwallis decided that English constitutional principles should form the basis of the system of government. In Cornwallis's view, these principles were entirely opposed to the authoritarian character of native Indian government. His purpose was to establish the rule of law instead of the law of the ruler – to provide something fixed and immutable in place of something variable and arbitrary. The corruption and misery of Bengal were, Cornwallis believed, the result of allowing too much discretion to underpaid Company servants, who fell easily into the ways of native Indian governments. Cornwallis's solution was to reduce the role of government. He opted for 'the introduction of a new order of things, which should have for its foundation, the security of individual property, and the administration of justice, criminal and civil, by rules which were to disregard all conditions of persons, and in their operation, be freed of influence or control from the government itself'.

The question of land revenue provided full scope for putting these views into action. Cornwallis ruled that the amount payable to the government should be permanently fixed, thus limiting interference by officials which, Cornwallis believed, took place when the revenue demand varied from year to year. One of the essential bases of Cornwallis's ideas was that the executive should be separated from the judiciary, and that the executive should itself be subject to the rule of law. This was a revolutionary suggestion, not only for Indians, but for the British in India who – following Indian practice – had made no division between the authority which made the law and the authority which enforced it. Even the men who collected the revenue possessed judicial powers. Cornwallis proposed to put an end to this. In his preamble to Bengal Regulation II of 1793, he wrote: 'The collectors of revenue must not only be divested of the power of deciding upon their own acts, but rendered amenable for them to the courts of judicature; and collect the public dues, subject to a personal prosecution for every exaction exceeding the amount which they are authorized to demand on behalf of the public, and for every deviation from the regulations prescribed for the collection of it.' Like the good Whig he was, Cornwallis believed that the prosperity of the state rested on landed property, and his purpose was to see that this principle was irrevocably established in British India.

English political concepts were to be translated into the soil of India, and Indians were to be removed from the halls of government. With Cornwallis's admiration for English principles and institutions went a belief in the general superiority of Englishmen and the role they must play in preserving British rule in India. 'I think it must be universally admitted', he wrote, 'that without a large and well-regulated body of Europeans, our hold on these valuable dominions must be very insecure.' Indians were dismissed from all but the most minor offices. In Bengal, landholders who had had the right to employ armed retainers – and who were responsible for policing their districts – were deprived of this right. A British official, known as the Collector, was appointed to each administrative area in Bengal with the task of collecting the revenue. He had no political or judicial powers. Such powers were to be exercised by the man known as district judge and magistrate, who controlled the police and whose function was to administer the law, even against the Collector, if necessary.

Although the principle of separation of powers involved conscious anglicization of the forms of government, it was not intended to change Indian society. On the contrary, supporters of the principle – particularly Lord Wellesley (governor-general 1798–1805) – believed that, in it, lay the best protection for that society. Wellesley argued that the interests of the mass of the people were non-political, involving no principles of government. If the government refrained from interference in religion, customs and personal law, Indian society could maintain its domestic structure. But whatever Wellesley might believe, interference there was. The British concept of private property rights and their enforcement by legal process was a radical innovation, and its effects were to alter the structure of Indian society profoundly.

If the ideas of Cornwallis and Wellesley may be said to have had their roots in the Whig view of society, classically stated by John Locke, the ideas of the opposition stemmed from romantic sentiments about the 'noble peasant' as expounded by William Wordsworth. This did not, however, mean that the men of the opposition such as Thomas Munro (1761–1827), John Malcolm (1769–1833), Mountstuart Elphinstone (1779–1859) and Charles Metcalfe (1785–1846) – from whose thoughts and actions emerged an alternative to anglicized forms of government – were sloppy sentimentalists. Far from it. They believed in pragmatic, personal, and dynamic administration, free from the dead hand of impersonal government. While they did not deny that English constitutional principles were intrinsically good, they doubted their relevance to the Indian situation unless modified in their application.

The importance of these four particular men was that they were not abstract thinkers but active administrators who, because the frontiers of British India were still expanding, were able to exercise considerable authority independently of the government in Calcutta. The Bengal system – by now a settled administration in an area where British rule was undisputed – had become cold and passive. Inherently, it was a system of division, above all, of rejection, for its purpose was to avoid involvement in the lives of the people. To men actively engaged in empire-building beyond such settled territories, the system lacked both warmth and what might be called the bravura of involvement. They were by no means opposed to reform, but they could not accept the belief that miraculous changes could be wrought in human society merely by means of legislative action. To them, a division of society between ruler and ruled was the natural order, and they believed in the exercise of political power as of right.

Munro, Malcolm, Elphinstone and Metcalfe differed on points of detail, particularly in their attitude to native states and to the old aristocracy. Munro believed it to be good policy to conciliate the princes and others. Metcalfe was against it. But none of them expected that British rule would ever rest upon the affection of the masses. Their common aim was, not to engage in some vast operation designed to transform the Indian sub-continent into a vague simulacrum of British society, but to conserve traditional institutions. They were against innovation and fully aware of what its effects had been in Cornwallis's time. When a new move towards increased anglicization began in the 1820s, they feared the worst. 'The ruling vice of our government', wrote Munro in 1824, 'is innovation. . . . It is time that we should learn that neither the face of the country, its property, nor its society, are things that can be suddenly improved by any contrivance of ours, though they may be greatly injured by what we mean for their good.'

In spite of their superficial disagreements, Munro, Malcolm, Elphinstone and Metcalfe were preservationists. Except for Metcalfe – whose outlook had been soured by direct experience of dealing with Maratha princes – they believed that the Indian states should be preserved, not only as places where Indian culture could survive in the most natural milieu, but also as a refuge for those Indians who could find no place in the hierarchies of British India. A direct relationship between the ruler and the ruled was, they argued, the foundation of stability. There should be ease of accessibility between government and peasant – government by mouth rather than by pen, instant decision rather than a multiplicity of written forms and slow judicial processes. This, in practice, demanded not the separation of judicial and executive powers but their union. The four administrators considered that the Collector should have magisterial authority, control of the police, and, above all, the power to impose summary punishment. Although convinced of the need for efficiency and economy in government, they felt it would be better achieved by delegating authority to trusted individuals surrounded by the realities of everyday life than by a centralized and therefore remote administration. In essence, Munro, Malcolm, Elphinstone and Metcalfe were in agreement with certain of the views of English Utilitarian philosophers, who also believed in the union of judicial and executive powers, in a simple code of law and respect for custom. But they could not accept either the desire for uniformity or the rigidity of principle involved in the Utilitarian outlook.

Above all, the romantic school of Indian administrators in the first half of the nineteenth century were fearful of violent change. 'The most important of the lessons we can derive from past experience', wrote John Malcolm, 'is to be slow and cautious in every procedure which has a tendency to collision with the habits and prejudices of our native subjects. We may be compelled by the character of our government to frame some institutions, different from those we found established, but we should adopt all we can of the latter into our system. . . . Our internal government . . . should be administered on a principle of humanity not pride. We must divest our minds of all arrogant pretensions arising from the presumed superiority of our own knowledge, and seek the accomplishment of the great ends we have in view by the means which are best suited to the peculiar nature of the objects.' And he went on: 'All that Government can do is, by maintaining the internal peace of the country, and by adapting its principles to the various feelings, habits, and character of its inhabitants, to give time for the slow and silent operation of the desired improvement, with a constant impression that every attempt to accelerate this end will be attended with the danger of its defeat.'

Essentially, the systems of Cornwallis and of Munro (and those who thought like him) were to prove permanent in the different parts of the country in which they were established by their creators. The general structure of both systems remained untouched, although there were to be many modifications and sometimes violent change within the structures. Both systems were designed to limit governmental interference in society, but both were designed to be operated by British officials, and both imposed Western concepts of property rights backed by Western law. The control of the administration by British officials meant that those officials could become agents of revolution if the climate of opinion in British India, or in Britain, changed. And the effect of Western legal institutions on matters concerning land – the core of Indian society – could be used as an instrument to transform that society.

Cornwallis's attitude – which involved the removal of Indians from positions of authority and the rejection of traditional administrative forms – was grounded fundamentally in a sense of racial superiority and its corollary, contempt for others. As the British in India ceased to be merchants and became empire-builders, they acquired a strong sense of exclusivity, occupying that special isolation which is characteristic of all conquerors. This was reinforced by a growing belief, not only that the British were racially superior to Indians and possessed of infinitely better political institutions, but that their religion was superior too. This assumption would not have meant very much if it had not been intimately associated with missionary zeal on the part of a number of people with influence in Indian affairs. The most important of these was Charles Grant, who had been one of Cornwallis's advisers in India and who, after his return to England, became chairman of the Court of Directors of the East India Company. His view, which illuminates the new mission that he and his associates proposed for Christianity, he summed up in these words: 'In considering the affairs of the world as under the control of the Supreme Disposer, and those distant territories [i.e. India] providentially put into our hands . . . is it not necessary to conclude that they were given to us, not merely that we might draw an annual profit from them, but that we might diffuse among their inhabitants, long sunk in darkness, vice and misery, the light and benign influence of the truth, the blessings of well-regulated society, the improvements and comforts of active industry? . . . In every progressive step of this work, we shall also serve the original design with which we visited India, that design still so important to this country – the extension of our commerce.'

The evangelicals – as Grant and his friends, who included William Wilberforce and the father of the future Lord Macaulay, were called – dismissed not only the religion of India as 'one grand abomination', but also by implication every aspect of Indian society from its arts to its institutions. Except in one particular area, however, these views had very little effect upon the Company's administration, because the evangelicals believed that society could not be reformed by legislation, but only by a change in individual morality. They intended a campaign to free the Indian mind from the tyranny of evil superstition, a sort of Indian counterpart to the European Reformation. Their instrument was to be education, for only through access to God's revealed word could the Indians be raised out of their darkness and idolatry.

The evangelicals believed that the future prosperity of the British connexion and the future happiness of the Indians themselves depended upon complete anglicization of Indian society. 'Let us endeavour to strike our roots into the soil,' said Wilberforce, 'by the gradual introduction and establishment of our own principles and opinions; of our laws, institutions, and manners; above all, as the source of every other improvement, of our religion, and consequently of our morals.'

This view represented a real challenge to the East India Company's continuing attitude of non-interference. The British in India, though conscious of their power, were equally conscious that it depended on the acceptance of the large mass of the people who did not particularly care who governed them as long as their customs and religion were not interfered with. Any attempt to convert Indians to Christianity promised to subvert the very foundations of civil peace by offending the most deeply entrenched religious prejudices. The Company's administration had endeavoured to maintain a sense of continuity with the past, to emphasize that – though it was an alien administration – it contemplated no revolutionary changes in the lives of the people. The truth of this was most apparent to Indians in that very area attacked by the evangelicals, namely the Company's religious policy.

This policy was essentially concerned with not giving offence and it was taken to such lengths that, until 1831, Indian Christians were actively discriminated against by the government. They could not hold appointments in the Company's judicial service, nor were they permitted to practise as lawyers in the Company's courts. In contrast, the government not only tolerated Hindu and Muslim festivals but allowed troops and military bands to participate in them. In 1802, for example, as a thanksgiving for the conclusion of the Treaty of Amiens between Britain and France, an official government party went in procession with troops and military music to the principal shrine of the Hindu goddess, Kali, in Calcutta, and presented the goddess with a substantial sum of money.

The British had also assumed certain of the responsibilities of previous governments in relation to religious endowments and buildings and the control of pilgrim traffic to the many Hindu shrines. The issue of a Regulation in 1817 was followed by government administration of a large number of temples and their funds. The pilgrim taxes levied by the Company were used for the repair and upkeep of temples. In fact, the government's involvement left its servants wide open to the criticism of supporting idolatry and acting, in the picturesque language of one observer, as 'dry-nurse to Vishnu'. As late as 1833, the Madras government was still responsible for the administration of some 7,500 temples and their funds. British officials played an intimate role in the material life of the temples – assessing and ordering repairs, and even, on occasion, press-ganging men to pull the temple cars.

The Charter Act of 1833 was to change this, though many years passed before it took effect and it was not until 1863 that the government finally severed its connexion with the administration of religious endowments. Many Indians were to look upon this ultimate dissociation of the government from involvement in the administration of temples and their funds

– an involvement which was a traditional function of India's rulers – as an abdication of one of the principal functions of government, and a deliberate repudiation of a duty incumbent upon all rulers, whatever religion they professed. More important still, it was to appear as yet another act of withdrawal, separating the government from the people and dramatizing for Indian society the uniquely alien nature of British government in India.

The evangelicals had their first triumph in 1813 when, by the Charter Act of that year, the Company was forced to appoint a bishop whose headquarters were to be in Calcutta and his see the whole of the British dominions; to open up the country to Christian missionaries; and to appropriate an annual sum for education. The Charter Act of 1813 also forced open the door of the Company's commercial monopoly, although many evangelists were, like Charles Grant, staunch supporters of a Company monopoly. Most of them possessed a vested interest in its maintenance, and ironically enough, believed they could reform the government of India without impinging upon the mercantilist conception of political dominion, which saw its *raison d'être* as the drawing-off of tribute. The rational extension of their view, which can briefly be summed up as 'assimilation and profit', was, in fact, free trade, colonization, and capital investment – not the drawing away of wealth, but the creation of prosperity. The Company, however, was already an anachronism as a trading corporation. Ever since its occupation of Bengal after 1757, trade had taken a low second place to revenue-control and the transformation of revenue-surplus into dividends for the Company's stockholders back in Britain. But the expansion of British dominion in India soon produced a burden of debt instead of a revenue surplus. By 1813, the Company had become basically a military and administrative power. It paid its way by using the profits of the opium monopoly in India to finance trade in China tea – from whose sale in Europe the shareholders' dividends were actually paid. Nevertheless, the Company resisted the breaking of its monopoly in the India trade, primarily on the grounds that free trade would lead to attempts to 'improve' Indian conditions and this would, it believed, endanger internal stability. In any case, it was convinced that no sudden improvement was possible.

The Company's attitude, however, ran counter to the spirit of the times, and, by the time the charter came up for renewal in 1833, evangelical opinion coincided with that of the free traders. By then, the evangelicals had witnessed some years of attempted improvement and social reform in India. The free traders had also gained an insight into India's profitability; the Company had lost its trading monopoly (except that with China) in 1813, and the extent of private trade – particularly in manufactured cotton textiles – had amply justified the hopes of the free traders. But their very success raised doubts about the future. Indians were poor and their purchasing power was strictly limited. If this were to be changed, it would necessitate the widest use of British expertise as well as considerable financial investment. Such a programme would call for the abolition of restrictions on European ownership of land and of discriminatory inland transit dues.

All this could be achieved – and was achieved – by political lobbying in Britain. But the creed of the apostles of free trade embraced more than the expansion of commerce. They firmly believed that the industrial revolution which was investing Britain with the commercial leadership of the world resulted from a superior civilization, and the passing on of its benefits was not only good business but a heaven-ordained duty. The only way this could be carried out was by spreading English institutions and English education. One of the results was that a Law Commission was appointed to codify Indian law according to Western principles. Another was that, in 1835, it was decided that English education in the English language should receive the principal support of the government of India. Essentially this denoted a *mission civilisatrice* rather than a philosophy of conquest. As Macaulay said: 'To trade with civilized men is infinitely more profitable than to govern savages.'

Paradoxical though it may appear, evangelicals and liberals such as Macaulay still wished to restrict government interference in the everyday life of the people of India. They believed that it was the government's duty to create a climate of change – but not to bully people into changing. To offer the means of change – but a means suitably protected by a hedge of English institutions. To persuade by example – but not to coerce by legislative action. They believed, however, that the government should be unmistakably British, demonstrating that its superiority stemmed from its civilization. Indeed, the general movement towards anglicization was aimed as much at the government of India as at Indian society. While legislation in London could be used to change the government's attitude, Indian society was expected to transform itself as knowledge of Western civilization was diffused by English education.

There were other thinkers who did not agree with the propositions of the evangelicals and liberals, who had little faith in the regenerative qualities of English education, and who saw very clearly that the *real* instrument by which a radical transformation of Indian society could be achieved was the system of land revenue, its determination and assessment. Some of these men – generally called Utilitarians – were in a position to influence India's administration. James Mill, for example, had been appointed to a senior post in the East India Company's headquarters in London in 1819; in 1830, he became the Examiner, or chief executive officer. Jeremy Bentham was the intellectual *animateur* of Lord William Bentinck, the reforming governor-general (1828–35). William Empson, a confirmed Benthamite, was professor of 'General Polity and Laws' at the Company's college at Haileybury, where its administrators received their initial training. Although none of the principal Utilitarian philosophers had any personal experience in India, they knew instinctively that it was quite as bad as, if not worse than, the descriptions of Charles Grant. James Mill, comparing India with China (which he also knew only at second hand), found that 'both nations are, to nearly an equal degree, tainted with the vices of insincerity; dissembling, treacherous, mendacious, to an excess which surpasses even the usual measure of uncultivated society. Both are disposed to excessive exaggeration with regard to everything relating to themselves. Both are cowardly and unfeeling. Both are in the highest degree conceited of themselves, and full of affected contempt for others. Both are, in the physical sense, disgustingly unclean in their persons and their houses.'

Both the evangelicals and the Utilitarians shared a fundamental contempt for Indian institutions, a contempt which became institutionalized as the nineteenth century progressed. But they shared little else. The difference between them lay in their concept of the operative law. The evangelicals believed in God's law, immutable and evident. In their view, all that was needed was to make knowledge of this law available to all; example could then be expected to do the rest. The Utilitarians expelled God from the equation. To them, sin was not original but a product of poverty, and poverty was – wrote James Mill – 'the effect of bad laws and bad government; and is never characteristic of any people who are governed well'. Mill had no faith in schoolmasters as purveyors of revolution. That savoured of placing the cart before the horse. 'It is necessary,' he went on, 'before education can operate to any great result, that the poverty of the people be re-dressed; that their laws and government should operate beneficently.'

This was a cold and mechanist view of social change, and one which did not appeal to the messianism of the new English middle class. For one thing, it did not support their essentially patriotic view of the value of British civilization. Mill and the economist Ricardo even threw doubt on the fundamental belief that free trade was the creator of happiness. What was even worse – at least from the point of view of the British mercantile community in India – was that Mill disapproved of the Cornwallis system which restricted the executive authority of government and relied on purely conservative application of the law to protect private property.

In the case of the law itself, Bentham opposed the jury system and glorified summary procedures. Mill believed that, in the Indian interior, both British and Indians should be subject to the same laws and the same courts. As well as offending the deep-seated prejudices of the mercantile community, the Utilitarians repelled the liberals who believed that Indians should play a part in the administration of their own country. Mill argued that the people of India wanted cheap and efficient government and did not really care who operated it as long as these criteria were satisfied. He rejected the idea even of a legislature representing the British in India. Mill's remedy for India's ills was quite simple. 'The mode of increasing the riches of the body of the people is a discovery no less easy than sure. Take little from them in the way of taxes; prevent them from injuring one another; and make no absurd laws to restrain them in the harmless disposal of their property and labour. Light taxes and good laws; nothing more is wanting for national and individual prosperity all over the globe.'

It was an essential of Mill's thesis that, as in Munro's system, there should be no middlemen between the state and the actual cultivator of the land. But he also called for a code of law which would be universal in its application and mode of procedure and – even more important – for a strong central authority and an end to the semi-independent status of the Madras and Bombay presidencies.

At the heart of the Utilitarian theories about India, however, lay the question of land revenue. Every level of Indian society, outside the urban areas, depended in one way or another upon the land. Before the fundamental rights of a rural community could be protected by the law, these rights had to be determined and recorded – a procedure which could be satisfactorily achieved only by means of Munro's *ryotwari* system, where the administration had a direct and unimpeded relationship with the cultivators of the soil. But of even more importance than the definition of rights was the method of taxation which, according to Mill, was one of the great forces which in conjunction with the form of government and the administration of justice moulded all human society.

Mill maintained that the state was, in effect, the universal landlord. This view was supported by Indian tradition, but was also a rebuttal of both the Cornwallis and the Munro systems, which sought by implication to remove the state from that position. The problem, as Mill saw it, was to determine the rent payable to the universal landlord. In its correct setting – i.e. the general chaos of Indian circumstances – Mill's apparently simple solution to the country's ills appears in its true light as a vast programme of reform. It entailed the establishment of a strong central government possessing exclusive legislative authority for the whole of British India; the embodiment of all law into a set of scientific codes; a total reorganization and expansion of the judicial system; a complete overhaul and reshaping of the administrative service; the survey and registration of all land-holdings; and a scientific assessment of land revenue based on detailed statistics of agricultural production. Yet – over a period of many years, and certainly not in its pure form – Mill's programme was actually carried through. It was to be diluted partly for environmental reasons and partly because the coldness of Utilitarian ideas did not appeal to the liberal-modernizers who were to carry out administrative and judicial reforms in India. Environment was a factor because two distinct revenue systems already existed – the *zamindari* and the *ryotwari* (see pages 94–9). The *zamindari* system was firmly established in Bengal, Bihar and Orissa, but for functional reasons could not be extended to newly acquired territories in the Deccan and the north-west; the *ryotwari* system had created its own administrative organization. Utilitarian influences were, however, to be found in both systems, and in the sixties and seventies of the nineteenth century they coalesced to produce a uniform administration in which Mill's basic ideas were largely realized.

The real effect of Utilitarian ideas during the period of Company rule depended upon two factors – Mill's position as a senior official of the Company in London, and the activities of certain men in India who had been converted to Utilitarian principles. By the time James Mill gave evidence before a parliamentary committee in 1831, he was able to reveal that, for many years, instructions from London concerning the amount of the revenue assessment had stipulated that it should be restricted to the limits of the net produce – i.e. the surplus after the payment of wage-labour and the natural profits of capital – which the Utilitarians called 'rent'. Mill also revealed, however, that there had been and still were immense difficulties involved in ascertaining rent and that, although this was partly due to the absence of statistics, the main difficulty lay in the fact that the revenue-administrators themselves did not understand Mill's 'doctrine of rent'. But there was at least one person in a position of authority in India who did – the Secretary to the Supreme Government in the Territorial Department at Calcutta, one Holt Mackenzie. Mackenzie had produced a memorandum in 1819 outlining a new system of land settlement for those areas in northern and central India which were later to be called the North-Western Provinces. Although the governor-general accepted the system in 1822, the Regulation embodying it (VII of 1822) was in practice largely ignored because of the difficulty of estimating the proceeds and expenses of cultivation. Local custom operated such a bewildering series of restrictive practices – including price-fixing – that the law of supply and demand did not exist.

There was opposition to the new system. John Malcolm considered it too academic, ignoring reality because it was too concerned with rigid principles. An assessment based on net produce was, in fact, carried out in Bombay in 1828, but in spite of (or even, perhaps, because of) its detailed statistical framework, it was generally considered – though not by Mill and the Directors in London – as too high. The assessment was abandoned in 1835. In general, after 1833, another less doctrinaire and far more empirical method of revenue assessment came into favour.

The failure of Utilitarian methods of revenue assessment was almost entirely due to the inadequacy of the administration. The searching investigation and detailed statistics necessary if they were to operate properly demanded more men – and more qualified men – than the administration possessed. Theoretically, however, the net produce criterion was never abandoned, though it was considerably modified in practice.

In their effect on society, perhaps the most important aspect of Mill's views and their embodiment in the revenue system of northern and western India was that they had an essentially anti-landlord bias. Indeed, in the North-Western Provinces, discrimination against the landlord – or, as the Utilitarians called him, the rent-receiver – and the upheaval this caused in the social order, helped to bring about civil involvement in the essentially military mutiny of 1857.

The concept of private property rights and their alienation for debt lay at the heart of every Western system – whether it was that of Cornwallis, Munro, or the Utilitarians – and it was this that was to dissolve the traditional social order. The moment land acquired realizable value either in outright sale or as security for loans, any tradition of communal interdependence as exemplified by joint proprietorship or co-sharing village-owned land tended to be eroded. There was a movement towards individual ownership supported, through the proper registration of title, by precise and legally enforceable definition instead of unwritten and therefore legally unenforceable custom.

This affected the whole of British India. But there was no uniformity in the matter of assessment or in the definition of land tenures. Before 1858, too much depended on the individual preferences of local administrators bound only by the Company's general instruction to maintain a moderate assessment. In a real sense, India was a series of laboratories for experiments in political economy.

The movement towards codification of the law was slow, principally because after 1835 the British were engaged in a succession of wars both inside and outside India which left successive governors-general with little time – and, frequently, less inclination – for contemplating major reforms. Nevertheless, the conclusions of the Law Commission (see page 92 ff.) and the code drafted by Macaulay laid the foundations for realizing the second great element in Mill's system – a code of law which would be universal in application and procedure.

There remained Mill's third reform, a strong central

government. There was an essential conflict between the two systems of government operating in India, whose leading protagonists were Cornwallis and Munro. This lay in the question of separation of powers. The paternalist school, represented by Munro, Malcolm, Elphinstone and Metcalfe, believed implicitly that executive and judicial functions should be combined. So did Mill and Bentham, although not for the same reasons. To the paternalists, the union of these powers – and a wide discretion for the officials actually operating them – was a preservationist link with traditional Indian practice. To the Utilitarians, the union of these powers was a matter of simple and rational common sense. That both attitudes were compatible was demonstrated in Elphinstone's administration of Bombay (1819–27), when he followed the Munro system but underwrote it with a precise and careful delegation of authority. Elphinstone also attempted to codify Hindu law, but ultimately had to be content with producing a consistent system of English law.

Widespread administrative reform, however, had to await the arrival in India in 1828 of Lord William Bentinck. His instructions were to try to put the Company's administration into some sort of order in preparation for 1833, when the Company's charter came up for renewal. There was a substantial annual budget deficit, and it had been obvious for some time that the civil administration was, to put it charitably, less than efficient. In certain parts of the country, in fact, administrative collapse seemed imminent. This was a result of the absence of knowledgeable supervision. In the North-Western Provinces, for example, the provincial boards of revenue were expected to exercise control over the district revenue administration by means of correspondence. They were unable to do so.

Before Bentinck's arrival, a suggestion had been put forward in India that new officials should be appointed, each of whom would be given full responsibility in a district of manageable size where he could keep a personal eye on the activities of his subordinates. These officials – District Commissioners, as they came to be called – were, in turn, to be accountable for everything that went on in their districts. They were to be, not executives, but inspectors. Both the Utilitarians and the paternalists believed in personal government at the level of action, carried on by experienced and practical men linked to higher authority by a precise chain of command. The plan for District Commissioners, responsible individuals operating within an area in which inspection and control could effectively be exercised, conformed excellently with Utilitarian and paternalist ideas.

In 1829, the plan was put into action in the Bengal Presidency. The boards of revenue were replaced by the new commissioners, who took over control of the police and also became judges of circuit and session. A chief board of revenue was formed at Calcutta to act as the highest controlling authority.

In Bengal, the commissioners exercised judicial functions only in matters concerning land revenue, but, as the system spread elsewhere, the union of powers desired by both Utilitarians and paternalists was achieved. In time, the commissioner system spread throughout the whole of Britain's colonial empire. What had begun with Bentinck's Regulation I of 1829 as a method designed (except in the initial case of Bengal) to facilitate immediate control of newly-acquired territories in India became the orthodox pattern of colonial government.

These changes in the executive arm of the government also made possible reforms in the administration of justice – a matter of some urgency, since the courts were clogged with arrears. But the movement towards reform once again aroused the controversy over the functions of the executive power and the rule of law as instruments of social change. It is important to recognize that, in the minds of the paternalists, orthodox Utilitarians, and liberals, the mechanics of government and the social purposes of governmental action were inseparable. The ideas of administration propounded in both Britain and India were concerned with wider matters than producing cheap and efficient administration as such, or even with erecting a system which could collect the maximum revenue in the most expeditious fashion. Some thinkers and administrators in India insisted that the function of government was to protect and preserve. Others believed that social change should be brought about by executive action. Others, again, were convinced that the rule of law itself, by its efficient operation, would naturally bring into being an individualist, competitive society such as had given Britain her dominating position in the world. The Bentinck reforms of 1831, which completed those of 1829, struck a kind of balance amongst all three attitudes, not so much by uniting the executive and judicial powers as by making them interdependent. In Bengal, each district was to have a collector-magistrate with control of the police and summary jurisdiction in rent cases, while a district judge was to try criminal cases committed for trial by the collector-magistrate and hear civil appeals from the courts of Indian subordinate judges, who were to be given extensive new powers of jurisdiction. The latter provision went some way towards satisfying such men as Macaulay that Indians were not to be excluded from official positions. The reforms also affected Madras and Bombay, and there was a considerable extension of the use of Indian subordinate judges in both these presidencies.

Bentinck succeeded in achieving the increased administrative efficiency which had been his brief on appointment. But there remained one overwhelming problem. This was not so much the very obvious lack of uniformity between different parts of the British dominions as the inability of the governor-general to impose uniformity. The governor-general's field of authority – and that of the presidency governments – had been fixed by the British parliament and could only be changed by it. It was clear to most people that, lacking any single legislative authority, the government of India was in confusion. This situation, and the absence of a single system of law, resulted in the major provisions of the Charter Act of 1833, which created a real government of India, complete with legislative council. The governor-general was now to become the 'Governor-General of India', and not, as previously, the 'Governor-General of Fort William in Bengal'. The new title made quite plain that the governor-general was to exercise supreme authority, and it was expressly stipulated that the former presidency governments no longer had the right to make their own laws. They were merely authorized to submit to the governor-general-in-council 'drafts or projects of any laws or regulations which they might think expedient'.

Reform in the government of India was brought about in the face of powerful but essentially helpless opposition. The paternalists were naturally opposed to the concentration of power at the centre and a uniform administration for the whole of British India. They favoured *delegation* of authority and wide discretionary powers for local officials. There was, they agreed, a need for administrative and legal reform. They believed, however, that codification, for example, should be pursued with intent to provide not a uniform law throughout India but a series of comprehensive bodies of law designed to protect local rights and customs from the alien and disruptive effect of English law. The paternalists were convinced that local experiments in administration were infinitely better than an all-India uniformity. But their views ran counter to the general feeling of the time.

Other opposition centred on the composition of the legislative council. Most opinion in India favoured a body with some popular basis, one which might include not only the members of the governor-general's executive council, two judges, and representatives of the presidencies, but also possibly a number of 'unofficial native gentlemen'. This dimly democratic concept ran counter to all Utilitarian principles. Mill maintained that a small body of experts was preferable on grounds of efficiency, and also argued that it would be more amenable to the influences of public opinion. Essentially, however, his view was that the business of government should be left to specialists who were not encumbered by the passions of what Bentham called 'the untaught and unlettered multitude'. Though Mill did not get exactly what he wanted, the Charter Act did accept the principle of small bodies of experts when it established the Law Commission, of four members (see page 92 ff.), and added a Law Member to the governor-general's three-man executive council. The Law Member acted as a member of council only when legislative matters were in question, and was not to be an employee of the Company. When he was present, the body of four was known as the Legislative Council. The Law Member was, however, to be more than just an expert on drafting legislation. 'His will naturally be the principal share', wrote Mill, on behalf of the Directors, 'not only in giving shape and connexion to the several laws as they pass, but also in the mighty labour in collecting all that local information, and calling into view all those general considerations which belong to each occasion, and of thus enabling the council to embody the abstract and essential principles of good government in Regulations adapted to the peculiar habits, character, and institutions of the vast and infinitely diversified people under their sway.'

The first man to occupy the position of Law Member was Thomas Babington Macaulay. Unlike the Utilitarians, he professed no general theories of government. His mind was essentially practical. He rejected the Utilitarian belief that society could be changed by the exercise of a universally applicable theory. He retained the old Whig suspicion of political power but, true to his times, accepted a large role for the state in the pursuit of limited aims. Macaulay believed that free enterprise and voluntary action were the springs of progress, and he was therefore strongly opposed to the authoritarian elements in the Utilitarian ideal. Nevertheless, although he consciously rejected Utilitarian principles, he had assimilated many of the practical attitudes of Utilitarian political science. To Macaulay, reform of the law was a rational and immediate objective, a matter of efficiency rather than of social engineering in the interests of fundamental improvement in Indian character and society. In effect, Macaulay's arrival in India removed the threat to the Cornwallis system of minimum interference, for his aim was to recondition, not to destroy.

Utilitarian theorists believed that legislation should be simply expressed and that 'public opinion' should be made aware of the reasons behind it. Bentham maintained that the best way of limiting abuse of power by the executive was to give the widest possible publicity to these reasons. In his Minute of May 11th, 1835, Macaulay supported this view which had been stated by a member of council, Alexander Ross. It was particularly important in India to explain the reasons for legislation, he said, because India was 'perhaps the only country in the world where the press is free while the Government is despotic. In all other despotic States, writers are afraid to criticize public measures with severity. In all other States where free political discussion is allowed, there is some public assembly in which the authors of laws have an opportunity of vindicating those laws. If the emperor of Russia puts forth an ukase, no Russian writes about it except to defend it. If an English or French minister brings forward a law, he has an opportunity of arguing for it in Parliament or in the Chambers, and his arguments are read by hundreds of thousands within a few hours after they have been uttered. We [the English in India] are perhaps the only rulers in the world who are mute on political questions, while all our subjects are unmuzzled. Our laws are the only laws which are exposed naked and undefended to the attacks of a free press.'

Though Macaulay's point was a good one, it must be remembered that the press in India at this time was almost entirely European-owned and in the English language. Generally speaking, it reflected only the entrenched interests of the British community. The 'public opinion' which was in any way influenced by the press was that of an extremely small minority, and it was certainly not *Indian* public opinion except in the case of the few Indians who could read English.

It was, however, decided that, when legislation had passed into law, it should be translated into a number of Indian languages. This, of course, was 'for information only'. There was no real question of inviting public criticism of proposed legislation before it was passed; *draft* legislation was to be published only in English. The views of the governor-general-in-council were succinctly expressed in a letter, sent to the government of Bengal, outlining the method of publicizing legislation. 'It would seem also advisable that the drafts of Acts should be made known to the native community before they are passed into law by which means the Governor-General-in-Council doubts not that many valuable suggestions might be offered to Government; but his Lordship in Council apprehends that this object could not be attained except by the sacrifice of much time, for it is obvious that the ordinary period of six weeks' notice would be far from sufficient for this purpose. There may besides be other objections in the present state of society to invite the opinions of the entire native community of the legislative projects of Government.' Efficiency was the watchword, and though there are indications that Macaulay himself would have liked to consult a much wider spectrum of public opinion, it was certainly quite impractical to do so without some machinery for surveying that opinion.

By 1838, the age of reform in India was over. After Bentinck's departure in 1835, little progress was made. Indeed, there was some regression. In Bengal, the Cornwallis system returned temporarily and the offices of collector and magistrate were separated – although they were to be reunited once and for all in 1859. Macaulay's draft legal code was referred to the judges in the presidencies for their comments. The government – as one writer lamented in the *Edinburgh Review* in 1841 – was so preoccupied with external problems that it had 'no adequate leisure for civil concerns of the utmost importance to the happiness of millions'. But there was more to it than just preoccupation on the part of the government of India. As the intellectual climate had earlier created a desire for reform in India, so a change in that climate brought about a change of attitude. When James Mill died in 1836, there died with him the eighteenth-century belief in man's perfectibility and the power of political institutions to produce it. The Victorians were not quite so sure of themselves, nor quite so ambitious to change the world overnight. Certainly, they were optimistic. But they were cautious, too.

The Utilitarian ideal, however, did not vanish into limbo in India. In Sind (annexed 1842) and the Punjab (finally absorbed in 1849), the form of government used was very close to the pattern of Bentham and Mill. There was no division between executive and judiciary. A highly disciplined body of men ruled the country. The Punjab administration was planned on military lines and, though in matters of executive strategy the man on the spot had discretion to act, his actions could be appealed against to higher authority. To ensure the validity of this right to appeal, each officer had to keep records, and any case sent for higher decision resulted in a demand for a personal report on the officer's part. The District Officer was also subject to inspection. The Punjab system, in fact, had its origins in the methods used by Charles Metcalfe – a paternalist by conviction – when he administered the newly-acquired Delhi Territory in 1811–19 and 1825–27. But the Punjab system was not a resurrected paternalism, although the men who operated it have often been shown, particularly by nineteenth-century British historians and their followers, as almost Biblical figures, striding about like Old Testament prophets, insisting upon 'simple' values, and exhibiting a patriarchal sentiment for the 'eternal' Indian village. Their system was a highly efficient and rigidly controlled military government designed to impose, in the shortest possible time, the scaffolding of a civilized state. The Utilitarian ideal was most apparent in the system of regular reports and collection of statistics, and the *animateur* of the system was not so much John Lawrence, who has received most of the praise, as Lord Dalhousie (governor-general 1848–56).

Dalhousie was an authoritarian reformer in the Utilitarian mould, but he admitted no slavish adherence to abstract political theories. He was an active modernizer. He expanded the area of direct British rule. He considered the remaining native states to be anachronistic, and would have been delighted to annex them all. Primarily, however, Dalhousie was determined to transform India into a modern state. He created new, all-India departments to deal with civil engineering works, telegraphs, railways and the post office. Uniformity of management and unity of authority were his guiding principles – and the phrases themselves have the authentic Utilitarian sound. But paradoxically, Dalhousie also encouraged the transformation of the Legislative Council into a sort of parliament, and advocated the appointment of Indian members to the council.

By the time the Charter Act came up for renewal in 1853, most opinion, both British and Indian, was opposed to Dalhousie's plans. The Act tinkered with the administration, but it was obvious that the Company's tenure was running out and that the day was not far distant when the Crown would take over the direct administration of India.

Despite the anticipated change in the relationship between Britain and India, which gave rise to some uncertainties, the general movement of reform associated with the name of Dalhousie continued to influence the existing system. The movement had the guarded approval of all who maintained an interest in India, whether they were theoreticians of government or businessmen anxious to enhance their profits. It represented, in effect, a new climate of optimism in England, where the industrial troubles of the Hungry Forties were over and a new wave of prosperity had hit the manufacturing classes. Again, the ideals and hopes which had inspired the first reformers produced the heady vision of an anglicized India. Again, too, education appeared as the key to happiness and greater markets for British goods. Now, too, had come the great single tool of material progress – for India was about to enter the railway age. Charles Trevelyan, who had written in 1838 of the regenerating virtues of English schooling, hailed the railway as the means by which 'the whole machinery of society will be stimulated' and 'every other improvement whatever, both physical and moral' intensified. The renewed belief in the *mission civilisatrice* of commerce and education was even to survive the shock of the Mutiny of 1857.

## LAW

Though pre-British India had its systems of law and legal institutions, both Hindu and Muslim, they had generally speaking ceased to function or been distorted by the operation of irresponsible force during the collapse of the Mughal empire. The village *panchayat*, the most widely surviving judicial institution, had no precise code of law, and its actions were governed by customs and precedents which were often purely local in character and acceptance. In the strict sense, the *panchayat* was not a court of law but of arbitration. It functioned only with the consent of those involved in a dispute, and had no powers of enforcement. Nevertheless, it did have certain techniques of coercion. These were known as *takaza* and *dharna*. Both were a form of blackmail. If one of the parties involved in a dispute refused to have it heard by the *panchayat*, the other party might begin by employing *takaza*. This method was described by Mountstuart Elphinstone in 1819. 'If a man have demand upon his inferior or equal he places him under restraint, prevents his leaving his house or eating, and even compels him to sit in the sun until he comes to some accommodation. If the debtor were a superior, the creditor had first recourse to supplications and appeals to the honour and sense of shame of the other party; he laid himself on his threshold, threw himself in his road, clamoured before his door, or he employed others to do this for him.' If *takaza* failed, *dharna* might be employed – a method which involved the gods. A person 'sitting *dharna*' would fast on the other party's doorstep, on the principle that, if the man fasting died, his death was the responsibility of the other and would bring down the wrath of the gods upon him. This was a method frequently used by Maratha troops in an endeavour to extract arrears of pay from their masters.

At the same time as Hindu law, there existed the Islamic system which had been introduced into India by the Mughal conquerors. The civil system applied only to Muslims, and was never at any time imposed on Hindus. Like Hindu law, it was mainly concerned with personal relations – marriage, property, and so on. But, under the Mughals, Muslim *criminal* law applied to both Muslims and Hindus. By and large, in the eighteenth century, the Muslim penal code was far more enlightened than English law. The death penalty was rarely imposed, at a time when in England it was the punishment for over one hundred and fifty offences. The Mughals, however, made no attempt to develop an organized system of law designed to regulate disputes between members of the two principal religious communities in India, nor did there exist any machinery of justice – for there was no law of evidence, or of procedure.

The first concern of the British when they came to establish their rule was to organize the administration of justice. The foundations were laid during the government of Warren Hastings in Bengal and, with modifications, the system then established survived until the end of British rule. Hastings' first principle was that courts should be open to all, whatever their religion. Such courts (*mafassal*) were set up in the administrative areas known as 'districts', and two other courts (*sadr*), civil and criminal, were created to act as courts of appeal. The courts were Company institutions, first established in Bengal and then, as British dominion spread, in the other provinces. Further Supreme Courts were set up first in Calcutta and later in Madras and Bombay, which were intended by the British parliament as instruments to control the excesses of the Company's servants in India. The Calcutta Supreme Court was instituted by the Regulating Act of 1773, and its chief purpose, according to Edmund Burke, 'was to form a strong and solid security for the natives against wrongs and oppressions of British subjects resident in Bengal'. This court, and those later established in Madras and Bombay, were independent of the governor-general and were known as King's Courts. They administered English law, but their jurisdiction was limited to the three towns. Furthermore, to Indians they were required to apply customary law, either Hindu or Muslim. This dual system of law, English and customary, was maintained until 1861.

The British parliament had been deliberately vague about the range of the Supreme Court's jurisdiction – a fact whose implications, according to Warren Hastings, posed a real threat to indigenous Hindu and Muslim law. 'The people of this country [Bengal]', he maintained, 'do not require our aid to furnish them with a rule for their conduct or a standard for their property.' This was an emotional judgement, for it was not based upon any knowledge of the real nature of Hindu or

Muslim law, and Hastings set about supplying the deficiency by encouraging the translation of Hindu and Muslim law books.

The principle was established that, in all disputes concerning family relationships and religious institutions, communal laws should be applied. But the discovery of what those laws actually were was a slow process. Ancient texts and commentaries were translated, and the British assumed – particularly in the case of Hindu law – that they represented an organized system and applied them as such. It took some time for the British to discover that there was no uniformity of practice or interpretation, and that the Hindu treatises they had translated represented ideal systems expressed in the vaguest terminology, systems which had never – within living memory at least – dictated common usage. The texts so laboriously translated by such oriental scholars as Sir William Jones were crushingly described by James Mill as 'a disorderly compilation of loose, vague, stupid or unintelligible quotations and maxims: selected arbitrarily from books of law, books of devotion, and books of poetry; attended with a commentary which only adds to the absurdity and darkness; a farrago by which nothing is defined, nothing established'.

During the period of British expansion, the problems of that expansion – including warfare and the pacification of annexed territories – kept justice, as well as government, on the level of improvisation. The British did not want to interfere with the customs of the country, partly because they only slowly discovered what these actually were, and partly because they were unwilling to create antagonism to their rule by interfering with what, in essence, was the religion of the people.

With modifications, Muslim criminal law was applied in those areas where it had previously been practised. The modifications took considerable time to become effective. As late as 1789, for example, robbers were still being punished in Bengal by having an arm or a foot lopped off.

In areas which had been subject to Maratha rule, criminal law had ceased to exist and had been replaced by a variety of local customs. Rather than restore the Hindu penal system – if it had been possible to do so, which is doubtful – English law was applied. In civil matters, where custom was known, this was respected. Where none existed, judges were expected to settle the matter according to equity.

An enquiry made preparatory to the renewal of the Company's charter in 1833 revealed a situation of confusion and disorder, and the Charter Act took the first steps towards codifying the law of British India. The aim, in the words of Lord Macaulay who presided over the Indian Law Commission set up in 1834, was to prepare a body of law which, while deferring to Indian conditions of religion and caste, would secure 'uniformity where you can have it, diversity where you must have it, but in all cases certainty'.

Until the new codes came into force after 1858, the British tried to retain and improve on the criminal law they had found when they began to exercise power in India. 'The foundation of our criminal law', wrote Sir George Campbell in 1852, 'is still the Mahommedan [i.e. Muslim] code; but so altered and added to by our regulations, that it is hardly to be recognised; and there has, in fact, by practice and continual emendative enactments, grown up a system of our own, well understood by those whose profession it is, and towards which the original Mahommedan law and Mahommedan lawyers are really little consulted. Still the hidden substructure on which the whole building rests is this Mahommedan law; take which away, and we should have no definition of, or authority for punishing, many of the most common crimes'.

By the time the Law Commission began its work, a great deal of Muslim and Hindu criminal law had been overlaid by Regulations – i.e. laws passed by the governor-general – though, as the commission reported with specific reference to Muslim law, it retained 'enough of its original peculiarities to perplex and encumber the administration of justice'.

The incompatibility of Muslim criminal law and Western practice had been discovered at an early stage. Muslim law, for example, permitted a 'blood price' to be the punishment for murder, a fine whose amount varied according to the murderer's ability to pay. Under Muslim law, a crime against the person was *not* a crime against the state. No Muslim could be prosecuted on the evidence of a non-Muslim (which placed non-Muslims in an inferior position before the law). No Muslim could be punished for murder if he could prove that the murder took place while he was attempting to convert his victim to Islam.

In 1790, Cornwallis had instructed all Muslim judges to take into account the motive, nature, and circumstances. He also established the principle that a crime of any sort was an offence against the state, and ordered judges to take notice of every crime, even if – as was permitted by Muslim law – the injured party did not wish to take action. In 1797, fines were made payable, not to persons, but to the state which then decided how they should be disposed. Modifications in Muslim legal practice continued to be made.

In 1827, Bombay promulgated a statutory penal code applicable to all. In 1832 in Bengal, Muslim criminal law ceased to be applied to non-Muslims. Elsewhere, however, all persons except European British subjects were amenable to Muslim criminal law as modified by various local Regulations. The result was that there was no punishment standard throughout British India for any specific crime. A counterfeiter, for example, was well advised to pursue his trade in Bombay rather than in Madras or Bengal, where the punishment was almost twice as severe. In Bengal, a man selling stamps without a licence was subject only to a fine; in Madras, to a short term in jail. The purchaser went unpunished. In Bombay, however, both seller and purchaser could be sentenced to corporal punishment and five years' imprisonment. It was such inconsistencies as these which offended the Law Commission.

Macaulay, the real *animateur* of the commission, hoped to produce a code which was entirely new rather than a patchwork of others, European and Indian. It was to be a system of law based on universal principles. In his pre-occupation with universality of outlook instead of the narrow requirements of a particular society, Macaulay echoed the views of the eighteenth-century *philosophes*.

The Law Commissioners agreed that they were looking for something new, neither English nor Indian in origin, and remarked that 'the system of penal code which we propose is not a digest of any existing system and . . . no existing system has furnished us even with a groundwork'. The draft code they produced, however, was influenced by the *Code Napoleon* and by Livingston's *Code of Louisiana* – both of which claimed to represent a universal rather than a particularist approach. In spite of this, Macaulay's code – and in essence it was of his devising – was described by Fitzjames Stephen as 'an entirely new and original method of legislative expression'. Its principal, and revolutionary, virtue was that it was clear, precise and exact, and this spirit dominated the whole pattern of subsequent Indian codes. Nevertheless, it took almost thirty years for Macaulay's draft to become the law of British India.

### *The Law relating to Land*

In a country where the vast majority of the inhabitants are engaged in agriculture, laws relating to landholding and tenancy rights are of paramount importance, not only to the people involved but to the government, which depends on the land for its primary source of revenue. Generally speaking, during their period of empire-building in India the British improvised regulations as they went along, to satisfy the needs of everyday administration. One important measure of the period, however, proved to be of lasting character. This, Bengal Regulation I of 1793, was commonly known as the Permanent Settlement.

The situation which resulted in the enactment of this Regulation can be summarized as follows. More than half the revenue of Bengal was derived from the land by way of a tax payable on all ground capable of cultivation. When the British assumed direct rule in Bengal, the tax had been collected for over fifty years by men known as *zamindars* who were responsible for remitting to the government the taxes raised on fixed areas, which varied in size. This system undoubtedly encouraged corruption, but the method of tax collection was continued by the British until 1772 for the simple reason given by Robert Clive: 'In the infancy of the Acquisition we were under the Necessity of confiding in the old officers of the Government, from whom we were to derive our knowledge, and whom we therefore endeavoured to attach to our Service by the Ties of Interest, until Experience should render their Assistance less necessary. Policy required we should pursue every Step likely to conciliate the Natives to our Government.'

Under Hastings' administration, however, it was decided that the *zamindars* could be regarded merely as officials of the former administration and therefore ignored. The right to collect revenue on behalf of the government was then auctioned to the highest bidder. As a result, revenue collection fell into the hands of a large number of speculators intent on squeezing a profit from the taxpayer. This, not unnaturally, led to a decline in the revenue. The British next attempted to collect directly through their own agents. This, too, proved unsatisfactory, as the Company's agents knew no more about the land, the system of tenure, or the methods of cultivation than did the British who employed them.

The real problem facing the British was to decide who actually exercised proprietorial rights. They could not tolerate the existence of a society based on custom and tradition, both of which lacked precision. Without an exact definition of private rights and private property incorporated in some written document, how could the role of the state and the individual be adequately circumscribed? The English Whig view was that government existed fundamentally to administer justice, and its basic task was to ensure that the law operated in the interests of the maintenance of private property. It was ingrained in the Whig outlook that landed property was almost part of the law of nature. From landed property, there sprang the natural stratification of society into ranks and classes. To the Whigs, government did not order society; it merely guaranteed that society functioned in a proper and equitable manner. As Lord Cornwallis, who was responsible for the Permanent Settlement, put it in Regulation II of 1793: 'Government must divest itself of the power of infringing, in its executive capacity, the rights and privileges, which, as exercising the legislative authority, it has conferred on the landholders.'

The title of 'landholders' had finally been conferred on the *zamindars*, the men who had collected the land revenue before the days of British rule. Regulation I of 1793 declared that the *zamindars* were to have permanent, heritable and transferable property rights in their estates. But before this decision was arrived at there had been much controversy amongst the British in Bengal. One side maintained that, by the law of India, all land belonged to the ruler, the *zamindars* being merely state officials. The other side insisted – in the words of Sir John Shore, its chief spokesman – that 'the rents belong to the sovereign, the land to the *zamindars*'. Neither of these propositions was fully supported by either Hindu or Muslim law.

Generally speaking, what could be derived from such Hindu law treatises as the *Code of Manu* (composed some time between 300 BC and AD 150) and later works suggested that the ruler was entitled to a share in the produce of the land and that this right was based upon his position as 'protector of the soil'. Other sources did state that the king was the 'lord of land and water'. As with all Hindu law, there was confusion and lack of precision, but in practice it seems to have been generally accepted that the ultimate ownership of the land lay with the ruler. Those who 'possessed' land did so until they were dispossessed – by force. There was nothing in Hindu law to indicate that the possessor-cultivator of land could sell or otherwise mortgage his holding for cash or any other form of payment. Ownership, in the modern sense, was totally unknown to Hindu law. But the cultivator's right to occupy the land he cultivated was as traditional as the ruler's right to a proportion of the produce.

Muslim law did recognize property rights, but it was not precise in matters of land. The law relating to conquered territories differed according to the code of law applied. That which was effective in India – the *hanafi* – permitted the conqueror, instead of dividing up the land among his troops, to leave it in the possession of its present occupants on the understanding that they paid a tax (*kharaj*) of twice the amount which would have been payable by a Muslim. According to the *hanafi* code, once this took place the state had renounced its claim to ownership and recognized the occupants as proprietors. If payments, in kind or cash, were not made as decreed by the state, the land could be taken over by the state or sold to a third party. This was the law. But in practice, the Muslim rulers of India acted as if they were the true owners of the land.

In the Permanent Settlement of Bengal, the British accepted the proposition that the state had been the ultimate proprietor of the land, and then apparently rejected the system in their own case by creating a landlord class vested with absolute proprietory rights. The recipients of this new status – one quite alien to Indian tradition – included tax-farmers, officials, and petty rulers with large estates.

Cornwallis himself was not particularly interested in the controversy over the ultimate ownership of the land or in the pre-British status of the *zamindar*. 'It is immaterial to government', he said, 'what individual possesses the land, provided he cultivates it, protects the *ryot* [cultivator] and pays the public revenue.' Although Cornwallis had been ordered by the Court of Directors to establish permanent rules for the collection of revenue '*according to the law and constitution of India*' (as the Act of 1784 phrased it), he had no alternative but to recognize the *zamindars* – regardless of their legal position in the Hindu or Muslim codes – since he did not have the means of collecting revenue direct from the cultivators.

In Bengal, the assessment of tax payable by the landholder was fixed. It bore no relation to actual economic conditions and was, in effect, a rent payable to the state which could foreclose if the rent were not paid, and sell up the land. One of the main objects of the settlement was to ensure that the revenue was paid, but the framers of the Regulation also hoped that a settled system would lead to agricultural expansion. This did not result. Widespread failure to meet the revenue demand led to the land being sold to rich merchants who had no real interest in the soil. It had been intended that tenant rights should be secured (as in the case of the newly created landlords) subject to the payment of rent, but the plan to give the cultivator the same security in relation to the *zamindar* as the *zamindar* had been given in relation to the state was a failure. The intention had been that the rights of the cultivators should be upheld by a special court, but this proved ineffective primarily because of the difficulty of establishing what the cultivator's rights actually were.

The Regulation enacting the Permanent Settlement was followed by a flood of litigation which almost submerged the judicial process altogether. Delays were so considerable that taking a dispute to court meant virtually abandoning any hope of reaching a decision. In this way, the interests of the cultivators were lost to view, while those of the *zamindars* were entrenched.

As the British expanded their rule, the Bengal system was applied elsewhere in India, although only in those parts of the country where it was possible – however inadequately – to identify some individual or corporate body as the proprietor of the land. In certain parts, notably in Bombay and the southern region of Madras, such a class did not exist. Elsewhere, there was a *zamindari* class which could be recognized as landholders. In Madras, it was proposed that villages should be grouped together into estates which could then be sold by auction, so creating landholders where none had existed before. This was in fact done in certain districts, but after 1802 this form of permanent settlement was progressively abandoned, to be replaced by another system known as *ryotwari* [from *ryot*, or cultivator].

The *ryotwari* system was based on a permanent assessment of the rent payable on all arable land, determined after a survey of fields and other small units. The sum involved was to be paid to the government by annual agreement between the government and the cultivator. The purpose was in fact the same as Cornwallis's – to establish individual property rights in the land. But the type of proprietor was very different. Fundamentally, the *ryotwari* system reflected a completely different concept of relations between the state and the individual. As Sir Thomas Munro, who was responsible for introducing the settlement in Madras, put it: 'Supposing the amount of property to be the same, it would be better that it should be in the hands of forty or fifty thousand small proprietors, than four or five hundred great ones.' There was more to it, however, than a dislike of large landholders. Cornwallis, the Whig, had wanted to protect the individual from state interference. Munro, on the other hand, insisted that the individual both deserved and stood in need of the state's protection. In effect, however, the two systems created a legally protected landholding class – on the one hand, landlords in the English sense; on the other, peasant proprietors.

*Personal Law*

In general terms, the British accepted the view that Hindu and Muslim personal law should not be subject to legislative interference. Such interference as did take place was mainly confined to those areas of custom which offended the conscience of the British, and these are examined in the chapter on 'Social Policy' on pages 116–32).

Nevertheless, personal law had to be administered, and it had to be administered by British courts. In the case of Muslim law, interpretation was comparatively simple as its provisions were much more precisely defined than those of Hindu law. The laws relating to marriage, divorce and inheritance – as well as other matters stemming from these – were categorically laid down in the Koran. As the conquests of Islam had spread, generations of scholars and jurists had attempted to adapt the laws of the Koran to suit different conditions. By the end of the eleventh century, Muslim law had petrified into the forms the British discovered when they arrived in India. It had become excessively rigid. And though legal rigidity is not socially desirable, it did mean that fairly clear-cut answers to specific problems were to be found. British judges had no need to fall back upon their own standards of equity when adjudicating on matters in which there was no written precedent.

Hindu law relating to personal matters was, as in the case of Hindu law concerning land, imprecise and variable. The first written records were (and are) the *smritis*. These records included the *Code of Manu* and later commentaries, of which the most important were those of Vijnanesvara (eleventh century), Hemadri (fourteenth century), and Jimutavahana (fifteenth century). Though this body of law books and commentaries often contained conflicting statements, each was assumed to be of equal authority – though not in every part of India. One commentary would be preferred in a certain part of the country, and there it would have become the settled law.

Until 1864, British judges had no responsibility for making interpretations of Hindu or Muslim law. They were compelled to accept the pronouncement of the Hindu or Muslim law officer attached to the court. The judge was merely a mouthpiece for the law officer. On this basis, the law was applied as though it were contemporary law instead of a dubious collection of variables which were probably obsolete even as customary law and certainly, in large part, irrelevant to the conditions of the day.

The administration of Muslim and Hindu personal law may have been less than adequate, but the dual system left important sections of the population without any law at all outside those areas subject to the jurisdiction of the Supreme Courts. Armenians, Parsees, Jews, Portuguese, and even Eurasians had *no* discoverable system of law. Yet the administration of justice required that the 'customs of the people' should be respected. When problems arose concerning the right of succession to land owned by Armenians, the matter had to be 'dealt with by reference to the customs of the people as they were supposed to have existed in former times and by reference to their priests who advise upon their customs, but there is no established law'. According to the Law Commission, some judges apparently applied English law, some their own idea of equity, and some made vain attempts to take advice from Armenian clerics.

The confusion over personal law and approaches to its administration persisted until after the assumption of power by the Crown, and though a large number of suggestions for settling the problems were made by the Law Commission, no results appeared on the Statute Book until after 1858.

# 3

# *Indian India: Areas of Impact*

## ECONOMIC LIFE

### *Agriculture*

THE confusion over proprietorial rights in the land has already been discussed in 'The Law relating to Land' (page 94 ff). The general purpose of the government's land legislation was to define proprietorial rights as a necessary step towards the efficient collection of revenue. High assessments undoubtedly affected rural solvency, and the ideological implications of the two land systems – *zamindari* and *ryotwari* – resulted in much social disorder and many changes in the rural hierarchies. But, though they produced a great deal of individual misery, the reforms instituted under Company rule did not seriously disturb the traditional agricultural economy. As Britain's rule expanded, rural security grew, freed from irresponsible tyranny and banditry. At the same time, the alien revenue and judicial procedures which were introduced into village life tended to stifle initiative.

In the areas where a permanent settlement on the *zamindari* principle was made, it led to considerable changes in the character of the land-owning classes. The number of absentee and essentially non-rural landlords increased, and the special relationship between landlord and peasant suffered accordingly. The area of land under cultivation increased rapidly, partly because of the changes in ownership and the need for larger cash returns, and partly because of population pressures. But the cultivators themselves did not benefit in any way. In *zamindari* settlement areas, the tendency was towards large estates, which led to a substantial increase in the proportion of landless labourers. This was not the case in *ryotwari* areas.

The social side-effects of Western judicial and revenue procedures helped to petrify existing agricultural techniques, and it was not until the second half of the nineteenth century that the government made any really large-scale attempt to improve them. Nevertheless, within the limits of the Company's finances, some work was done to clean up and refurbish existing systems of irrigation, which had fallen into decay during the troubled years which preceded the expansion of British dominion.* Renovation of canals was only one aspect of the government's activity. Another was the construction of protective embankments designed to prevent rivers from overflowing into low-lying fields during the monsoon. This work was begun in northern India in the 1820s and in southern India in 1834. Unfortunately, in many areas the rise of subsoil water levels led both to salination – which destroyed soil fertility – and to a high incidence of malaria as a result of increased breeding of the anopheles mosquito in stagnant waters.

The company's main agricultural innovations consisted of attempts to exploit, and in some cases introduce, exotic commercial crops such as indigo, opium, cotton, jute, and tea. The production of these crops was almost entirely a European monopoly. Indigenous indigo production was expanded, particularly in Bengal, and the export figures reached about 10,000,000 lb. in 1848–49. The production of tea – whose large-scale cultivation began with the importation of plants and seeds from China and the almost simultaneous discovery of wild plants in Assam – quickly expanded to reach approximately 22,000 lb. in 1851. Opium, which remained a government monopoly until the end of British rule, contributed substantially to the total revenue; £3,309,637 in 1849–50. The importance of the opium trade with China had led to the so-called Opium War of 1839–42. During this war, which was intended to force the Chinese government to allow uninterrupted trade in opium, the Company's opium revenue fell to about £300,000. After its successful conclusion, however, John Capper was able to report (in 1853) that 'at no

* See appendix, 'Irrigation Works', page 114.

period of the history of this article has the trade in it to China been carried on so successfully and so extensively as during the last few years'.

As early as 1788, the Court of Directors of the East India Company had urged the government of Bengal to encourage the growth of cotton. The short staple of Indian cotton was not suitable for machine spinning, and attempts were made to introduce new, long-staple varieties. But shipments of these to Britain declined while imports into Britain from the USA showed a tremendous increase. Many people were convinced that the Company had not really tried. 'The Honourable Company', wrote John Capper, 'have, during a period of about seventy years, introduced a dozen American planters, a score of ploughs, a few hundred bushels of seed, opened a model farm or two, offered some paltry premiums, and lately despatched two hundred cotton-gins for distribution amongst two millions of cultivators; and when all these gigantic efforts, paraded through whole hecatombs of despatches that would supply ample fuel for a hundred suttees – when these have all failed, the red-tapists protest that all has been done that can be done!' In fact, there was considerable resistance to growing long-staple cotton on the part of the cultivators, who preferred to produce an indigenous variety for sale in local markets. Indian cotton continued to have a substantial market in China and other parts of South-east Asia.

All these principally European activities affected agriculture only in that they gave employment to a large number of landless labourers. They were, too, purely local in scale. Indeed, no general statement on the effects of British rule on Indian agriculture before 1858 has any validity. The true index of impact should be the rise or fall in the standard of living, and it has been suggested that a long-drawn-out depression between 1825 and 1854 adversely affected the standard of living in rural India. This seems highly unlikely, but there are no adequate statistics in support of either view. The standard of living cannot, however, be used as a touch-stone, since before the construction of roads and railways, rural India consisted of a vast number of isolated areas which were virtually self-contained and affected only by natural calamities and strictly local disturbances. Trade in agricultural produce was conducted at small local markets, and prices varied from place to place. Bumper crops produced local surpluses and depressed local prices; in the absence of adequate transport facilities, surpluses could not be moved for sale elsewhere. Nor could local shortages be remedied by purchase from other areas.

Local shortages were frequently severe, and famine struck at various parts of India. It brought intense local suffering. An eye-witness of the terrible famine in the Guntur district of Madras in 1833 said: 'The description in *The Siege of Corinth* of dogs gnawing human skulls is mild as compared with the scene of horror we are daily forced to witness in our morning and evening rides. . . . It is dreadful to see what revolting food human beings may be driven to partake of. Dead dogs and horses are greedily devoured by these starving wretches; and the other day, an unfortunate donkey having strayed from the fort, they fell upon him like a pack of wolves, tore him limb from limb, and devoured him on the spot.' Nearly half the population died and more than two-thirds of the livestock. Some relief works were begun, and substantial remissions were made in the revenue demand, but the government had no general famine policy. A similar famine occurred in northern India in 1837. The government's attitude to local scarcity, however, was based upon economic principles and the sacred law of supply and demand which *ought* to have moved food from surplus to scarcity areas and should not be interfered with. Unfortunately, lack of communications inhibited the operation of this law, and relief works usually came too late.

On the whole, governmental interference in the traditional sector of agriculture was confined to the pursuit of policies which were not directly economic in purpose. The effect of the policies varied from place to place and depended, to a large extent, on the ignorance or over-enthusiasm of local British officials. In certain areas, land ceased to be cultivated because of over-assessment or even of brutality on the part of subordinate revenue officers. This state of affairs was only temporary, however, and by 1858 the difficulty was less to produce revenue than to find land for cultivation. Where government policies did have an effect was on the composition of the property-owning classes, the incidence of rural indebtedness, and – by default – the preservation of social customs which tended to reduce the economic viability of landholdings.

There were a number of reasons for the negative attitude taken by the Company's government. There was Britain's attachment to the economic principles of *laissez-faire,* which condemned government interference in the mechanism of supply and demand as particularly mischievous. There were the problems of security facing an alien minority whose principal aim was to preserve civil peace. Direct interference in the modes of traditional agriculture would have meant interference in long-established social customs, and this, in turn, would have led to resentment and possibly revolt – which would have interrupted the collection of that revenue on which the administration depended. The principal reason, however, was that the government was indifferent to indigenous agriculture. Commercial crop production was almost entirely in European hands (though until 1837 Europeans could not own land in India), and the Company itself was more interested in trade until it had to surrender its commercial functions under the Charter Act of 1833.

### *Trade, Industry and Transport*

Before the East India Company conquered Bengal, it had been obliged to send out from England large amounts of bullion (between £400,000 and £500,000 a year) with which to buy goods for export from India. After it gained control of the revenues of Bengal, however, it stopped sending out bullion and used part of the revenues to buy goods. According to Charles Grant, 'in the thirty years following the acquisition of the Bengal provinces, this nation [Britain] by public and private channels, derived from them alone, exclusive of its other Eastern dependencies and of the profits of goods remitted, fifty millions sterling'.

The Company did its best to restrict the activities of British private traders in India, but encouraged foreign traders – because they paid in bullion to the Company's agents. British traders were allowed to transport their goods to Europe only in Company ships. The Company did, however, encourage inland trade. This was in its own interests, since any general rise in prosperity increased Company revenue. On the other hand, by encouraging competition in this way, it was undermining its own monopoly.

The Company's attitude towards British traders, and to its own servants, encouraged clandestine investment. Before 1772, the Company's servants had made substantial profits to the detriment of their masters' profits. When the Company forbade this activity, it was forced to go underground. Native merchants were used as a trading front, and foreign traders as the means by which what were, in effect, illegal profits could be remitted to England. The use of native merchants in this context was to be of supreme importance in helping to create an Indian commercial middle class. The merchants played an extremely active role as middlemen, and the benefits they gained were not only material.

Clandestine European investment in Indian trade had a comparatively short life. The administration continued to restrict direct participation in trade by the Company's servants, and this helped to create new avenues of investment. A number of Company servants left their employment and began mercantile careers, attracting the investments of friends who remained in the Company's service. The need to provide some mechanism for investment led to the creation of the agency house system. The agency houses accepted investment from the Company's military and civil employees and used it for trading in India instead of remitting it home. In these houses, Indians received training in European business methods, and many of them later set up their own organizations on the joint stock principle. They succeeded mainly because the Company prohibited European private merchants from residing in the interior; the agency houses did their business with Indian merchants.

Thomas Bracken was a partner in the largest of the agency houses. 'The commerce of Calcutta', he said, 'was in the hands of a very small number of houses before the opening of the present charter [of 1813]; previous to that time the houses were chiefly formed of gentlemen who had been in the civil and military services, who, finding their habits perhaps better adapted for commercial pursuits, obtained permission to resign their situations, and engage in agency and mercantile business. They had of course a great many friends and acquaintances in their respective services, and from those gentlemen they received their accumulations. They lent them to others, or employed them themselves, for purposes of commerce; they were, in fact, at first the distributors of capital rather than the possessors of it. They made their profits in the usual course of trade, and by the difference of interest in lending and borrowing money, and by commission. In the course of time, carrying on a successful commerce, many became possessors of large capital and returned to this country [Britain] leaving the most part of it there [India]; but the persons who succeeded generally came in without capital of their own, the same system being continued, and those houses became the usual depository of the savings and accumulations of the military and civil services in India.'

Before 1813, the Company's attitude remained, generally speaking, biased against British private merchants. Theoretically, this should have stimulated the business of British agency houses, who could – and were encouraged to – operate on behalf of foreign merchants who brought bullion into the country. But it was the Indian agency houses which benefited, for they transacted business at lower rates than the British. The Americans, for example, who were by far the largest group of foreign merchants operating in the India trade, usually employed Indian firms.

The Company's policies, if they can be dignified as such, were contradictory. The Company held a trading monopoly, but continually encouraged everyone except British merchants to break it. It actively promoted the large-scale production of plantation crops such as indigo and cotton, but prohibited

Europeans from directly owning land. It forced British merchants to use only Company ships, which could not carry the increased cargoes, so the business went to foreign instead of British ships. By denying British merchants access to the interior, the Company allowed itself to be cornered by a new Indian commercial class, which brought goods and produce to Calcutta where the Company had to pay cash for them.

The Charter Act of 1813, however, opened up the India trade to British private enterprise, though some restrictions remained until the Company's economic role was completely abolished in 1833. The opening up of the country was a qualified disaster for indigenous industry. Indian exports of cotton piece-goods declined, after 1815, to a negligible figure, while imports of machine-made cloth from Lancashire, through private traders, rose very substantially. This virtually destroyed the indigenous cotton industry, for the handloom could not compete with the machine, even when that machine was several thousand miles away.

As its commercial activities declined, the Company became convinced that something ought to be done about Indian industry. The Court of Directors, in a despatch of June 11th, 1823, attributed the decline in cotton manufacture to 'the improved state of machinery in Europe, and the protection which the countries in Europe and the United States of North America are giving to their own manufactures by heavy duties on foreign goods or by absolute prohibition' and recommended 'the removal of all unnecessary charges from the native manufacture, especially when it is considered that the piece-goods of Great Britain are introduced into India at a rate of duty considerably lower than that to which the native manufactures are liable on transit within India'. Some transit dues were abolished, but the evidence given by Sir Charles Trevelyan to a Select Committee of the House of Commons in 1840 made it obvious that any remedies would be too late. 'The peculiar kind of silky cotton formerly grown in Bengal, from which the fine Dacca muslins used to be made, is hardly ever seen; the population of the town of Dacca has fallen from 150,000 to 30,000 or 40,000 and the jungle and malaria are fast encroaching upon the town. The only cotton manufactures which stand their ground in India are of the very coarse kinds, and the English cotton manufactures are generally consumed by all above the very poorest throughout India . . . Dacca, which was the Manchester of India, has fallen off from a very flourishing town to a very poor and small one; the distress there has been very great indeed.'

The real decline in indigenous Indian industry began with the increase of imports in cotton goods and continued throughout the nineteenth century. But the decline was patchy. Generally speaking, handicraft industries suffered severely, and there was no way in which the unemployed artisans could be absorbed into the economy except as landless labourers. English handloom weavers had suffered in the same way as Indians by the coming of the machine, but they had found a place (though not without misery) in the new machine-textile industries of Lancashire. In India, it was to be many years before such an industry was established. It was an outstanding feature of the pattern of Indian economic life under British rule that that pattern should be profoundly disturbed by an industrial revolution taking place many thousands of miles away in Britain, without absorbing any of the compensating benefits which would have flowed if the revolution had taken place in India. Nevertheless, the forces of capitalist enterprise reached India and brought profit to the commercial middle classes who were later to develop interests in Indian industry.

Before this came about, however, there was to be a radical change in the overall pattern of India's external commerce. This was brought about partly by the withdrawal after 1824 of the Company's trading investment – which ran at about £2,000,000 per annum – and partly by the severe financial crises of the 1830s, during which a number of agency houses collapsed. The subsequent shortage of capital helped to produce a complex and extremely shaky system of barter. Credit would be obtained in London for, say, a consignment of Manchester cloth, on the basis of a post-dated bill to be settled after the consignment had been sold in India. With the proceeds of the sale in Calcutta, Indian goods would be bought and shipped back to England. These having been sold, the bill could be paid, and the whole uncertain process begun again.

The collapse of the agency houses led to mercantile and managerial functions being separated from the financing side. A number of banks were established, and ultimately, because of the shortage of bullion, paper currency came into being. The establishment of Western-style banking institutions led to a considerable decline in the commercial activities of native bankers. Nevertheless, the economic activities of the Company and of private individuals continued to benefit the growing Indian middle class.

The Hindus of Bengal had been among the first to profit from the introduction of British trading methods, but the Parsee community of Bombay was not far behind. 'The Persees', wrote William Milburn in 1813, 'rank next to the Europeans. They are active, industrious, clever, and possess considerable local knowledge. Many of them are very opulent, and each of the European houses of agency has one of the principal Persee merchants concerned with it in most of their foreign speculations. They have become the brokers and banians [traders] of the Europeans. The factors belonging to these different houses resident in China, Bengal, &c., are generally Persees, and the correspondence is carried on in the country language, so that the British merchant knows no more than they communicate to him.'

The general decline in the Company's commercial activities after 1813 left the expansion of trade in private hands. After 1833, inland transit duties were progressively abolished, as were a number of export duties. In 1848 the double duties which had been imposed on foreign shipping entering Indian ports were abandoned. Once more, the general expansion of trade benefited Indians rather than Europeans, as the Company's restrictions on European immigration remained in force – though in a modified form. In 1852, the number of male Europeans resident in India was only about 6,000 (excluding the army), and of these some 2,000 were in the Company's employ. Except for those engaged in planting, most non-official Europeans remained in the major towns. The extension of commerce resulted in more openings for employment for Indians and gave increased incentive for the establishment of Indian-owned organizations.

Perhaps one of the most significant results of the extension of private trade was the growth of the mercantile community, both Indian and British, as a pressure group. The Calcutta-merchant interest and its influence in Britain has already been mentioned (see page 72) but, as trade organizations were established, it was also able to bring pressure to bear on the government of India. The first such organization, the Calcutta Trade Association, was founded in 1830, and the Calcutta Chamber of Commerce followed four years later. They pressed the government of India for improvements in transport and the building of roads and railways. They demanded that trade should be freed from restrictions, and what they achieved they achieved not only for themselves but for all Indian traders. There was, in fact, a profound identity of interests between the newly-emerging Indian middle classes and the British mercantile community, and this was to have political consequences.

The growth of factory and heavy industry in India was inhibited by Britain's desire to retain India for as long as possible as a market for British manufactures. The Company did help an Englishman establish a modern iron foundry in 1825, but the enterprise failed because supplies of charcoal were inadequate, and coal was not available. It was not until 1855 that a Dundee jute manufacturer brought machinery out to Bengal and established a mill to process the cloth on the spot. An American named Landon built a cotton mill at Baroach in 1853, and another was established in Bombay a year later by a Parsee. Before the end of Company rule, there was considerable expansion in both jute and cotton manufacture.

The late arrival in India of the advanced technology of the industrial revolution resulted in the late emergence of an Indian industrial middle class. But there were other factors peculiar to India which also contributed. In the cotton industry for example, there was little capital. Indian weavers were wage-earners who had little opportunity for saving. Even more important, artisans were a caste and sons followed fathers in their trade because there was no other possible occupation for them within the functional system of caste. There was lack of occupational mobility and there was also a restriction on the mobility of ideas. Techniques improved little, if at all, because 'a ritual law in which every change of occupation, every change in work technique, may result in ritual degradation, is certainly not capable of giving birth to economic and technical revolutions from within itself, or even of facilitating the first germination of capitalism within itself.'

This situation was perpetuated by the lack of control over production; there was no management in a modern sense. The trader, whether he was a European or an Indian middleman, was more interested in keeping up supplies than in technological progress. This conservative attitude petrified traditional methods. Such change as *was* achieved under Company rule owed most to the Company's own servants, who were prepared to invest capital in industrial or quasi-industrial undertakings, in the knowledge that they could use their official positions to protect their investment. For private traders and commercial undertakings, the risk was greater. When private capital did become more adventurous, it confined its investment almost entirely to plantation industries, particularly after 1837 when Europeans were permitted to own land. Industrial investment by Indians was extremely slow in expanding, mainly because Indians had no way of hedging their risks.

The expansion of inland trade – both in indigenous and imported goods – and the parallel expansion of an Indian manufacturing industry were entirely dependent upon the creation of an adequate system of communications. The foundations of such a system were laid during the last years of Company rule, but the advantages were not significantly felt until after the assumption of power by the Crown.

Despite the fact that roads, in any modern sense, were non-existent before the 1830s – and the same could be said for most European countries – British goods did penetrate even to some of the remotest parts of India. In some areas, rivers were extensively used for transport, and steam vessels made their appearance as early as 1828. Away from navigable rivers, such tracks as existed were usually unsuitable for wheeled traffic and disappeared altogether in the rainy season. The government constructed its first road (between Bombay and Poona) in 1830, and in 1839 took the momentous decision to construct a continuous highway from Calcutta to Delhi – linking such roads as already existed, bridging smaller rivers and streams, and supplying ferries and pontoons on the larger ones. This highway became the famous Grand Trunk Road, stretching for over a thousand miles across northern India. Other roads were constructed from Madras to Bombay (800 miles) and from Bombay to Agra (900 miles). Since much of the road-building was dependent on the enthusiasm of District Officers, some areas were better provided for than others.

In 1844 the first serious proposals were made for constructing railways in India. The initiative came from the European business community. The Directors in London were doubtful whether railways could be successfully built in India, because of the difficult terrain and wild extremes of climate. Since Hindus would possibly be barred by their caste customs from travelling by train, it was also open to question whether railways would pay. Although orthodox opinion, when consulted, did not support this theory, the Directors would not agree to do more than sanction the construction of a number of short experimental tracks in the first instance. In 1853, however, the governor-general, Lord Dalhousie, persuaded them that railways would bring very considerable economic advantages. Less than three hundred miles of track were finished before the Mutiny of 1857, but a notable step had been taken towards progress in the years to come.

## *Appendix*

### Irrigation Works

In the general chaos of the eighteenth century, the extensive canal system which had been created by the Muslim rulers of northern India fell into disuse and decay. In 1810, after the Company had acquired the Delhi Territory as a result of the second Maratha war, a committee of survey was set up to discover the state of the canals, but no acceptable plan for renovation could be agreed. In 1815, the governor-general, Lord Hastings, after seeing the situation for himself during the course of an up-country tour, ordered work to be begun on the Western Jumna canal. A general superintendent of irrigation was appointed to Delhi in 1823, and work on the canal – 445 miles in length – went on rapidly. The Eastern Jumna canal was next to receive attention, and work on it was completed in 1830.

The most important irrigation project begun under Company rule was the Ganges canal, which by April 1856 extended to nearly 450 miles of main trunk and feeder branches. In the Punjab, which was finally annexed in 1849, several canals were found to be in good working order, and plans were drawn up for restoring others. The only major construction undertaken there was the Bari Doab canal; 325 miles of this had been excavated by 1856.

In the Bombay presidency, little was attempted. In Madras, a few irrigation works were, however, carried out – entirely because of the enthusiasm of Arthur Cotton, an engineer officer. Against much opposition, he began to build a dam across the Coleroon river in 1836. In 1853, a dam across the Krishna (Kistna) river was also begun.

All the Company's irrigation works were financially profitable. Water dues and, in some cases, increase in the revenue assessments, adequately covered costs. Nevertheless, the Company's attitude remained parsimonious and – even though, after the first major works on the Western and Eastern Jumna canals, it became clear that there was a strong probability of substantial returns – the Directors authorized expenditure only with reluctance and, generally speaking, under the strongest pressure from administrators in India.

## SOCIAL POLICY

### *The objects of Social Legislation*

Even in the first uneasy years of their dominion, the British in India did have a concept of governmental responsibility for the welfare of the people they ruled. It was a concept which had emerged out of the years immediately following the battle of Plassey, when the people of Bengal had suffered from the plundering by the Company's servants. The Regulating Act of 1773 was designed to control the activities of the Company's servants, its chief purpose being, in the words of Edmund Burke, 'to form a strong and solid security for the natives'. Nevertheless, the government was anxious to avoid interfering in the social order. The Court of Directors put it precisely in a despatch sent in 1808 to the governor-general, Lord Minto, on the subject of Christian missions. 'It will be your bounden duty,' they said, 'vigilantly to guard the public tranquillity from interruption and to impress upon the minds of all the inhabitants of India, that the British faith, upon which they rely for the free exercise of their religion, will be inviolably maintained.' It was the government's function to establish peace and order, to create a climate of justice for all, to *protect* the people from government and its servants, and, in effect, to *preserve* the social order rather than to reform it.

This was the continuing paternalist view of responsibility. But towards the end of the eighteenth century, there had begun to grow in Britain a degree of pressure in favour of opening up the Company's dominions to Christian proselytism (see page 70 ff.). There was a sure conviction that Indian society was in desperate need of reform. This attitude frightened the Company, especially when it was expressed in such uncompromising terms as those used by Charles Grant. 'We cannot avoid recognizing in the people of Hindostan,' he wrote, 'a race of men lamentably degenerate and base; retaining but a feeble sense of moral obligation; yet obstinate in their disregard of what they know to be right, governed by malevolent and licentious passions, strongly exemplifying the effects produced on society by a great and general corruption of manners.' The evangelicals – in Britain, at least – did not believe that man could be reformed by legislation, but they did believe that certain practices which offended against 'moral law' should be removed by act of government. William Wilberforce and his associates procured the cessation of the slave trade, and it was necessary – necessary, that is, to the conscience of British Christians – that the government of India should proceed against similar evils.

The Company resisted both missionaries and reform, but the terms of the Charter Act of 1813 compelled it to allow some Christian activity in Company territories. It did its considerable best, however, to impede what it regarded as the unsettling work of missionaries. Nevertheless, some of the Company's own servants, both civil and military, were becoming so conscious of their 'Christian duty' that one of the leading protagonists of non-interference, Sir Thomas Munro, was driven to protest in 1821 that he could not share the faith 'in the modern doctrine of the rapid improvement of the Hindoos, or of any other people. The character of the Hindoos is probably much the same as when Vasco da Gama first visited India, and it is not likely that it will be much better a century hence. When I read, as I sometimes do, of a measure by which a large province had been suddenly improved, or a race of semi-barbarians civilized almost to Quakerism, I throw away the book.'

The government's policy, however, could not fail to be influenced by the general pressure against its toleration of the less humane practices of Hindu society. Slavery had early attracted the attention of British administrators. In 1774, Warren Hastings had expressed the opinion that it must be abolished – though two years earlier a law had been passed decreeing that the families of convicted bandits (dacoits) were to be sold into slavery. This had been defended on the grounds that slaves were very well treated in India. Sir William Jones, in an address to a Calcutta jury in 1785, discounted this argument: 'Hardly a man or woman exists in a corner of this populous town who hath not at least one slave child, either purchased at a trifling price or saved for a life that seldom fails of being miserable. Many of you, I presume, have seen large boats filled with such children coming down the river for open sale at Calcutta. Nor can you be ignorant that most of them were stolen from their parents or bought for perhaps a measure of rice, in time of scarcity.' In 1789, Lord Cornwallis tried to put a stop to slave trading by issuing a proclamation forbidding the collection of adults and children for export overseas or to parts of India not under British control.

The British parliament's anti-slavery legislation of 1807 led to renewed interests in Indian slavery. Conditions differed throughout India, but there could be no doubt that slavery was widespread or that the slave trade was extremely profitable. The government moved slowly, however, unwilling to alienate the powerful commercial interests involved in the trade. In 1811, it went so far as to forbid the importation of slaves into British India, but Charles Metcalfe observed in 1812 that the number of slave merchants in Delhi was actually increasing. He took action first and informed the government afterwards. 'Being satisfied that it was not the intention of the Government that this iniquitous traffic should be encouraged,' he reported, he had taken steps to prohibit 'this abominable commerce ... the sale of Human beings in the town and country of Dihlee [Delhi].' He was severely censured for extending his prohibition to include the resale of slaves, 'a measure which his Lordship in Council was not prepared to sanction'. Persons already slaves were to remain subjects to resale.

In 1832, the purchase or sale of slaves between one administrative district and another was prohibited, but transactions within a district still remained legal. In 1833, the Charter Act required the governor-general to abolish slavery – but only when it was practicable and safe to do so. In fact, the sale of children continued even in Calcutta, the seat of government, until an Act was passed in 1843 prohibiting the legal recognition of slavery. This was an attempt at indirect abolition, but it was only when the new penal code was enacted after the assumption of power by the Crown that the trade in, and possession of, slaves finally became illegal. The effects of even this legislation were slow. There was no emancipation of slaves, and only the most lethargic drift away to other occupations.

The problems of human sacrifice and female infanticide first attracted government action in 1802. After an investigation made by the Baptist missionary, William Carey, into the religious background of the custom of throwing Hindu children to the sharks at Saugor island in Bengal, Lord Wellesley had the practice suppressed. Female infanticide was discovered to be more widespread, existing not only among some so-called primitive tribes but also among certain Rajput castes. By a Bengal Regulation (XXI) of 1795, the practice was declared to constitute murder, and the territory to which the Regulation applied was extended in 1804. But the practice continued, and it was extremely difficult to suppress without actually penetrating into people's homes. The energy of a number of administrators slowly wore the practice down, both in British India and in some princely states where the British were even more reluctant to interfere, but although a number of states prohibited female infanticide, it still proved impossible to stamp it out completely. William Sleeman, making a journey through the independent kingdom of Oudh in 1849–50, asked a respectable Rajput landowner about infanticide and was told that the custom of destroying female infants was of great antiquity. One of the reasons for it, he was told, was that it was impossible for a child to marry outside her own caste. Sleeman thought the custom 'a misfortune, no doubt', but felt that it 'could not be got rid of'. Mothers 'wept and screamed a good deal when their first female infants were torn from them, but after two or three times giving birth to female infants, they become quiet and reconciled to the usage, and say "do as you like"; that some poor parents did certainly give their daughters for large sums to wealthy people of lower clans, but lost their caste for ever by so doing; that it was the dread of sinking, in substance from the loss of property, and in grade from the loss of caste, that alone led to the murder of female infants; that the dread prevailed more or less in every Rajput clan, and led to the same thing, but most in the clan that restricted the giving of daughters in marriage to the smallest number of clans.'

The infant was usually destroyed in the room where it was born. According to Sleeman, the juice of a particular shrub was placed in the child's mouth, which was then covered with the faeces which first passed from its bowels. When the child was dead – and sometimes when it was not – it was buried in the earth that formed the floor of the room. The floor was then covered with cow dung, an antiseptic. On the thirteenth day after the burial, the family priest cooked and ate a meal in the room. 'He is provided with wood, ghi, barley, rice and tilli (sesamum). He boils the rice, barley and sesamum in a brass vessel, throws the ghi over them when they are dressed and eats the whole. This is considered as a burnt-offering, and by eating it in that place the priest is supposed to take the whole sin upon himself, and to cleanse the family from it. . . . After the expiation the parents again occupy the room, and there receive the visits of their family and friends, and gossip as usual.'

It was demonstrated by another Rajput landowner, who came to Sleeman with a petition relating to other matters, just how automatic female infanticide could be. He himself had saved his daughter from death two years earlier. 'When she was born he was out in his fields, and the females of the family put her into an earthen pot, buried her in the floor of the apartment where her mother lay, and lit a fire over the grave; that he made all haste home as soon as he heard of the birth of a daughter, removed the fire and earth from the pot, and took out his child. She was still living, but two of her fingers which had not been sufficiently covered were a good deal burnt. He had all possible care taken of her, and she still lives; and both he and his wife are very fond of her. . . . He had given no orders to have her preserved, as his wife was confined sooner than he expected; but the family took it for granted that she was to be destroyed, and in running home to preserve her he acted on the impulse of the moment. The practice of destroying female infants is so general among this tribe, that a family commonly destroys the daughter as soon as born, when the father is from home, and has given no special orders about it, taking it to be his wish as a matter of course.'

The practice of female infanticide was generally confined to Rajputs, and was regarded with some loathing by other castes. In most cases, however – as the Rajput was generally the landlord – his tenants were reluctant to talk to Sleeman about it. 'Our lives would not be safe for a moment were we to say anything, or to seem to notice such crimes.' This was, perhaps, exaggeration – a case of telling the Englishman what he wanted to hear. Human life in India at the time was held at no great value. Woman was like any other piece of property, a mere chattel, and the fate of a girl child was a matter more for indifference than for horror or sympathy.

As late as 1870, the government was compelled to pass yet another Act attempting to enforce the registration of births and regular verification of the fact that girl children were still alive. Gradually, however, the practice of infanticide was dying out.

Among other abuses which offended against the 'universal moral law' was suttee. The word is an Anglo-Indian one, derived from *sati* (meaning virtuous one), which described the women who performed the rite. The rite itself should properly be called *sahamarana*, 'dying in company with'. The practice was of long standing in India, and virtuous widows usually died in company with their husbands by allowing themselves to be burned to death on a funeral pyre. In general, the rite was confined to high-caste Hindus. The Muslim invaders of India had found it particularly objectionable, and the Mughal emperors had tried to discourage it. In the late seventeenth century, Aurangzeb issued an order that no women should be allowed to immolate themselves by fire. But the practice continued, particularly (as in the case of female infanticide) in the Rajput states. In 1780, the deceased Raja of Marwar was joined in death by sixty-four wives. A Sikh prince of the Punjab took with him ten wives and no less than three hundred concubines.

Such holocausts as these were not offensive to Hindus. Indeed, a suttee was a popular semi-religious festival. Although a number of individual British officials interfered at various times to prevent particular cases of suttee, this was not official policy. In 1803, Lord Wellesley had proposed to abolish suttee in the Company's territories but he had first referred the idea to the Supreme Court in Calcutta. The court's answer was cautious and pedantic. The government, it suggested, would be well advised to be guided by 'the religious opinions and prejudices of the natives'. The government therefore compromised with half measures; in 1812 officials were instructed to permit the rite in cases where it was 'countenanced by their [the Hindu] religion and to prevent it in others in which it is, by the same authority, prohibited'. This simply meant that suttee voluntarily embarked on by a widow over sixteen years of age and not pregnant would be permitted, although police were to ensure that the suttee *was* voluntary and that women were neither drugged nor consigned forcibly to the flames. Understandably, the government's attitude was ineffective in reducing the number of suttees. In fact, the presence of a police official at a widow-burning appeared to give government sanction to the affair. The number of suttees officially reported in Bengal increased from 378 in 1785 to 839 in 1818.

However, the enforced presence of an official at these unpleasant rites brought a strong movement in the 1820s in favour of prohibition. Evidence began to pour in on the government. One Mr Ewer, superintendent of police in Lower Bengal, submitted in 1818 a report on a suttee which is well worth quoting at length, since it gives a good description of what most suttees were like. 'There are very many reasons for thinking that such an event as a voluntary suttee rarely occurs; few widows would think of sacrificing themselves unless overpowered by force or persuasion, very little of either being sufficient to overcome the physical or mental powers of the majority of Hindu females. A widow, who would turn with natural instinctive horror from the first hint of sharing her husband's pile, will be at length gradually brought to pronounce a reluctant consent because, distracted with grief at the event, without one friend to advise or protect her, she is little prepared to oppose the surrounding crowd of hungry Brahmins and interested relations. . . . In this state of confusion a few hours quickly pass, and the widow is burnt before she has had time to think of the subject. Should utter indifference for her husband, and superior sense, enable her to preserve her judgement, and to resist the arguments of those about her, it will avail her little – the people will not be disappointed of their show; and the entire population of a village will turn out to assist in dragging her to the bank of the river, and in keeping her on the pile.'

The general disgust of the Company's servants, both civil and military, brought pressure to bear both on the government of India and on the Court of Directors in London. Religious and humanitarian societies in Britain published many pamphlets, some of them written by Indian administrators. But the government of India itself did little, although it allowed considerable discretion to its officials on the spot, who could permit or prevent a suttee as they thought fit. The government continued to submit a wide variety of reports to the Directors in London, from people who believed that such a long-established tradition should be left alone, and others who advocated complete and immediate prohibition. Suttee did, in fact, have some religious sanction, but many men other than Ewer were convinced that widows were encouraged to burn themselves by relatives anxious to increase their share in the dead husband's estate.

The Directors in London were under intensive fire, and on June 17th, 1823 they wrote to the governor-general. 'You are aware that the attention of parliament and the public has lately been called to the subject [of suttee]. It appears that the practice varies very much in different parts of India both as to the extent to which it prevails and the enthusiasm by which it is upheld. . . . It is upon intelligible grounds that you have adopted the rules which permit the sacrifice when clearly voluntary and conformable to the Hindu religion. But to us it appears very doubtful (and we are confirmed in this doubt by responsible authorities) whether the measures which have been taken in pursuance of this principle have not tended to increase rather than to diminish the practice. It is moreover with much reluctance that we consent to make the British Government, by specific permission of the suttee, an ostensible party to the sacrifice; we are averse also to the practice of making British courts expounders and vindicators of the Hindu religion when it leads to acts which not less as legislators than as Christians we abominate.' The Directors, however, left it to the governor-general's discretion to do whatever his 'superior means of estimating consequences may suggest'.

The governor-general, Lord Amherst, was convinced that the time was not right for abolishing suttee by legislative action. Hindus had presented petitions to the government protesting against preventive action on the part of officials. When the Bengali reformer, Ram Mohun Roy, wrote pamphlets to prove that suttee was not sanctioned by the Hindu scriptures, they aroused so much opposition that he went in fear of his life. Amherst preferred to wait and see, and to hope that 'the more general dissemination of knowledge among the better-informed Hindus themselves might . . . prepare gradually the minds of the natives for such a measure.'

When Lord William Bentinck arrived in 1828, however, there was a change of tempo. The Directors had instructed him to take steps to end the practice of suttee – whether gradually or immediately was for him to decide. Bentinck's own temperament inclined him towards instant reform. Though Ram Mohun Roy and a leading British orientalist, Horace Hayman Wilson, both submitted that a gradual approach would arouse no discontent and was much to be preferred, Bentinck could anticipate no such discontent from immediate abolition. Charles Metcalfe, who had prohibited suttee in Delhi when he was Resident there, was by now a member of the governor-general's council. Although he thought that abolition might possibly be used 'by the disaffected and designing to inflame the passions of the multitude and produce a religious excitement', he nevertheless believed that the time would come 'when it will be universally acknowledged by the people of India as the best act performed by the British Government. My only fears, or doubts, are as to its early effect, and those are not so strong as to dissuade me from joining heartily in the suppression of the horrible custom by which so many lives are cruelly sacrificed.'

On December 4th, 1829, suttee was declared illegal in the Bengal Presidency (Regulation XVII). By this Regulation, anyone assisting a voluntary sacrifice was to be held guilty of culpable homicide, and anyone using violence to force a widow to burn herself was to be liable to the death sentence. A similar resolution was passed in Madras on February 2nd, 1830, and action was also taken to make it effective in Bombay. The Regulation aroused considerable agitation in Bengal, and a petition was submitted to Bentinck, protesting strongly against it. The petitioners even went so far as to appeal to the Privy Council in London (January 1830). However, the Directors presented an overwhelming case in favour of abolition, and they were reinforced by Ram Mohun Roy, who took to England a petition supporting the abolition of suttee. He himself presented it to parliament. The appeal was dismissed, and there were no disturbances in India.

The practice of suttee lingered on for some time in various princely states, in the Punjab and the Rajputana, the last case occurring in Udaipur in 1861. As recently as 1932, however, the London *Times* reported a case of attempted suttee. At the last moment, the widow was saved from the flames by police action – in the course of which, ironically, three other persons were killed.

Another act of government aroused no public hostility, because its practical advantages were plain to everybody. This was the campaign for the suppression of Thuggee. The word 'thug' was probably derived from the Sanskrit verb *thagna* (to deceive), and the men who were called Thugs should more accurately be termed *phansidar*s (noose-holders), because strangulation was the method they used for murdering their victims before robbing them.

The practice of Thuggee was of considerable antiquity. It is mentioned in a fourteenth-century history, and probably dates back very much further. During the reign of Shah Jahan – the Mughal emperor who built the Taj Mahal at Agra – the French traveller, de Thevenot, reported that the road between

Delhi and Agra was infested by Thugs, 'the cunningest Robbers in the World . . . They use a certain slip with a running noose which they can cast with so much slight about a Man's Neck when they are within reach of him, that they never fail; so that they strangle him in a trice.' The British first began to realize that there was a murder organization operating towards the end of the eighteenth century, but they did not begin effective action against it until 1829.

The Thugs were not ordinary criminals who murdered simply for gain. Their activities and their methods were ringed by divine sanction. According to their legends, in the remote past a great demon had roamed the earth devouring man as he was created. The earth was empty; no life could exist. Then the goddess Kali, 'the black one' – another face and form of Parvati, wife of Siva – came to the rescue. She battled with the demon and cut him down, but from every drop of blood that spilled to earth another demon appeared. The more of these killed by Kali, the more appeared. At last, in desperation she turned to more subtle methods. Herself exhausted – for even the gods can suffer divine fatigue – she fashioned two men from the perspiration of her arms. To each she gave a square of cloth, and commanded them to kill the demons without shedding any drop of blood. Her command was obeyed, and soon all the demons were strangled. The two men, their task over, offered back the squares of cloth, but Kali refused them, bidding the men keep the cloths as a remembrance of her and use them as implements of a profitable trade.

It was William Sleeman who proved the existence of the powerful Thug confederacy operating over the whole of northern India. In 1829, in the course of his reforms, Lord William Bentinck authorized a special department to investigate and destroy the practice of Thuggee, and Sleeman was placed in charge of the whole operation in 1835. In 1839 he was appointed Commissioner for the Suppression of Thuggee and Dacoity. The Thug gangs were often protected by petty rajas and landowners, as well as by revenue-farmers who shared their profits. But the British were determined to suppress Thuggee once they had grasped its proportions. Revolted by the thought of murder for gain, and horrified by the supposed religious sanction given to it by Hinduism, they attacked the menace of Thuggee with single-minded energy – and stamped it out.

The process of suppression was complex and difficult, for the British were sticklers for legality. Evidence *was* collected, however, and between 1831 and 1837 more than three thousand Thugs were convicted. Five hundred of these saved their skins by becoming 'approvers', or informers. The approvers were detained in special prisons, the principal one being at Jubbulpore. Condemned Thugs appeared to suffer from no remorse. Indeed, one told an English officer that his only regret was that he had been caught before he had reached his target of a thousand murders. He was much upset at being halted at 719. By 1860, Thuggee was no more, though the office of Superintendent of Thuggee and Dacoity was maintained until 1904.

Once these great and rather dramatic exercises in reform had been initiated, the government felt it had interfered enough. Apparently, the reaction to reformist legislation had been slight; in fact, the impact was very real as was to be shown by the Mutiny of 1857. The general movement of reform became subsidiary to the government's military preoccupations from the end of the 1830s on, though there was little reduction in reformist pressures either in Britain or in India. Much of this agitation was concerned with the position of women in Hindu society.

The history of female education is dealt with in an appendix in Part Two. Broadly speaking, the government was not willing to provide education for women, and did not do so until the end of Company rule; most schools for girls were the product of missionary activity. In response both to missionary pressure and the infiltration of general ideas of Western liberalism, a certain amount of agitation did, however, grow up over the status of women in general and widows in particular. A number of Indians proposed legislation to raise the minimum marriage age, and to permit the remarriage of Hindu widows.

Although the government preferred not to initiate legislation itself, and generally resisted attempts to pressurize it into enacting legislation which it believed would interfere in religious matters, it allowed itself to be persuaded by Isvarchandra Vidyasagar to pass the Hindu Widows Remarriage Act of 1856.

Hindu polygamy was another matter which brought many petitions to the government between 1855 and 1857. In 1855, the Maharaja of Burdwan described the evils he believed should be legislated against. The particular offenders were a Brahmin caste in Bengal known as Kulins. 'Those Koolins,' wrote the maharaja, 'who cannot get persons of equal caste willing to effect matrimonial alliances with them, nor afford the large marriage gratuities which are demanded, are obliged to let their daughters arrive at old age without being married. Koolin Brahmins never marry without receiving large donations and multiply wives for the sake of obtaining those gratuities without knowing or caring what becomes of the women to whom they are united by the most solemn rites of their religion. They have been known to marry more than a hundred wives each; and it is customary with them, immediately after going through the nuptial ceremony and receiving their gratuities, to leave the houses of the girls they have married, never to see their faces more.' Legislation was drafted but the outbreak of the Mutiny held up proceedings, and when the lieutenant-governor of Bengal later asked the government of India to enact legislation it refused, on the grounds that it might set a precedent which might not be approved by others practising polygamy (principally Muslims) outside Bengal.

Of the period up to 1857, it can be said that certain essential reforms were achieved as a result of legislative action stimulated by a positive desire for reform. The limits of security, however, made the government distinctly reluctant to go further. Western ideas, both secular and religious, had their effect on Indian intellectuals, and Hindu reform movements emerged in response to both governmental reforms *and* the government's unwillingness to do more.

The reaction of the masses to innovation and reform is difficult to assess. There was certainly bewilderment and resistance. That legislation against infanticide, suttee and Thuggee was widely accepted was due, in the main, to the fact that the first two were not generally practised and the third was a physical menace which most people were glad to have removed. When it came to such matters as female education and widow remarriage, however, no legislation – however enlightened – could be enforced. Such legislation as was passed was mostly ignored.

There was undoubtedly a measure of real fear over certain aspects of Westernization. Macaulay's famous description of the effects of British justice, though exaggerated, rests on a basis of truth. The Supreme Court of the time of Warren Hastings, he wrote, began a reign of terror, 'of terror heightened by mystery; for even that which was endured was less horrible than that which was anticipated. No man knew what was next to be expected from this strange tribunal. . . . It consisted of judges not one of whom spoke the language, or was familiar with the usages, of the millions over whom they claimed boundless authority. Its records were kept in unknown characters; its sentences were pronounced in unknown sounds. . . . No Maratha invasion had ever spread through the province such dismay as this inroad of English lawyers. All the injustice of former oppressors, Asiatic and European, appeared as a blessing when compared with the justice of the Supreme Court.' During the campaigns against the Marathas in the early nineteenth century, it was said that people fled not from the British army but from fear of the civil court. They had every reason to fear it for its function was to deal with matters of property and property rights, the settlement of debts, and so on, and it was preoccupied with documentary proof in a country where written leases were unknown. This meant that the court's decision could easily lead to a peasant losing his land.

It was not long, however, before Indians learned how to manipulate the courts and, in particular, the European judges – who, as often as not, had little knowledge of the language and even less of customary law. 'Our Courts,' wrote Charles

Metcalfe in 1820, 'are scenes of great corruption. The European Judge is the only part of them that is untainted. He sits on a bench in the midst of a General conspiracy, and knows that he cannot trust any one of the Officers of the Court. Every one is labouring to deceive him and to thwart his desire for justice. The pleaders have no regard for truth.'

The law continued to appear strange and arbitrary. It was a menacing instrument breaking up the old pattern of life, placing traditional customs in peril, and threatening the livelihood of the peasant. Its mechanics brought into being a new class of oppressor, the pleaders, who were enabled by their superior knowledge of the law to take advantage of the peasant. Corruption lay about the courts of law until the end of British rule, and it did not vanish with independence. Instead of appearing as a tangible defence against injustice, the law itself seemed to be – and indeed, by default, acted as – an engine of tyranny. The very real protection that English law did offer could function only if it was asked for and accepted; but the general inclination of ordinary people in India was to avoid the courts.

The effects of the Company government's social policy cannot be divorced from the general effects of Western ideas. The administration and the law courts pressed equally heavily upon the people. Alien in spirit, and operated by aliens, they caused unease and apprehension even though they were not actively oppressive. In northern India, tensions grew inside society which were to be a contributory factor to the Mutiny of 1857.

### *Public Health*

The government of India did not accept any major responsibility for public health until 1880. Until that date, it confined its activities to providing a certain amount of medical relief, some medical education, and nothing more. The reasons for this were fairly straightforward, especially during the period of Company rule. In the first place, medical knowledge was not far enough advanced to do more than recognize the existence of different tropical diseases. Secondly, the British had little expertise in matters of sanitation. And thirdly, when pressure for public health legislation came, it emerged as the result of similar pressure in Britain – where the first national Public Health Act (dealing with sanitation, drinking water, street cleaning, and so on) had not been passed until 1848.

The East India Company had provided a doctor (known as a surgeon) in each of its early settlements. Hospitals were established at these settlements in 1664, but they did not have a particularly good reputation and it was generally believed that the odds on a sick patient recovering were infinitely greater if he stayed out of hospital. The services of the Company's doctors were confined to the Company's servants, soldiers, and the population of the local jail. Mortality was extremely high among Europeans, and contemporary medical science could do little about it. Towards the end of the eighteenth century, a hospital for Indians was opened in Calcutta, and others were established at Madras and Bombay about 1800. By 1840, there were a dozen hospitals in various large towns throughout the British dominions.

As far as indigenous medicine was concerned, there were two main systems. The *ayurvedic* system of the Hindus was of great antiquity and, in some areas, of considerable sophistication. The Muslim *unani* system was a mixture of Greek and Arabic medicine. Both systems had become rigid and unyielding, resistant to experiment as well as to the discoveries of other medical systems. They had become saturated with superstition and, in the eighteenth century, had largely fallen into decline. Early in the nineteenth century, however, the Sanskrit College at Benares and the Madrasa at Calcutta included the study of indigenous medicine in their curricula. In 1822, a separate school for training Indians in Western medical science was opened at Calcutta. It was intended to train assistants for the Company's medical officers. There was, however, 'only one teacher attached to the institution, and he delivered his lectures in Hindustanee. The only medical books open to the pupils were a few short tracts which had been translated for their use into that language; the only dissection practised was that of the inferior animals.... The knowledge communicated by such imperfect means could neither be complete nor practical.'

In the schools teaching indigenous Hindu medicine, there was no dissection of human bodies because of the Brahminical injunction against touching the dead. When the Calcutta Medical College was founded in 1835, most of its students were Muslims who had no prejudice against the practice of anatomy. A Hindu, Pandit Madhusudan Gupta, did, however, perform a dissection in January 1836 and though it aroused horror among the orthodox he was hailed as a hero by the progressive. The government even went so far as to fire a salute of guns from Fort William to mark the occasion. Within the next few years, medical colleges were also founded in Bombay (1848) and Madras (1852).

Indians graduating from these new colleges were expected to join the subordinate ranks of the government service. They were not permitted to become members of the Indian Medical Service itself – which was reserved for Europeans – and when Indians were unavoidably appointed to the medical charge of civil stations it usually caused difficulties, as most Europeans did not want to be attended by Indian doctors. Graduates did, however, find a demand for their services among 'natives of rank', and it was reported that 'men, after leaving the medical college, have refused appointments under the Government for the purpose of private practice'. Nevertheless, their services were confined to 'natives of rank' and to the principal towns. Neither government nor private practitioners offered any service to the mass of the people. The government could hardly have done a great deal more than it did, for the state of preventive medicine was not advanced enough for positive action. Inoculation against smallpox had been introduced into India early in the nineteenth century, but it was by no means widely accepted even among Europeans. Christian missionaries began some medical work before 1858 and established colonies for lepers, but they too were inhibited by the limits of medical knowledge.

## EDUCATION

The story of educational progress under Company rule divides conveniently at the year 1835, when it was decided that English should be the language of instruction in higher education and that the purpose of education should be to disseminate Western knowledge. This decision was to have far-reaching effects on India's cultural and political life, and before it was arrived at there was considerable and occasionally bitter controversy between the supporters of what was then called 'oriental education' – using Indian languages as the media of instruction – and the advocates of English. Of the British in India, those who favoured the use of English received strong support from the new Indian middle classes, especially in Bengal, which was the most advanced part of the British dominions. Those who supported the 'oriental' view were seeking, primarily, to perpetuate the attitude the Company had held since it assumed sovereign rights in India.

The type of education the British had found when they arrived in India was almost entirely religious, and higher education for Hindus and Muslims was purely literary. Hindu higher education was almost a Brahmin monopoly. Brahmins, the priestly caste, spent their time studying religious texts in a dead language, Sanskrit. There were a number of schools using living languages, but few Brahmins would send their children to such schools, where the main subject taught was the preparation of accounts. Muslim higher education *was* conducted in a living language – Arabic, which was not spoken in India. But there were also schools which taught Persian (the official language of government in India until 1837, when it was finally abandoned) and some secular subjects.

Hindu and Muslim education had much in common. Both used, in the main, a language unknown to ordinary people. Both systems stuck firmly to traditional knowledge. Muslim education, however, was more democratic than Hindu, for where the latter was confined almost exclusively to the Brahmin castes, the former was open to all Muslims. The state – as distinct from individual rulers – accepted no responsibility for education. Schools existed on private or community funds. As late as 1835, the ancient seat of Hindu learning at Nadia in Bengal still managed to preserve 'its character as a university' because the local rajas 'endowed certain teachers with lands for the instruction and maintenance of scholars.' This was not an isolated example. Muslim schools were similarly supported by Muslim rulers and communities.

By the time the British began to exercise power in Bengal, however, the general state of the country had to some extent reduced private endowments for educational institutions. The new government's first excursion into Indian education followed the traditional pattern of the country. In 1780, a Muslim teacher petitioned Warren Hastings on behalf of a number of leading Muslims and gave him the opportunity to demonstrate that the British were just as concerned with the patronage of education as their predecessors had been. In 1781, suitable quarters were found for a Muslim teacher (*maulvi*) and the Calcutta Madrasa was founded. What Hastings had done for Muslims was later to be done for Hindus. In 1792, a Sanskrit College was established at Benares, whose object was 'the preservation and cultivation of the laws, literature and religion of that nation [the Hindu] at this centre of their faith and common resort of all their tribes'. The scholars at the Sanskrit College were to be examined four times a year in the presence of the British Resident at Benares – except in such religious matters as were not supposed to be discussed in the presence of non-Brahmins. Neither the Muslim nor the Hindu institution proved successful; both were riddled with feuds, the funds were improperly used, and there were frequent reports of 'grave misconduct' and 'disorder'.

In 1811, as is apparent from a rather incoherent Minute (dated March 6th) of the governor-general, Lord Minto, the 'orientalist' school was uppermost. 'It is common remark that science and literature are in a progressive state of decay among the natives of India. . . . The number of the learned is not only diminished, but the circle of learning, even among those who still devote themselves to it, appears to be considerably contracted. The abstract sciences are abandoned, polite literature neglected, and no branch of learning cultivated but what is connected with the peculiar religious doctrines of the people. The immediate consequence of this state of things is the disuse, and even actual loss, of many valuable books; and it is to be apprehended that, unless Government interfere with a fostering hand, the revival of letters may shortly become hopeless from a want of books or of persons capable of explaining them.' Nothing was actually done until the Charter Act of 1813, when the evangelicals managed to have a clause inserted in the charter to the effect that 'it shall be lawful for the governor-general-in-council to direct that ... a sum of not less than one lakh [100,000] of rupees in each year shall be set apart and applied to the revival and improvement of literature and the encouragement of the learned natives of India, and for the introduction and promotion of a knowledge of the sciences among the inhabitants of the British territories in India.' The sum allocated was extremely small and no one seemed to have much idea about how it should be used. The Directors' instructions were, perhaps deliberately, vague and it was 1815 before Lord Moira (later Marquess of Hastings), who was governor-general 1813–23, was able to consider what action might be taken. Hastings' opinion was that there must be improvements in the education of the masses. 'The remedy,' he said, 'is to furnish the village schoolmasters with little manuals of religious sentiments and ethic maxims conveyed in such a shape as may be attractive to the scholars, taking care that while awe and adoration of the Supreme Being are earnestly instilled, no jealousy be excited by pointing out any particular creed.' There were other equally woolly suggestions for helping institutions of higher learning. The Director ignored them all, and for some years the education allocation was not disbursed.

Though the Government appeared incapable of formulating any educational policy, private individuals and organizations were anxious to establish schools. They, unlike the government, wanted to provide Western education in the English language – which, though not explicitly stated, had been the intention behind the clause in the Charter Act of 1813. In

1817, a number of Indians and British established the Calcutta School Book Society and the Hindu College. Their example was followed by others, and more schools teaching English were established, some sponsored by missionaries, others by Indians. Their motives differed. Most Indians saw English education as a passport to official appointments and as a tool of commerce. The missionaries, on the other hand, saw it as a means to conversion through which Indians 'now engaged in the degrading and polluting worship of idols shall be brought to the knowledge of the true God and Jesus Christ whom He has sent'.

The government's slowness in implementing the educational clause of the 1813 Charter Act was partly due to security considerations – for it believed that it was a dangerous policy to interfere in any way with traditional patterns of Indian society – and partly to the pressures of 'orientalist' opinion. It still did not consider it to be the government's duty to sponsor English education. In 1823 it established a General Committee of Public Instruction, whose function was to take charge of existing government educational institutions and to administer the educational grant. The committee was further to inquire into the educational situation and to advise on measures for the better instruction of the people and the 'improvement of their moral character'. But the committee soon found itself overwhelmed by its task. Taking the easy way out, it decided to spend the allocation on supporting Sanskrit and Arabic learning. There was considerable opposition to the government's decision in 1823 to found and support a new college for Sanskrit studies. Ram Mohun Roy, the Bengali reformer, in a letter to the governor-general expressed the sentiments of those who wanted the intellectual and material advantages which would result from their being given access to 'mathematics, natural philosophy, chemistry, anatomy, and other useful sciences, which the natives of Europe have carried to a degree of perfection that has raised them above the inhabitants of other parts of the world'. They were, Roy continued, horrified at the idea that they were to receive instead a school which could 'only be expected to load the minds of youth with grammatical niceties and metaphysical distinctions of little or no practical use to the possessors or to society'. If it was the government's policy to 'keep this country in darkness', establishing a Sanskrit college was the best way of going about it. But this and other protests had no effect. It was the committee's opinion that 'tuition in European sciences [is] neither among the sensible wants of the people nor in the power of the Government to bestow'.

The committee members' response may have been inspired by the radical political and social views expressed by the staff and students of the Hindu College, but, whatever the cause, they were fighting a losing battle. Not only was there a general desire among Indians – particularly in Bengal – for English education, but the influence of reformers and political thinkers in Britain was behind it too. The famous missionary, Dr Duff, recalled that in Calcutta 'the excitement for Western education continued unabated. They pursued us along the streets; they threw open the doors of our palankeens; they poured in their supplications with a pitiful earnestness of countenance which might have softened a heart of stone.'

The stone was already softening, and for sound ideological reasons. Lord William Bentinck, already engaged in a number of reforms, wrote to the Committee of Public Instruction on June 26th, 1829. 'Impressed with a deep conviction of the importance of the subject,' he said, 'and cordially disposed to promote the great object of improving India by spreading abroad the lights of European knowledge, morals, and civilization, his Lordship in Council has no hesitation in stating to your Committee and in authorizing you to announce to all concerned in the superintendence of your native seminaries that it is the wish and admitted policy of the British Government to render its own language gradually and eventually the language of public business throughout the country, and that it will omit no opportunity of giving every reasonable and practical degree of encouragement to the execution of this project.'

The committee at this time was evenly divided between orientalists and anglicizers. While they debated, private initiative continued to expand the number of schools teaching the

English language and Western subjects. The orientalists were, in fact, losing ground. Their essentially conservative attitude was quite alien to the new spirit which permeated Britain's view of her responsibilities in India. When Macaulay arrived in India, this spirit – already expressed by Bentinck – received powerful reinforcement. Macaulay's Education Minute of 1835 (extracts from which are given in the appendix, page 146) summed up the reformist attitude. The decision to make English the medium of higher education was announced in a brief resolution on March 7th, 1835. 'His Lordship is of the opinion,' said the first paragraph of the resolution, 'that the great object of the British Government ought to be the promotion of European literature and science among the natives of India, and that all the funds appropriated for the purpose of education would be best employed on English education alone.'

The decision to divert government funds to the provision of English education alone not only satisfied the demands of the growing Hindu middle classes but also met the fundamental problems of the economy. The government's resources were strictly limited. The cost of any project to translate textbooks into Indian languages, for example, would have been ruinously expensive. All practical considerations were in favour of using English textbooks. The same considerations demanded that the scope of education should be limited, though it was hoped that knowledge could be diffused. Once certain sections of the population had been given an English education, the government thought, they would be able to pass on the knowledge they had acquired to their countrymen – in their own languages. 'The rich, the learned, the men of business, will first be gained,' wrote Macaulay's brother-in-law, Charles Trevelyan. 'A new class of teachers will be trained; books in the vernacular language will be multiplied; and with these accumulated means we shall in due time proceed to extend our operations from town to country, from the few to the many, until every hamlet shall be provided with its elementary school. The poor man is not less the object of the committee's solicitude than the rich; but, while the means at their disposal were extremely limited, there were millions of all classes to be educated. It was absolutely necessary to make a selection, and they therefore selected the upper and middle classes as the first object of their attention, because, by educating them first, they would soonest be able to extend the same advantages to the rest of the people.'

The decision to concentrate on providing Western education in the English language was made from other motives than economy, though that was undoubtedly of first importance. But education had moral, political and commercial overtones in the eyes of such men as Macaulay. He, and those who thought like him, were following evangelical rather than Utilitarian principles. It was Charles Grant who was the prophet of English education in India, not James Mill. Indeed, Mill was highly sceptical about the effectiveness of *any* form of education in India. The moral overtones were, of course, Christian in character. They were reflected by Macaulay in a letter to his father in 1836, in which he forecast that in thirty years' time there would be not a single idolater among the respectable classes in Bengal, a situation which would be brought about merely by the diffusion of knowledge.

That many Indians were aware that there was a proselytizing purpose behind English education had been shown in their suspicion when such education was offered by missionaries. Bishop's College, for example, which had been established in Calcutta in 1820, would not admit non-Christians; its real function was to create missionaries who would go out and evangelize the heathen. It never attracted more than eleven scholars at any one time during the twenty-five years following its establishment. Though great pressure was brought to bear on the government, from both Britain and India, to introduce religious instruction into government schools, it refused to depart from its traditional neutrality in matters of religion until 1854, by which time it had become clear that Macaulay's hopes for conversion-by-example had not been realized. The moral motive also had a more immediate and practical application. With administrative reforms, a growing number of Indians were joining government service, with increasing responsibility and powers, particularly in the judicial and revenue branches. English education was intended to make them morally and intellectually 'fit' to perform their duties with efficiency and probity.

The commercial motive was also extremely powerful, and it gained for the cause of English education the full support of the mercantile community in Calcutta as well as in Britain. The economic activities of the British had already produced a commercial middle class in India, on whose cooperation the expansion of the economy depended. Cooperation was needed not only for exploiting India's natural resources; it was essential to the creation of that prosperity which would lead to the purchase and consumption of British goods. To people who thought in these terms, commerce was more important than conquest. Macaulay, who is so frequently the mouthpiece of his times, put the case in his great speech in the House of Commons on the Charter Act of 1833. 'The mere extent of empire is not necessarily an advantage. To many governments it has been cumbersome; to some it has been fatal. It will be allowed by every statesman of our time that the prosperity of a country is made up of the prosperity of those who compose the community, and that it is the most childish ambition to covet dominion which adds to no man's comfort or security. . . . It would be, on the most selfish view of the case, far better for us that the people of India were well-governed and independent of us, than ill-governed and subject to us; that they were ruled by their own kings, but wearing our broadcloth, and working with our cutlery, than that they were performing their salaams to English collectors and English magistrates *but were too ignorant to value*,* or too poor to buy English manufactures.'

Though Macaulay and others looked forward to a future in which Indians, having acquired a taste for 'European civilization', might demand European institutions and even independence from Britain, it was to a very distant future. In the meantime, there remained the essential problem facing an alien government – the avoidance of popular revolt. English education, it was believed, would play its part here too. 'The

* My italics—M.E.

political education of a nation is a work of time,' wrote Charles Trevelyan, 'and while it is in progress, we shall be as safe as it will be possible for us to be. The natives will not rise against us, we shall stoop to raise them; there will be no reaction, because there will be no pressure; the national activity will be fully and harmlessly employed in acquiring and diffusing European knowledge, and in naturalizing European institutions. The educated classes, knowing that the elevation of their country on these principles can only be worked out under our protection, will naturally cling to us. . . . The change will thus be peaceably and gradually effected; there will be no struggle, no mutual exasperation; the natives will have independence, after first learning how to make good use of it; and we shall exchange profitable subjects for still more profitable allies. . . . Trained by us to happiness and independence, and endowed with our learning and political institutions, India will remain the proudest monument of British benevolence; and we shall long continue to reap, in the affectionate attachment of the people, and in a great commercial intercourse with their splendid country, the fruit of that liberal and enlightened policy which suggested to us this line of conduct.'

Though there is the ring of arrogance in the statements of the liberal reformers, it is a mistake to think of them as hard and calculating men. They were not – for they were genuinely convinced that the transformation of India would be as good for Indians as it would be for themselves. Because their ideas of reform (and the consequences of these ideas) coincided with the self-interest of Britain's merchants and rulers, the reformers' moral view has often been dismissed as hypocrisy, as exploitation hidden behind humbug. But they saw no conflict between real altruism and a desire for commercial profit, for they did not place commerce and industry in a separate compartment. They viewed economics as they are viewed today, as a fundamental and indivisible part of the total structure of human happiness.

The theorists of 1835 were, however, unduly optimistic. They thought that, by converting the top levels of Indian society, they would in time convert the masses. In this they were sadly mistaken, for the desire so powerfully expressed by a certain section of Indian society for the boons of English education was by no means altruistic. The theorists thought they were creating missionaries of a new civilization when in fact they were stabilizing the existence of a new class.

In the early years at least, the reformers had some justification for optimism. Many thousands of Indians wanted to be enrolled in the new schools. The Calcutta School Book Society sold over thirty thousand books in English in two years. English education at government institutions was available to all without religious or caste distinctions, though among Hindus, not unnaturally, it was the Brahmin caste who took most advantage of it. Muslims did not respond to the new education with any enthusiasm. In fact, a vigorous protest was signed by eight thousand Calcutta Muslims when English was made the official language of government. Although an English-language class had been established in the Calcutta Madrasa as early as 1826, only two students passed the junior scholarship examination during the next twenty-five years. It was only after the Mutiny of 1857 that the Muslims became aware of the advantages they had let slip.

The greatest desire for English education was to be found in Bengal – and even then, it existed only in what might be called Bengal proper. Elsewhere in India, there was considerable opposition to the use of English as the medium of instruction. In Bihar, administratively a part of the Bengal Presidency, there was powerful resistance from Muslim landlords, and as late as November 1858 the Patna office of the inspector of schools was known as 'the devil's counting-house'. In the Bombay Presidency, there was little demand for English education, and by 1850 there were only ten government-aided or government schools with a total of about two thousand pupils. The Madras Presidency was even more backward; by 1854 it had only three government, or aided institutions. However, it was estimated that there were about thirty thousand pupils in establishments run by missionaries in India, which received no financial assistance from the government. According to statistics prepared for a report to the House of Commons, a total of

17,360 pupils was being educated at government expense in all parts of the British dominions in India on April 30th, 1845. Of these, 13,699 were Hindus, 1,636 Muslims, and 236 Christians.

In Bengal, government policy was to establish either an English or what was called an Anglo-Vernacular school – i.e. a school which used both English and the local language – at the headquarters of each administrative district. The best of these schools were given college status, and were linked with lower schools by a system of scholarships. Higher education was available at the Hindu College at Calcutta, which was finally taken over by the government in 1854 and renamed Presidency College. The standard of examinations was high. It required 'a critical acquaintance with the works of Bacon, Johnson, Milton and Shakespeare, a knowledge of ancient and modern history, and of the higher branches of mathematical science, some insight into the elements of natural history, and the principles of moral philosophy and political economy, together with considerable facility of composition, and the power of writing in fluent and idiomatic language an impromptu essay on any given subject of history, moral or political economy.' In the years 1845–49, only thirty-six students passed the examinations. Mission and privately-owned colleges complained that the government was deliberately discriminating against them, because it appeared that only students at government colleges could reach the required standard and therefore had an undue advantage when it came to the award of appointments in the government service.

The government did not entirely neglect vernacular education in Bengal, but an experiment in 1844 when 101 native-language schools were established proved a failure, almost entirely because – though local inhabitants were often willing to support a traditional school themselves – they expected the government to give them an English one. The situation in Bombay was very different. There, the board of education, established in 1840, had concentrated its efforts on establishing vernacular schools in every village of more than two thousand inhabitants, on condition that the people bore a share of the cost. By 1842, there were 120 such schools with about seven thousand pupils. The Madras government preferred to leave such activity largely in the hands of missionaries.

In the North-Western Provinces (created 1843), however, James Thomason, who was lieutenant-governor 1843–53, laid the foundations of a system of vernacular education which was to have some influence on the government's future policy. In effect, Thomason restated the paternalist position as opposed to the diffusionist. Where the anglicizers hoped to create an English-educated middle class, the paternalists looked towards what they conceived to be the general welfare of the masses. They, the paternalists maintained, stood in no need of 'European civilization' (which did not seem to be reaching them, anyway). What the peasant needed was a standard of literacy advanced enough for him to be able to understand village land records. He would thus have a weapon with which to defend himself against the moneylender, the landlord, and the lawyer, who – because they could read while the peasant could not – waxed fat upon his ignorance. Thomason's experiment was, however, on a small scale, and by 1853 only about one in three hundred of the population of the North-Western Provinces had received even the minimal education given in the rural schools. Elsewhere in the country, a report of 1856 recorded, 'a school, either Government or Missionary, is as rare as a lighthouse on our coast . . . three or four schools exist among three or four millions of people'.

In Sir Charles Wood's Educational Despatch of 1854, both liberal and paternalist strands were woven together into the proposed fabric of a complete system of education for India. Any really complete system was, of course, completely outside the financial resources of the government. Wood therefore proposed a grant-in-aid system, so that private institutions could take over the burden of higher education and release government funds for the education of the predominantly rural masses. Essentially, this was no more than a pious hope. The government's main aim was still to be the extension of English education, and it was proposed to establish universities in Calcutta, Bombay and Madras. The purpose of education was the same – to produce a high standard of government servant, and to increase commercial potential. The advancement of European knowledge, wrote Wood, 'will teach the natives of India the marvellous results of the employment of labour and capital, rouse them to emulate us in the development of the vast resources of their country, guide them in their efforts and gradually, but certainly, confer upon them all the advantages which accompany the healthy increase of wealth and commerce; and, at the same time, secure to us a larger and more certain supply of many articles necessary for our manufactures and extensively consumed by all classes of our population, as well as an almost inexhaustible demand for the produce of British labour'.

The matter of grants-in-aid to private institutions, which would include those run by missionaries, raised some doubts because of the possibility of political repercussions. Even men who had no particular liking for the type of Indian produced by a purely English literary education did not anticipate trouble from that source; their interests lay with the British. The real danger, if there was one, would come from those traditionalists who were offended by the reforming activities of the government. One distinguished British official regarded grants-in-aid to missionary schools as a dangerous breach in the government's attitude of religious neutrality, but he could mobilize no opinion on his side until after the traditionalist uprising of the Mutiny.

The leaven of English education, was, in fact, working amongst the Indian middle classes,* though it was not yet to produce an overt threat to British dominion. Among the English-educated classes, a spirit of nationalism was slowly growing. There is symbolic significance in the fact that modern India's first three universities were founded in the year the Indian Mutiny broke out.

*The education of women, under both the Company and the Crown, is dealt with on pages 291–6.

## *Appendix*

### Extracts from Macaulay's Minute on Education, 1835

We have a fund to be employed as government shall direct for the intellectual improvement of the people of this country. The simple question is, what is the most useful way of employing it?

All parties seem to be agreed on one point, that the dialects commonly spoken among the natives of this part of India contain neither literary nor scientific information, and are, moreover, so poor and rude that, until they are enriched from some other quarter, it will not be easy to translate any valuable work into them. It seems to be admitted on all sides that the intellectual improvement of those classes of the people who have the means of pursuing higher studies can at present be effected only by means of some language not vernacular amongst them.

What, then, shall that language be? One half of the Committee maintain that it should be the English. The other half strongly recommend the Arabic and Sanskrit. The whole question seems to me to be, which language is the best worth knowing?

I have no knowledge of either Sanskrit or Arabic. – But I have done what I could to form a correct estimate of their value. I have read translations of the most celebrated Arabic and Sanskrit works. I have conversed both here and at home with men distinguished by their proficiency in the Eastern tongues. I am quite ready to take the Oriental learning at the valuation of the Orientalists themselves. I have never found one among them who could deny that a single shelf of a good European library was worth the whole native literature of India and Arabia. The intrinsic superiority of the Western literature is, indeed, fully admitted by those members of the Committee who support the Oriental plan of education.

It will hardly be disputed, I suppose, that the department

of literature in which the Eastern writers stand highest is poetry. And I certainly never met with any Orientalist who ventured to maintain that the Arabic and Sanskrit poetry could be compared to that of the great European nations. But, when we pass from works of imagination to works in which facts are recorded and general principles investigated, the superiority of the Europeans becomes absolutely immeasurable. It is, I believe, no exaggeration to say, that all the historical information which has been collected from all the books written in the Sanskrit language is less valuable than what may be found in the most paltry abridgements used at preparatory schools in England. In every branch of physical or moral philosophy the relative position of the two nations is nearly the same.

How, then, stands the case? We have to educate a people who cannot at present be educated by means of their mother-tongue. We must teach them some foreign language. The claims of our own language it is hardly necessary to recapitulate. It stands pre-eminent even among the languages of the West. It abounds with works of imagination not inferior to the noblest which Greece has bequeathed to us; with models of every species of eloquence; with historical compositions, which, considered merely as narratives, have seldom been surpassed, and which, considered as vehicles of ethical and political instruction, have never been equalled; with just and lively representations of human life and human nature; with the most profound speculations on metaphysics, morals, government, jurisprudence, and trade; with full and correct information respecting every experimental science which tends to preserve the health, to increase the comfort, or to expand the intellect of man. Whoever knows that language, has ready access to all the vast intellectual wealth, which all the wisest nations of the earth have created and hoarded in the course of ninety generations. It may safely be said that the literature now extant in that language is of far greater value than all the literature which three hundred years ago was extant in all the languages of the world together. Nor is this all. In India, English is the language spoken by the ruling class. It is spoken by the higher class of natives at the seats of government. It is likely to become the language of commerce throughout the seas of the East. It is the language of two great European communities which are rising, the one in the south of Africa, the other in Australasia; communities which are every year becoming more important, and more closely connected with our Indian Empire. Whether we look at the intrinsic value of our literature, or at the particular situation of this country, we shall see the strongest reason to think that, of all foreign tongues, the English tongue is that which would be the most useful to our native subjects.

The question now before us is simply whether, when it is in our power to teach this language, we shall teach languages in which, by universal confession, there are no books on any subject which deserve to be compared to our own; whether, when we can teach European science, we shall teach systems which, by universal confession, whenever they differ from those of Europe, differ for the worse; and whether, when we can patronize sound Philosophy and true History, we shall countenance, at the public expense, medical doctrines which would disgrace an English farrier – Astronomy, which would move laughter in girls at an English boarding-school – History, abounding with kings thirty feet high, and reigns thirty thousand years long – and Geography, made up of seas of treacle and seas of butter.

It is said that we ought to secure the cooperation of the native public, and that we can do this only by teaching Sanskrit and Arabic.

I can by no means admit that, when a nation of high intellectual attainments undertakes to superintend the education of a nation comparatively ignorant, the learners are absolutely to prescribe the course which is taken by the teachers. It is not necessary, however, to say anything on this subject. For it is proved by unanswerable evidence that we are not at present securing the cooperation of the natives. It would be bad enough to consult their intellectual taste at the expense of their intellectual health. But we are consulting neither – we are withholding from them the learning for which they are craving; we are forcing on them the mock-learning which they nauseate.

This is proved by the fact that we are forced to pay our Arabic and Sanskrit students, while those who learn English are willing to pay us. All the declamation in the world about the love and reverence of the natives for their sacred dialects will never, in the mind of any impartial person, outweigh the undisputed fact, that we cannot find, in all our vast Empire, a single student who will let us teach him those dialects unless we will pay him.

It is said that the Sanskrit and Arabic are the languages in which the sacred books of a hundred millions of people are written, and that they are, on that account, entitled to peculiar encouragement. Assuredly it is the duty of the British government in India to be not only tolerant, but neutral on all religious questions. But to encourage the study of a literature admitted to be of small intrinsic value only because that literature inculcates the most serious errors on the most important subjects, is a course hardly reconcilable with reason, with morality, or even with that very neutrality which ought, as we all agree, to be sacredly preserved. It is confessed that a language is barren of useful knowledge. We are told to teach it because it is fruitful of monstrous superstitions. We are to teach false history, false astronomy, false medicine, because we find them in company with a false religion. We abstain, and I trust shall always abstain, from giving any public encouragement to those who are engaged in the work of converting natives to Christianity. And while we act thus, can we reasonably and decently bribe men out of the revenues of the State to waste their youth in learning how they are to purify themselves after touching an ass, or what text of the Vedas they are to repeat to expiate the crime of killing a goat?

It is taken for granted by the advocates of Oriental learning that no native of this country can possibly attain more than a mere smattering of English. They do not attempt to prove this: but they perpetually insinuate it. They designate the education which their opponents recommend as a mere spelling-book education. They assume it as undeniable, that the question is between a profound knowledge of Hindoo and Arabian literature and science on the one side, and a superficial knowledge of the rudiments of English on the other. This is not merely an assumption, but an assumption contrary to all reason and experience. We know that foreigners of all nations do learn our language sufficiently to have access to all the most abstruse knowledge which it contains, sufficiently to relish even the more delicate graces of our most idiomatic writers. There are in this very town natives who are quite competent to discuss political or scientific questions with fluency and precision in the English language. I have heard the very question on which I am now writing discussed by native gentlemen with a liberality and an intelligence which would do credit to any member of the Committee of Public Instruction. Indeed it is unusual to find, even in the literary circles of the Continent, any foreigner who can express himself in English with so much facility and correctness as we find in many Hindoos. Nobody, I suppose, will contend that English is so difficult to a Hindoo as Greek to an Englishman. Yet an intelligent English youth, in a much smaller number of years than our unfortunate pupils pass at the Sanskrit college, becomes able to read, to enjoy, and even to imitate, not unhappily, the composition of the best Greek authors. Less than half the time which enables an English youth to read Herodotus and Sophocles ought to enable a Hindoo to read Hume and Milton.

To sum up what I have said: I think it is clear that we are free to employ our funds as we choose; that we ought to employ them in teaching what is best worth knowing; that English is better worth knowing than Sanskrit or Arabic; that the natives are desirous to be taught English, and are not desirous to be taught Sanskrit or Arabic; that neither as the languages of law, nor as the languages of religion, have the Sanskrit and Arabic any peculiar claim to our encouragement; that it is possible to make natives of this country thoroughly good English scholars, and that to this end our efforts ought to be directed. In one point I fully agree with the gentlemen to whose general views I am opposed. I feel, with them, that it is impossible for us, with our limited means, to attempt to educate the body of the people. We must at present do our best to form a class who may be interpreters between us and the millions whom we govern; a class of persons, Indian in blood and colour, but English in taste, in opinions, in morals, and in intellect. To that class we may leave it to refine the vernacular dialects of the country, to enrich those dialects with terms of science borrowed from the Western nomenclature, and to render them by degrees fit vehicles for conveying knowledge to the great mass of the population.

I would strictly respect all existing interests. I would deal even generously with all individuals who have had fair reason to expect a pecuniary provision. But I would strike at the root of the bad system which has hitherto been fostered by us. I would at once stop the printing of Arabic and Sanskrit books; I would abolish the Madrassa and the Sanskrit college at Calcutta. Benares is the great seat of Brahmanical learning; Delhi, of Arabic learning. If we retain the Sanskrit college at Benares and the Mahomedan college at Delhi, we do enough, and much more than enough in my opinion, for the Eastern languages. If the Benares and Delhi colleges should be retained, I would at least recommend that no stipend shall be given to any students who may hereafter repair thither, but that the people shall be left to make their own choice between the rival systems of education without being bribed by us to learn what they have no desire to know. The funds which would thus be placed at our disposal would enable us to give larger encouragement to the Hindoo college at Calcutta, and to establish in the principal cities throughout the Presidencies of Fort William and Agra schools in which the English language might be well and thoroughly taught.

I believe that the present system tends, not to accelerate the progress of truth, but to delay the natural death of expiring errors. I conceive that we have at present no right to the respectable name of a Board of Public Instruction. We are a Board for wasting public money, for printing books which are less value than the paper on which they are printed was while it was blank; for giving artificial encouragement to absurd history, absurd metaphysics, absurd physics, absurd theology; for raising up a breed of scholars who find their scholarship an encumbrance and a blemish, who live on the public while they are receiving their education, and whose education is so utterly useless to them that, when they have received it, they must either starve or live on the public all the rest of their lives. Entertaining these opinions, I am naturally desirous to decline all share in the responsibility of a body which, unless it alters its whole mode of proceeding, I must consider not merely as useless, but as positively noxious.

## CULTURAL AND RELIGIOUS LIFE

### *Religion and Philosophy*

In the case of India's religions the impact of the West was confined to a minority of thinkers and philosophers. The religion of the masses, whether Hindu or Muslim, remained untouched except around the fringes of its social expression. Generally speaking, this only tended to reinforce traditional religious attitudes and acceptance.

On the intellectual level, however, Western ideas – and even the actions of the British government – supplied a means for reinforcing Hinduism and, to a much lesser extent, Islam. The challenge posed by Christianity, as well as the ethical content of its teaching, had profound effects. So, too, did the rediscovery and translation of the Sanskrit classics by European orientalists, a by-product of the administration's desire to know more about the customary law of the Hindus (see page 91 ff.).

The principal movements designed to revivify and purify Hinduism were initiated by reformers active in more practical fields. All reaffirmed the validity of Hinduism but demanded changes in its social expression so that it could be made more responsive to modern needs. All such movements therefore had social and political aspects which are dealt with separately (in the sections on Nationalism, pages 165 and 312 ff.). These aspects had important consequences for many people. The purely religious innovations, however, did not, primarily because their influence was mainly intellectual.

The first of the modernizers of Hinduism was that protean figure, Ram Mohun Roy (1772–1833). In his revulsion at the superstitions which had drowned the original beliefs of Hinduism, Ram Mohun turned to other religions, including Islam, Buddhism and Christianity, for aid. He did not accept any of these faiths. He had a particular hatred for idolatry, and could not accept the divinity of Christ, however impressed he might be by his ethical teaching. Searching for the basis of an ethical monotheism, he found it in some of the classical Hindu scriptures, and particularly in the *Upanishads* which he translated into Bengali.

Ram Mohun made no attempt to think out a religious system. His view of theism was very much that of the eighteenth-century European rationalist, and he found it expressed in the *Upanishads* where Brahma, the Supreme Being, exists outside thought and speech and cannot be reached either through prayer or meditation. This was a very intellectualized approach, as can be seen in a passage from his *Religious Instructions founded on Sacred Authorities*.

QUESTION: What is meant by worship?
ANSWER: Worship implies the act of one with a view to please another; but when applied to the Supreme Being, it signifies a contemplation of his attributes.
QUESTION: In what manner is this worship to be performed?
ANSWER: By bearing in mind that the Author and Governor of this visible universe is the Supreme Being, and comparing this idea with the sacred writings and with reason. In this worship it is indispensably necessary to use exertions to subdue the senses, and to read such passages as direct attention to the Supreme Spirit . . . The benefits which we continually receive from fire, from air, and from the sun, likewise from the various productions of the earth, such as the different kinds of grain, drugs, fruit and vegetables, all are dependent on him: and by considering and reasoning on the terms expressive of

such ideas, the meaning itself is firmly fixed in the mind.

The movement founded by Ram Mohun was originally called the Brahma Sabha, but the name was changed to Brahmo Samaj. At the beginning, there was no membership and no fixed creed, and the association's meetings were open to all. In 1830, the Samaj, which had first met in a private house in Calcutta in August 1828, was able to begin erecting its own building. It was opened two years later. The Samaj had the support of a number of wealthy men, the most important of whom was Dwarkanath Tagore, one of India's first Western-style capitalists. The trust deed of the Samaj's temple forms a précis of the religious ideas of Ram Mohun and his supporters. The temple was to be used 'as a place of public meeting of all sorts and descriptions of people without distinction as shall behave and conduct themselves in an orderly sober religious and devout manner for the worship and adoration of the Eternal Unsearchable and Immutable Being who is the Author and Preserver of the Universe but not under or by any other name designation or title peculiarly used for and applied to any particular Being or Beings by any man or set of men whatsoever and that no graven image statue or sculpture carving painting picture portrait or the likeness of anything shall be admitted within the said building . . . and that no sacrifice . . . shall ever be permitted therein and that no animal or living creature shall within or on the said premises be deprived of life . . . and that in conducting the said worship and adoration no object animate or inanimate that has been or is . . . recognized as an object of worship by any man or set of men shall be reviled or slightingly or contemptuously spoken of . . . and that no sermon preaching discourse prayer or hymn be delivered made or used in such worship but such as have a tendency to the promotion of the contemplation of the Author and Preserver of the Universe to the promotion of charity morality piety benevolence virtue and the strengthening the bonds of union between men of all religious persuasions and creeds.'

Despite the dryness of Ram Mohun's approach, he did offer

Hindus who were inspired by Christian teaching and revolted by their own religion in its popular form a way of accepting that part of Christianity which had most appeal – its humanitarian message – without being converted to Christianity. This in itself was a positive achievement, but the movement founded by Ram Mohun did not have many adherents until in 1843 Dwarkanath Tagore's son, Debendranath (1817–1905), merged an association of his own with it and gave the Samaj a new sense of purpose.

In 1838, Debendranath had gone through a profound religious experience. In the following year, he founded the Tattvabodhani Sabha (truth-teaching society) which met weekly for religious discussions. As his father's heir, Debendranath would have inherited his wealth and business ventures. But he was drawn into the heart of Hinduism and away from the material world. 'My father was in England', he wrote in his *Autobiography*: 'The task of managing his various affairs devolved upon me. But I was not able to attend to any business matters properly. My subordinates used to do all the work, I was only concerned with the Vedas, the Vedanta, religion, God, and the ultimate goal of life. I was not even able to stay quietly in the house. My spirit of renunciation became deeper under all this stress of work. I felt no inclination to become the owner of all this wealth. To renounce everything and wander about alone, this was the desire that reigned in my heart.' Nevertheless, there was need for action of some sort.

Debendranath continued Ram Mohun's work, opposing both the idolatry of popular Hinduism and the attempts of Christian missionaries at conversion. A Scottish missionary, Alexander Duff, had arrived in Calcutta in 1830, and under his influence a number of Hindus educated at mission schools were turning to Christianity, partly because Duff maintained that the highest form of education was a Christian education. The combination of a daily scripture lesson with Western intellectual and scientific training convinced many young Hindus that they could not have one without the other. Debendranath called a meeting in Calcutta at which funds were raised to found a school which did not have Christian teaching built into the curriculum. But Debendranath was fundamentally a quietist, not a man of action. In his attempt to set monotheism firmly into the frame of classical Hinduism, he tried to find authority in the *Vedas*. Unable to do so, he fell back on intuition. He arranged a series of extracts from the Hindu scriptures, mainly from the *Upanishads*, for use in public and private devotions. Later, too, he produced a set of ceremonies to replace the idolatrous ones used in Hindu homes on such occasions as births and marriages.

Outside Bengal, similar fears existed over the threat to the educated classes posed by Christian conversion, though they were not felt quite so intensely. A number of Hindus were beginning to re-examine their religion, although not in order to assimilate Western ideas, to create a synthesis, or even to supply a retreat for intellectuals. European influences were to have little effect upon them. But they too reflected – sometimes overtly, though more often subtly – the Indian reaction to the general pressure of Western ideas and missionary activity.

The frontal attack on Hinduism had begun in the Company's dominions after the country was opened to missionaries by the Charter Act of 1813. The aim was to convert the upper castes through education, and it was to this threat that the Brahmo Samaj responded. Elsewhere, particularly in the south where Christian missionaries – mainly Danish and German – had been active since the early eighteenth century, missionary activity had its main impact on the lower castes. By 1851, there were 90,000 Protestant Christians in India, and about 200,000 of all denominations, including Catholic families of long standing who had been converted by the Portuguese.

Early Lutheran and Anglican missionaries had accepted the Catholic view that caste was a secular and not a religious institution, but this attitude changed after 1833. Christian activities carried with them not only Christian teaching but the superficialities of European culture – European clothes, new names, new food habits. It seemed as if what made a Christian was wearing a hat, eating beef, and drinking liquor.

The outward Europeanization of Christian converts contributed much to the belief that the activities of the government (a Christian government, whatever it might say) were designed to remake the Hindu personality in a European image.

The two basic Hindu reactions – religious reform, in response to the ethical content of Western religious and political ideas, and religious revivalism, as a rejection of Europeanization – owed much to missionary activities.

The effect of Western ideas and Christian mission work on Islam was comparatively slight. Hinduism is essentially tolerant, holding to no rigid dogma, but Islam was already monotheistic and possessed a sacred book containing ultimate statements of belief and action. Muslims, too, had the sense of a nationalist past ended by British conquest. It was a past which they, unlike the Hindus, had no need to rediscover, only to preserve. When Hindus accepted Western education, this merely reinforced Muslims in their conviction that they should remain isolated from it. It was only after the Mutiny – which opened the eyes of some Muslims to how dangerous the rejection of Western ideas might be to their community – that the Muslim religious revival began.

### *Art and Architecture*

Throughout the whole period of the Company's connexion with India, artists continued to paint in traditional styles. Many of them lived and worked in the princely states, outside the sphere of direct British influence. Until 1858, large areas of India remained remote from Europeans and European ideas, and traditionalist schools of painting flourished under the patronage of rajas and princes. In such places as Rajasthan and the hill states known today as Himachal Pradesh new styles were developed based firmly on tradition. In British India, too, new styles emerged in response to new patronage – that of the British. Though these were rooted in tradition, they reflected British rather than Indian taste. The reaction of the British to Indian painting was one of highly-qualified pleasure. They admired the delicacy of the workmanship, but regretted the absence of perspective, the lack of light and shade.

The coastal towns in which the British first established themselves were not centres of artistic activity. These were mainly inland, at the princely courts. But the collapse of the Mughal empire destroyed many such courts and put the court painters out of work. The anarchy of the late eighteenth century destroyed much of the *luxe privée* which the artist not only contributed to but drew upon for his inspiration. Deprived of the patronage of princes, artists moved towards the coastal towns in the hope that the British might be interested in their work.

The painters' chances of success depended on two things – that the British should have some reason for employing them, and that the artists should be willing to adapt their technique to the requirements of new patrons. Quite early in the British connexion, artists were employed as house decorators. They were soon to be found, too, on surveyors' staffs, drawing maps and views. But perhaps the two most important reasons for the growth of British patronage were that Indian portrait miniatures were cheap compared with the prices charged by European artists in India and that the British wanted 'picture postcards' of exotic festivals and ceremonies to send to friends or preserve in albums.

The first development of an art designed to suit British taste seems to have begun at Murshidabad, the former capital of Bengal. The Nawabs of Bengal had employed local artists who usually painted in the Mughal imperial style. As the power of the Nawabs declined after 1757 and the British population in Murshidabad increased, artists turned to the latter for employment. They produced portrait miniatures on paper and – much more exotic – paintings on thin sheets of clear mica. From about the middle of the 1770s on, mica painting was extremely popular with the British. The demand for sets showing local festivals was so high that patterns for producing them at greater speed were prepared. This 'industry' seems to have flourished until about 1850, by which time the number of British residents in Murshidabad had considerably decreased.

Murshidabad painting, though it obviously reflected British

taste, remained essentially Indian in character. The painters of Patna (in present-day Bihar), however, consciously adapted British techniques. They produced sets of 'occupations', a new subject for Indian painters. They developed perspective. They used watercolours. The paintings they produced have a great deal in common with the contemporary aquatints of Thomas and William Daniell (see page 60). The Patna school flourished under the patronage of local British residents and British visitors who passed through the city in appreciable numbers. Sir Charles D'Oyly – who was Opium Agent at Patna until 1833, and a competent artist and lithographer – encouraged at least one known artist, Jairam Das, and helped to familiarize other artists with European techniques. Some of D'Oyly's own work was copied and included in sets of views produced by native artists. Mica painting, which was imported by artists from Murshidabad, became popular with the British and remained so until the late nineteenth century. Towards the 1870s, Patna painters were forced to rely more and more upon Indian customers, and their style of colouring changed from the sombre tones of English watercolours to the more vivid tints of traditional painting. By the beginning of the twentieth century, the trade in Patna paintings had almost disappeared.

Wherever there was a British colony, there were usually artists to supply what the British wanted – picturesque mementoes of a picturesque country. Things were slightly different in Lucknow, however. Oudh, of which it was the capital, did not form part of the British dominions until 1856, and there were rich opportunities for Europeans at its corrupt court. Painters arrived in the wake of the adventurers, and many works by European artists were freely copied by Indians. The influence of the European (and mainly, in fact, British) artists who were continually patronized by successive rulers of Oudh can be seen in the changing colours, from the brilliant richness of Mughal art to the pale delicacy of English water-colours.

In Delhi, for long the capital of the imperial Mughals, the British found a flourishing traditional style and yielded to its appeal. They encouraged artists to produce copies of earlier

Mughal works. But they also demanded picturesque views, understandably, since the Delhi area was full of the monuments of the past. About 1830, painting on ivory came into vogue, both for portraits and views. The coming of photography only increased the demand – at least for a time – and, in making copies of photographs, the artists to a large extent abandoned the somewhat rigid style they had formerly favoured.

In southern India, the beginnings of Indo-British art were centred on the town of Tanjore, where a group of Mughal-style painters from Hyderabad had settled about 1770. They brought with them a tradition peculiar to Hyderabad at that time, of painting subjects which appealed to Europeans – festivals, forms of transport, and so on – in which there had been trade with the Dutch settlements on the west coast from the late seventeenth century. The style, however, had not been influenced by European tastes. The painters at Tanjore, though they derived their art from the Mughal tradition of Hyderabad (known as Deccani style), made certain changes, and these increased as British influence in Tanjore expanded. The raja, Serfaji, was partly responsible for this, as he had been educated by a Lutheran missionary in Madras and returned to Tanjore in 1798 with strong European tastes. In the new pictures, flat backgrounds disappeared, white and blue skies were broken by jagged clouds, and there was a receding foreground – all unmistakably European in origin.

The two main and lasting effects of British patronage on Indian art were in technique – the use of water-colour instead of the traditional tempera – and in subject matter, which broke away from court scenes and aristocratic portraits and began to represent ordinary people and ordinary life.

In architecture, during the period of Company rule, the princely rulers and the ordinary people continued to use traditional Hindu and Mughal styles when they built their palaces and hovels. But the architecture of the British, first classical and then neo-Gothic, inevitably inspired imitation. Lucknow remains to this day a monument to the eclecticism of its rulers. Mughal and classical styles are mixed in a kind of Indian rococo. In fact, that astute observer, Bishop Heber, thought Lucknow resembled Dresden, though its main thoroughfare reminded him of the High Street at Oxford. In the south, Serfaji of Tanjore built himself a palace in a mixture of European and Indian styles, while in the urban centres – notably Calcutta – the growing Indian middle classes demonstrated their Westernization by adorning their homes with Corinthian columns in the contemporary fashion.

### *Literature*

The West influenced Indian literatures by means of two principal instruments, the printing press and English-language education.

Before the arrival of the British, the anarchic state of the country had had its effect on indigenous literatures. Though a virile tradition of ballads, folksongs, adaptations of Sanskrit works, and so on, existed in the native languages of India, such intellectual works as were composed were written in Sanskrit or, in the case of the Muslims, in Persian or Arabic. These languages were, to some extent, the *linguae francae* of the intellectuals. As the world of Western ideas was slowly opened to Indians, it became clear that neither the intellectual nor the vernacular languages of the country possessed a vocabulary suitable to express them. This was part of the reason why Indians demanded Western education in the English language. Not surprisingly, educated Indians acquired a deep interest in English literature as well as in Western science and Western political ideas.

The first effect was to encourage Indians and, in particular, Bengalis, to write in English themselves. Ram Mohun Roy wrote an elegant and lucid English prose. Henry Derozio (see page 165) was strongly influenced in style by the English romantics, though his subject matter was distinctly Indian. Within a very short time in the nineteenth century, English came to be looked upon as a new *lingua franca*, the common speech of the educated throughout India. Much of what was written by Indians in English was prose, and mainly concerned with social and political matters. On the whole, creative writing in English was meretricious, as even among educated

Indians there were few who could handle the English language with real fluency.

The desire to imitate English models in an Indian language also first showed itself in Bengal. The introduction of printing freed poetry from the oral tradition and from religious or quasi-religious subject matter. This freedom from past forms encouraged experiment and, in the decades following 1830, there was considerable innovation and adaptation in verse form. Michael Madhusudan Dutt adapted blank verse and sonnet forms from Milton. In the work of the men who followed him, the influence of Byron and Scott is particularly marked, especially in their narrative poetry.

Other vernaculars were very slowly influenced by English forms. Missionary activity resulted in the preparation of simple textbooks and translations of the Bible. The Baptist mission at Serampur, under the guidance of William Carey (1761–1834) produced a large number of grammars and translations, many of them by Carey himself, of some of the Sanskrit classics. The majority of the books translated, however, were of European and, specifically, English origin. Bunyan's *Pilgrim's Progress* and Aesop's *Fables* were among the first. Most of the translations were no more than serviceable. Few could have been called works of art. But in any case, they were primarily designed for use in schools. Before Indian literatures could really be fertilized by Western ideas, those ideas had to be assimilated, and that could only result from the acquisition of English – the only key to major works of literature and ideas. Early translations were almost entirely the product of Christian missionary endeavour and were therefore largely confined to Christian works or to works purveying simple moral precepts.

Outside Bengal, the first generation to assimilate and then to transfer English forms and ideas into creative (and non-imitative) vernacular literature did not really emerge before the end of Company rule. In Bengal itself, the main effect – except in the case of a few men like Madhusudan Dutt and Bihari Lal Chakravarti, who between them contributed new and essentially English rhythmic devices to Bengali poetry –

was on prose writing. In the creative sense, that too was not to flower until after 1858. The real significance of the Company period was that it secularized literature and made available a wide range of subject matter which had previously been unknown in the literature of Bengal. In this process, the newspaper and periodical press played an extremely important role, especially in the dissemination of ideas.

The first newspaper in India was published in Calcutta by James Hicky in 1780. This was the *Bengal Gazette,* and two years later it was suppressed by Warren Hastings. After this, the government's attitude towards newspapers scarcely changed. It was contemptuous of newspapers and their editors and convinced of the need to keep them under tight government control. The English-language press was, of course, originally intended for British readers, and its qualities and vices were those of contemporary journalism in Britain. Many of the newspapers which appeared were, in fact, merely digests and reprints of British newspapers. Many of the English-language journals, too, resembled their British contemporaries by being highly critical of the government and government personalities. They did not hesitate to attack both in the most scurrilous language.

In 1823, the government passed two regulations which securely gagged the press. The regulations were directed against English-language and British-owned newspapers; there were, at that time, only one or two Indian-language papers in existence. But it was, in fact, Indians who reacted positively against the new regulations. It was safer for them to do so than for a European, since one of the government's most frequently used weapons against English journalists was deportation – a weapon which could hardly be used against Indians. Nevertheless, the protest was made, inevitably (in the circumstances of the time) by Ram Mohun Roy. He and five other distinguished Bengalis, including Dwarkanath Tagore, failed in their appeal first to the Calcutta Supreme Court and then to the Privy Council in London, but it was the first demand made in India for liberty of the press, and it was made on sound European principles.

Of the vernacular papers then in existence, one of the first had been founded by a Serampur missionary, Joshua Marshman, in 1818. It began as a monthly, but proved so popular that it was decided to publish a weekly as well. The first issue of the *Samachar Durpan* ('mirror of the news') with Marshman as editor appeared on May 23rd, 1818. The *Samachar* carried both Indian and foreign news. In 1829 it became bilingual, running English and Bengali in parallel columns. The paper survived a number of vicissitudes, only to disappear in 1852.

It was only natural that Ram Mohun Roy, intent on disseminating Western ideas as part of his campaign for reform, should turn to the press as a vehicle. He did not see journalism merely as a process of collecting and commenting on news. Indeed, the *Sambad Kaumudi* ('moon of intelligence') – which he founded in December 1821 – expressed Ram Mohun's liberal ideas so powerfully that one of the staff left in protest against his agitation for the abolition of suttee. The dissenting employee set up a rival paper. The success of another rival, the *Samachar Chandrika*, forced the *Sambad* to close down in 1822, but it was revived in the following year. Ram Mohun also established a paper in Persian, the *Mirut-ul-Akhbar* ('mirror of news'), in 1822 and closed it down in protest at the press regulations of 1823.

Bombay had its first weekly paper in Gujarati, the *Moombaina Samachar* ('Bombay news') in 1822, and this was followed by others. The first paper in Hindi, the *Benares Akhbar*, appeared in 1845. In south India, a monthly magazine in Tamil was started by missionaries in Madras in 1831. Most of the papers and periodicals in existence in south India in 1858 had, in fact, been founded by missionaries and were primarily missionary in purpose.

As well as making available a wide range of Western learning and ideas, the Indian-language periodical press had a profound and vitalizing effect on the *use* of Indian languages. The straightforward simple prose needed to express alien ideas with accuracy helped to replace the old, allusive, over-ornamented literary language with a new, colloquial style.

## NATIONALISM

In the political field, India's response to British rule followed two main lines, one Indian and revolutionary, and the other Western and gradualist. The first expressed the reactions of entrenched traditional classes – political, cultural and religious – to an alien conqueror. The second represented the assimilation of Western liberal ideas by new social classes which were themselves a product of Western economic, educational and administrative systems.

The resistance of the traditional ruling elites culminated in the Mutiny of 1857, when an attempt was made to retrieve the old territorial jurisdiction lost in the course of British conquest. The British recognized the strength of traditionalist sentiment and the value of maintaining quasi-independent princely states, and therefore neutralized this brand of nationalism by giving it a place within the structure of the Indian empire and protecting it from change. Cultural and religious nationalism, however, could neither be neutralized nor protected from the impact of alien ideas. Towards the end of Company rule, a revulsion against Western ideas developed among certain sections of the middle classes and began to give a new political direction to cultural and religious nationalism.

Bengal, the foundation province of the British Indian empire, was the epicentre of the earthquake of Western ideas. But the effect there was not to create Indian nationalism; it was to create *Bengali* nationalism. The first important figures were Henry Derozio (1809–31) and Ram Mohun Roy (1772–1833).

Derozio was a Eurasian who had been reared as a Protestant Christian. When he was seventeen, he wrote some romantic poems which made him the talk of intellectual Calcutta, and two years later he became assistant headmaster of the Hindu College (see page 136). There, his expression in Indian terms of the patriotic sentiments and aspirations of his poetic masters – the English romantics, Byron and Shelley – gave him tremendous influence over the minds of young Bengalis. His views, essentially English in character, were expressed in English verse:

> Expanding like the petals of young flowers
> I watch the gentle opening of your minds,
> And the sweet loosening of the spell that binds
> Your intellectual energies and powers,
> That stretch (like young birds in soft summer hours)
> Their wings, to try their strength. O, how the winds
> Of circumstances, and freshening April showers
> Of early knowledge, and unnumbered kinds
> Of new perceptions shed their influence;
> And how you worship truth's omnipotence.
> What joyance rains upon me, when I see
> Fame in the mirror of futurity.
> Weaving the chaplets you have yet to gain,
> Ah! then I feel I have not lived in vain.
> Your hand is on the helm – guide on, young men,
> The bark that's freighted with your country's doom.
> Your glories are but budding; they shall bloom
> Like fabled amaranths Elysian, when
> The shore is won, even now within your ken,
> And when your torch shall dissipate the gloom
> That long has made your country but a tomb,
> Or worse than tomb, the priest's, the tyrant's den.
> Guide on, young men; your course is well begun;
> Hearts that are tuned to holiest harmony
> With all that e'en in thought is good, must be
> Best formed for deeds like those which shall be done
> But you hereafter till your guerdon's won
> And that which now is hope becomes reality.
>
> *Sonnet to the Pupils of the Hindu College*

Under Derozio's influence, Bengali middle-class youth studied Francis Bacon, Hume, and Tom Paine. The latter's *Age of Reason* – a hundred copies of which had been advertised for sale by a Calcutta bookseller – was soon the subject of a flourishing black market and copies were changing hands at five times the original price. Part of the book was later reprinted in a Bengali-language magazine.

In 1828, Derozio founded the Academic Association for discussion of advanced social and political ideas. The subjects considered included 'free will, free ordination, fate, faith, the sacredness of truth, the high duty of cultivating virtue, the meanness of vice, the nobility of patriotism, the attributes of God, and the arguments for and against the existence of the Deity as these have been set forth by Hume on the one side, and Reid, Dugald Stewart and Brown on the other, the hollowness of idolatry and the shams of the priesthood'.

The numbers of students who had access to, and discussed Western social and political ideas were extremely small. In 1828, there were only 436 students on the rolls of the Hindu College – but they formed a seminal minority. They were almost entirely Western in their outlook, so much so that the Calcutta newspaper, *The Englishman,* reported in May 1836 of former students of the Hindu College that 'in matters of politics, they are all radicals, and are followers of Benthamite principles. The very word Tory is a sort of ignominy among them. They think that toleration ought to be practised by every government, and the best and surest way of making the people abandon their barbarous customs and rites is by diffusing education among them. With respect to the questions relating to Political Economy, they all belong to the school of Adam Smith. They are clearly of opinion that the system of monopoly, the restraints upon trade, and the international laws of many countries, do nothing but paralyse the efforts of the industry, impede the progress of agriculture and manufacture and prevent commerce from flowing in its natural course.'

The students of the Hindu College published a number of magazines, most of them concerned with political, social and scientific matters. The views they expressed were far in advance of those of Ram Mohun Roy, who was not infrequently attacked in their pages. One of Ram Mohun's projects was that a colony of Englishmen should be established in India.

This idea was ridiculed in a paper given at a meeting of the Hindu Literary Society. 'No sooner did the benevolent inhabitants of Europe behold the sad condition of the natives', the author of the paper remarked, 'than they immediately got to work to ameliorate and improve it. They introduced among them, *rum, gin, brandy* and the other comforts of life, and it is astonishing to read how soon the poor savages learnt to estimate these *blessings*.'

Though the views of Ram Mohun Roy were liberal, he did not reject religion. On the contrary, he wanted to reform Hinduism rather than to reject it for a wholesale acceptance of Western ideas, as was the case with many students of the Hindu College. He sought to demonstrate that the humanitarian ideas of Western Christianity were already present in Hinduism, though they had become overlaid by superstition and corruption. He attacked Hindu idolatry as a later accretion to the simple and basically monotheistic concepts of the classical Hindu scriptures. Ram Mohun was, in fact, the first of the cultural and religious nationalists to see – though without rancour or racial arrogance – the humanitarian concepts of Western liberalism (even, indeed, the seeds of Western science) in Hindu civilization. Replying to an attack made on him by Christian missionaries because he rejected the divinity of Jesus, Ram Mohun stated his viewpoint. 'If by the "ray of intelligence" for which the Christian says we are indebted to the English, he means the introduction of useful mechanical arts, I am ready to express my assent and also my gratitude; but with respect to *science, literature,* or *religion,* I do not acknowledge that we are placed under any obligation. For by a reference to History it may be proved that the world was indebted to *our ancestors* for the first dawn of knowledge, which sprang up in the East, and thanks to the Goddess of Wisdom, we have still a philosophical and copious language of our own which distinguishes us from other nations who cannot express scientific or abstract ideas without borrowing the language of foreigners.'

Nevertheless, Ram Mohun believed that India could benefit from Western ideas and was a firm supporter of English education. There was no hesitation, on his part, about accepting anything the British had to offer that was not present at a similar level of sophistication in Hindu society. This did not, however, entail accepting the ideological basis of Western society as well.

Ram Mohun's purpose was to reform Hinduism, but the followers of Derozio rejected religion altogether. Both reactions were fundamentally intellectual and lacking in popular appeal. Ram Mohun Roy and the organization he founded to put forward his ideas (the Brahmo Samaj) aimed at influencing the progress of social reform. The followers of Derozio were more concerned with political action. One sought to reinstate the identity and the dignity of the Hindu world. The other sought to identify as completely as possible with an alien civilization.

These two strands in Bengali thought could not, however, remain entirely apart. When the time came for positive political action, they joined forces, often uneasily, united only in the desire to get rid of the British who denied them political power. But that still lay in the future.

The first overt political move was an Indian demand for association in the administration, which a number of declarations by the British had led the middle classes to believe was their right. The general preference of the government of India, in fact – whatever it might say to the contrary – was for the old governing classes. Macaulay had, however, stated that at some time in the very distant future a new anglicized class would demand and deserve self-government. This was rhetoric, not policy, but educated Indians – many of them afire with Western liberal ideas – chose to believe him.

The first political organization was the Zamindari Association of Calcutta, founded in 1837. It was principally a body of landholders and the name was soon changed (in 1838) to Landholders' Association. Its organizers were Raja Radhakant Deb Bahadur, a bitter opponent of Ram Mohun's proposals for reform, and Prasanna Kumar Tagore, a renegade disciple of Ram Mohun. According to *The Reformer* (a journal published by former students of the Hindu College) of November 14th, 1837, 'the only instruction with which the members of the provisional committee [set up to decide the rules and regulations of the Zamindari Association] were charged was that in preparing the rules, they should bear in mind that the Association was intended to embrace people of all descriptions, without reference to caste, country or complexion, and rejecting all exclusiveness, was to be based on the most universal and liberal principles; the only qualification to become its member being the possession of interest in the soil of the country'. The association was, in fact, a self-interest body designed to defend landlords against what were believed to be the pro-peasant tendencies of the government.

The association received support from a number of Englishmen and from the British India Society which was founded in London in 1839. They suggested that the name gave the impression of much too sectional an interest. In 1843, an entirely new organization, the Bengal British India Society, was founded. Its objects, according to the *Bengal Hurkuru,* were to be 'the collection and dissemination of information relating to the actual condition of the people of British India, and the laws and institutions, and resources of the country, and to employ such other means of peaceable and lawful character as may appear calculated to secure the welfare, extend the just rights, and advance the interests of all classes of our fellow subjects'. The meeting at which the society was constituted pledged its loyalty to Britain and disclaimed any desire to 'subvert legal authority or disturb the peace and well-being of society'. The Landholders' Association maintained its separate existence, but by 1851 both organizations were moribund.

In that year, a new body, the British Indian Association was formed, partly to channel protest against legal discriminations and partly to make representations to the British government when the Company's charter came up for renewal in 1853. The association professed to welcome all classes, but the subscription was so high that only the wealthier could afford it. The association was – and remained – an upper-class body representing powerful landholding and merchant interests. Branches were soon established in Madras, Poona and Bombay. The association memorialized the government on almost every conceivable subject, though it was fundamentally concerned with the removal of discriminatory tariffs and the admittance of Indians to the legislatures and the civil administration.

At the first annual general meeting of the Bombay branch, one speaker made a prophetic speech. 'The British Government,' he said, 'professes to educate the Natives to an equality with Europeans, an object worthy of the age and of Britain. But if Englishmen after educating the Natives to be their equals continue to treat them as their inferiors – if they deny the stimulus to honourable ambition, and show the Natives that there is a barrier over which superior Native merit and ambition can never hope to pass, and that these are considered traits which a Native can not hope to exhibit – are they not in effect undoing all that they have done, unteaching the Native all that he has been taught, and pursuing a suicidal policy, which will inevitably array all the talent, honour and intelligence of the country ultimately in irreconcilable hostility to the ruling power.'

These first political associations represented moderate and gradualist views, but by the end of Company rule there was a growing sense of frustration among the educated middle classes. The younger elements among the Western-educated were beginning to turn away from whole-hearted identification with Western ideas and ambitions, and the alienation from traditional society to which such identification inevitably led. They were moving towards a new sense of being Indian – or, more precisely, of being Hindu.

It is important to remember that there was no real concept of an *Indian* nationalism in the geographic or ethnic sense. This was mainly because British dominion did not spread throughout India until just before the Mutiny. Linguistic and cultural differences, too, separated the various parts of the country from each other. Modern communications did not exist, and there was little exchange of ideas between the intelligentsia of the provinces of British India. When there was, its effect was confined to a minority of the urban middle classes in the presidency capitals. Bengali nationalism, however, *was* taking root, and so was a particularly Hindu nationalism. This was not unnatural; the majority of the Western-educated were in fact Hindus. The Muslims were basically indifferent to the West, and their indifference was reinforced not only by their religion but by the fact that they had been dispossessed from their rule by the British. Generally speaking, they lived withdrawn from the effects of Westernization, though this was to change after 1858. In pre-Mutiny Delhi, however, there was considerable interest in Western ideas, and a group of scholars set out to translate into Urdu something of the science and learning of the West. This brought some diffusion of liberal ideas, but the movement came to an end with the Mutiny.

By the end of Company rule, the main attitudes nationalism was to take in India already existed. All were responses to Western influences, and even those which appeared totally to reject Western ideas and values were motivated by them. All were attempts to declare some sort of identity, either in the conqueror's terms or in those of indigenous religions and cultures. In a very real sense, the Mutiny cleared the decks, crystallized emotions, and laid down the order of battle.

# ENTR'ACTE

## *The Mutiny as the Meeting of Two Dying Systems*

# *The Mutiny as the Meeting of Two Dying Systems*

BASICALLY, the revolt of 1857 originated in the reaction of a conservative, tradition-loving section of Indian society to the modernizing zeal of their British conquerors. As the British consolidated their power in India, they also seemed to be intent on reforming Indian society both morally and politically. In creating a rational and efficient administration, they threatened much of the traditional order. Princes and landowners, the principal representatives of that order, felt themselves under sentence of extinction.

Under the governor-generalship of Lord Dalhousie, both the princes and landowners had felt the heavy hand of government. Dalhousie wished to remove as many feudal states as he could, leaving only a few of the larger ones nominally independent but actually under the control of the central government. The plan was laudable in many senses, for it was designed to lead to better government and a happier situation for the peasantry who, under their feudal princes, had no rights or protection against the whims of the ruler. Dalhousie first used his powers to annex states where there was no direct heir, refusing to accept the custom that a childless ruler had the right to adopt an heir. Satara, Jhansi, Nagpur, and a number of minor states were annexed. The kingdom of Oudh, which had been grossly misgoverned for many years, was also made a part of British India.

Dalhousie's second objective was to expropriate land from landlords without 'proper' title to their estates. Some twenty thousand were confiscated in the Deccan alone.

Because the government was a foreign government, and its agents foreign, too, with only a slight understanding of customary law and even of local languages, there were many cases of injustice which the government did little to remedy. The reforms were carried out ruthlessly, with little or no attempt to consider the feelings of those involved. It is little wonder that those who suffered were angry, or that those who expected to find themselves in the same position were frightened.

Indians only had to look around them to see the British interfering at every level of life. In the twenties and thirties of the nineteenth century, a number of reforms had been carried out. Suttee had been banned, infanticide suppressed, and a campaign mounted against the Thug gangs who robbed and murdered in the name of Kali. These warts on Hindu society had been regarded with horror by the British, who had also allowed themselves to view the Hindu religion as a barbaric, pagan creed, beneath contempt. Many officers in the Company's army took this attitude and grasped every opportunity of trying to persuade their men to become Christian.

Some of the sepoys felt that an attempt would be made to break their caste in such a way as to cut them off from their religion. Hinduism, unlike Christianity, is indivisibly part of the social order. Man's place in society is carefully ordered by the mechanism of caste. Break a man's caste, and not only is his place in society destroyed but he stands on the threshold of a damnation far worse than the Christian concept of hell. A Hindu believes that reincarnation continues until the highest caste – the Brahmin – is reached after the soul has returned many times and has suffered much. When a Brahmin dies, his reward is oblivion, the heaven of the Hindus. Many of the sepoys in the Company's army were Brahmins and therefore felt that they had everything to lose from the Christianizing activities of the British. There had, in fact, been mutinies based on similar fears before 1857.

In Vellore in south India, the sepoys had revolted in 1806 after being ordered to wear a new style of headdress, to trim their beards, and to give up wearing caste marks. This, they believed, was an attempt to make them Christians. The mutiny was brutally suppressed. In 1824, a sepoy regiment which had been ordered to Burma refused to move because it felt its caste was endangered by an official refusal to supply special transport for cooking pots; caste usage compelled each man to have his own set. Guns opened fire on the sepoys on the parade ground where they were assembled, and next morning six of the ringleaders were hanged, while hundreds were condemned to fourteen years' hard labour on the public roads. Five more men were later executed and their bodies hung in chains as an example to their fellows. In 1852, another regiment refused to cross the sea to Burma. This time, however, the sepoys were simply marched away to another station. A number of other mutinies and near-mutinies had taken place, all with some basis of fear that the British were trying to break the sepoys' caste and make them turn Christian.

By the end of 1856, the whole of India – and particularly the north – was uneasy. Nearly every class had been shaken in some way by the reforms and political changes instituted by the British. Only the most Westernized Indians were unaffected by fear. The newly emerging middle class had no wish to preserve the old order unchanged, and during the Mutiny they remained actively loyal to the British. But the dispossessed had been awaiting their opportunity. Those princes who had lost the territories they felt to be rightly theirs, the king of Oudh, the last sad descendants of the Mughal emperors at the twilight court of Delhi – all were awaiting the opportunity to rise in rebellion. Their agents were active among the sepoys, playing upon their fears and exciting their apprehensions, recalling the tale that a hundred years after the battle of Plassey would come the day that saw the end of British rule. The fuel was ready for the fire; all that was needed was a spark. The British themselves provided it.

In 1857 it was decided to replace the old musket known as Brown Bess with the new Enfield rifle, which had a much longer range and infinitely greater accuracy. To load the new rifle entailed biting a greased cartridge. The sepoys believed, with some justification, that the grease was made from cow or pig fat – the first, from an animal sacred to the Hindus, and the second from an animal regarded as unclean by the

Muslims. The Hindu sepoys saw this as yet another attempt to break their caste as a preliminary to making them all Christians. Slowly at first, but with increasing momentum, sepoy regiments refused to accept the new cartridges and finally broke into open mutiny. To them rallied the disaffected. At last the opportunity had come to make a stand against the British and, with the Bengal army at their backs, the disaffected seemed to have every chance of success.

Essentially, the Mutiny which had been triggered by dissatisfaction in the Bengal army was a feudal reaction to the pressures of British dominion which had been felt at all levels of the community. Behind the rebels there temporarily coalesced a wide and conflicting range of interests. There has been much controversy – engendered in the main by Indian historians – about the 'national' character of the Mutiny. There was none. Among the feudal elements involved, there was merely a desire to return to things as they had been before the coming of the British. The sepoys rebelled in what they believed was self-defence. Not unnaturally, other elements took advantage of the breakdown of law and order. In some areas, there were distinctly Luddite overtones when mobs attacked and destroyed factories and machinery. This may well have been partly a product of class antagonisms, for there was a general tendency to attack those who had benefited from British rule – bankers, moneylenders, and the like, who were also merchants and entrepreneurs.

One of the principal factors in the suppression of the Mutiny was the fact that most of the leading rebels were united only on one simple issue, the ejection of the British. When this seemed impossible to achieve, everything else fell to pieces. The sepoys fought on – not for any ideal, but because the British had made it quite clear to them that the chances of death if they surrendered were about as high as, if not higher than, they would be if they went on fighting. Most of the civilian leaders either disappeared, were killed in battle, or executed. The men who had taken impromptu advantage of the effective collapse of British rule faded into the background from which they had emerged.

The Mutiny represents a divide in the history of British India. It was, in general terms, the violent meeting of two dying systems, of British India as a 'country' power – an essentially oriental government with strong European overtones – and of traditional India, trembling with unresolved and frequently unstated fears, obsessed with the past and unable or willing to accept the modernizing tendencies of the British. The Mutiny and the process of its suppression created no gulf between the Indians and the British, for the reforms of the 1830s and the changing attitude of the administration had already succeeded in alienating the rulers from the mass of the ruled. But it did crystallize and reinforce the division by increasing the distrust of both sides.

PART TWO

# *The Indian Empire 1858–1947*

# Historical Framework

ONE of the results of the assumption of power by the Crown in 1858 was that, generally speaking, the internal political boundaries of India became fixed. This removed the princes' fears of expropriation and identified their interests with those of the British. The result was the petrification of the frontiers of over five hundred princely states, occupying nearly two-fifths of India. The reasons for this new attitude by the British were that most of the princely states had stood firm or at least neutral in the Mutiny, and the British hoped they would stand as firm in the future against any internal rebellion; furthermore, the British were unwilling to endanger their position by continuing a policy of political and social reform which had, they believed, contributed to the outbreak of the Mutiny. After 1860, there were no further annexations, but the princely states had to accept the overriding authority of the government in Calcutta.

So, too, the government of India was now subject to the overriding authority of the secretary of state in London. Though the Act of 1858 set up a Council of India in London, which included members with Indian experience, to advise the secretary of state, it was essentially a consultative body. As parliament took little interest in Indian affairs, the secretary of state wielded virtually unlimited and only infrequently questioned powers.

This authority really became effective after the construction of the Red Sea telegraph in 1870, which brought Whitehall and Calcutta into direct communication. Though strong viceroys were still able to get their own way in some matters, the government of India was fundamentally helpless. In everyday matters it had considerable freedom of action, but in constitutional issues affecting the government of India, the government in London often imposed its ideas in defiance of the administration in India. In the government of India itself there were a number of changes immediately after the Mutiny. The Central Legislative Council was enlarged in 1861 by the addition of non-official members, amongst whom were two Indians. The council had virtually no legislative function and no control over the executive. It was the first of many quasi-democratic devices designed to give an appearance of responsibility to institutions of a parliamentary character. Councils were established in the provinces on the same basis as at the Centre. These legislative councils supplied the framework for later demands for constitutional changes. In 1892 the principle of election was established, though only for special-interest groups such as municipalities, chambers of commerce and universities. The Viceroy's Executive Council, however, remained entirely official in character.

Fear of external aggression still dominated many minds in India, especially in the army. Russian expansion in Central Asia raised the possibility of an attack upon India through Afghanistan. Similar fears had led in 1839 to the disasters of the first Afghan war. History virtually repeated itself – though without any serious military reverse – when in 1879 British troops once again entered Afghanistan. A new Liberal administration in Britain, however, replaced the viceroy, and the campaign was brought to an end.

Though the problems of Afghanistan and the Russian threat to India temporarily receded, they remained the axis on which much of the government of India's policy revolved. Frontier affairs, both in their imperial aspect and in the local problem of frontier tribes, offered a continuing excuse for drastic administrative actions, as well as a valid argument for retaining large numbers of well-armed British troops in the country, ostensibly for the defence of the frontier. Apart from the drain on Indian finances, preoccupation with the North-West Frontier led to the neglect of other frontiers and to a specialization in military training which was found to be useless in 1942 when India was really threatened with invasion.

The last major aggression by Britain in Asia has certain similarities to events in Afghanistan, only with France instead of Russia as the rival power. France was expanding in Indo-China and there was some apprehension in Calcutta and London that French influence was growing in Upper Burma. The death of King Mindon, who had ruled since 1853, led to a dispute over the succession, and Thibaw was placed on the throne as a pliable tool of the ministerial party in 1879. In that year, the British withdrew their Resident from the Burmese capital. Six years later an enormous fine was imposed on the British-owned Bombay-Burma Trading Corporation, which had refused a loan to Thibaw. At the same time, a French envoy was endeavouring to obtain the management of state monopolies and the right to construct a railway. A British ultimatum (1885) was ignored by the Burmese, and war was declared by the British. Thibaw surrendered within two weeks and the country was annexed. The Indian system of administration was put into practice, and Burma became a province of the Indian empire.

From the Mutiny until the 1890s was a period of civil peace in India, but this was broken towards the end of the period by outbursts of extremist and revivalist nationalism. The history of India from the last decade of the nineteenth century until the end of British rule is virtually that of the conflict between the government of India and the principal nationalist movement, the Indian National Congress. Its principal events are a series of constitutional concessions by the British government.

The first of these was the Indian Councils Act of 1909, usually called (after its authors) the Morley-Minto reforms. Briefly, its provisions increased the membership of the Central Legislative Council from sixteen to sixty, twenty-seven of whom were to be elected mainly by special-interest groups. Perhaps the most important change was the recognition of the Muslim community as the most important of these groups, and the dangerous principle of communal representation was incorporated into the Act.

The members of councils were made up of three groups – elected members, officials, and non-officials nominated by such bodies as trade associations, landholders, and universities. In the provinces, non-officials outnumbered the officials, but in the central council there was an official majority. The councils, however, could offer only criticism and advice.

These concessions did not satisfy nationalist opinion, and agitation for further reform continued. In 1917, an announcement was made of further concessions. These were embodied in the Government of India Act of 1919, known as the Montagu-Chelmsford reforms. The Act, which came into force in 1921, was a major step forward in the technique of responsible government but not in its practice, for though in theory the powers of the new legislatures were extensive, the governor-general remained the real authority; he could 'certify' measures rejected by the legislatures, and if necessary rule by ordinance. A wide range of debate was therefore encouraged, but only listened to if it suited the executive. A system known as 'dyarchy' was introduced in the provinces. By this was meant the division of the departments of administration into 'reserved' and 'transferred' sectors. Generally speaking, law and order, revenue and finance, were reserved – i.e. administered by the provincial governor – while local government, sanitation, education, and economic development were transferred to elected ministers. Again, the concession of the forms of government without real responsibility led to further demands for reform.

In external affairs, there was once again trouble with Afghanistan. In 1919, the Amir was assassinated and his son, Amanullah, taking advantage of civil disturbance in the Punjab, attempted to invade the North-West Frontier Province by raising the tribesmen. The campaign lasted for only a few weeks.

India also began to take her place in international affairs. Indian representatives appeared at the League of Nations and at many international conferences.

The disturbances in the Punjab, of which Amanullah had sought to take advantage, were the result of the delay in putting the new reforms into action. In 1919, martial law was declared in the Punjab, and a number of security ordinances were passed by the government which seemed at variance with the supposed spirit of the new reforms. The consequences of a massacre of unarmed people at Amritsar by troops under the command of Brigadier-General Dyer convinced Congress nationalists that the British government did not intend to allow the new reforms to work. The result was the first non-cooperation campaign of the new Congress leader, Mahatma Gandhi.

The campaign resulted in the abstention of nearly two-thirds of the eligible electorate from voting for the new legislatures. English cloth was burnt in public, and the jails were crowded with 30,000 political prisoners. The Prince of Wales, brought out to India to arouse the enthusiasm of the masses for the Crown, was greeted by a *hartal* (suspension of business) which faced him with empty streets.

At the session of Congress held at Ahmedabad in 1921, Gandhi was given the sole authority to lead the nationalist movement. Mass demonstrations were called off after the destruction of a police station and the murder of twenty-two policemen in a town in the United Provinces. The frustration which resulted and the failure of the Swaraj party formed by C. R. Das and Pandit Motilal Nehru to contest the elections and to wreck reforms from within, helped to revive Hindu-Muslim conflict. Communal riots, undoubtedly provoked, broke out in 1923, and the Muslim League which had been virtually moribund since 1916 was revived in the following year.

One of the provisions of the 1919 Act was that its results should be examined after ten years. In 1927, a Conservative government in Britain appointed a commission of investigation consisting entirely of British members of parliament under the chairmanship of Sir John Simon. The commission visited India in the following year, but was boycotted by nationalist leaders. Its report was issued in 1930. In the meanwhile, however, a Labour government had taken office, and the viceroy – who had been recalled for consultations – announced on his return to India that the British government envisaged that constitutional progress would lead in time to dominion status for India. He also announced that a conference representing all sectors of Indian life, including the princes, would meet shortly in London.

The boycott of the Simon commission in India might have given the opportunity for an alliance between the Muslim League and Congress. However, Congress refused to accept claims put forward on behalf of the Muslims by M. A. Jinnah at an all-party conference held in 1928. Both the all-party conference and later Congress agreed to accept dominion status by December 31st, 1929, at the latest, despite the latter's declaration in 1927 that its aim was complete independence. However, Congress, in a session at Lahore in December 1929, again declared that its aim was complete independence, and decided to boycott the forthcoming conference in London and begin a civil disobedience campaign. The campaign was inaugurated by Mahatma Gandhi on April 6th, 1930, with his famous march to Dandi in western India and his making of salt from sea-water in protest against the government's salt monopoly. This was followed by mass strikes, the boycott of British goods, and violence. The government reacted with such vigour that 103 people were killed, 420 injured, and 60,000 imprisoned in less than a year. These repressive measures proved unsuccessful, and conciliation was attempted.

The first session of the Round Table Conference in London was adjourned on January 2nd, 1931. On March 4th, the so-called Gandhi-Irwin pact between the Congress leader and the viceroy was concluded. The government abandoned its repressive measures and released political prisoners, and Congress called off the civil disobedience campaign and agreed to join the conference when it re-assembled. Gandhi attended as the only representative of Congress, and proved unwilling to agree on any subject. The government decided that it must proceed without the approval of the Indian National Congress. In January 1932, Gandhi was arrested and Congress was declared an illegal organization. By March of the following year, more than 120,000 people had been arrested in India and, according to a report of a delegation of the India League (published in 1933), there were 'wholesale violence, physical outrages, punitive expeditions, collective fines on villages, and seizure of lands and property'.

Civil disobedience continued until May 1934, when Congress decided that it would work within the framework of the forthcoming Government of India Act of 1935 which was to come into force in 1937. The provisions of the new Act were as follows. (1) The provinces, then numbering eleven, were to be given full responsible government, subject to certain reserved powers in the hands of the governors to be used only in the event of complete breakdown of law and order. (2) At the centre, a federal structure was to be set up. The central legislature was to consist of two houses, made up for the first time of representatives not only from the provinces but from the princely states. The viceroy's executive council was to consist of ministers responsible to the central legislature, with the exception of the portfolios of foreign affairs and defence, which were to remain in the hands of the viceroy, who also retained certain reserve powers like those of the provincial governors to be used in the case of emergency. As for dominion status, it was officially stated that the clauses of the Act – i.e. the retention of reserve powers – which precluded full self-government were merely transitional, and that India would, by usage and convention, quickly acquire all the freedom, external and internal, enjoyed by the other dominions.

That part of the Act concerning a federal structure never came into force, as the princes could not agree to any lessening of their sovereignty. The federal principle was also denounced by both Congress and the Muslim League. Thus the government of India remained what it always had been, an autocratic government with the executive only responsible to the secretary of state in London.

The elections held early in 1937 resulted in Congress ministries in seven out of the eleven provinces. In some provinces, the Muslim League wanted to form coalition ministries with Congress, but Congress refused. Congress administrations were reasonably successful, and the prestige of the organization had grown to such an extent that its membership reached five million by the end of 1939.

When the second world war broke out, Congress refused to cooperate with the government, and all the Congress ministries resigned in October and November 1939. But with the

German armies apparently victorious in Europe, Congress offered to cooperate with the British government if a provisional national government was established at the centre. This was refused in August 1940, but an offer was made (1) to set up after the war a body to prepare a new constitution, (2) to enlarge the viceroy's executive council with more Indian members, and (3) to create a War Advisory Council of representatives from British India and the princely states. Congress rejected the offer, and a new civil disobedience campaign – not on a mass scale, but by individuals only – was begun.

After the fall of Rangoon to the Japanese in March 1942 and the possibility of an immediate attack on India, the British cabinet minister, Sir Stafford Cripps, was sent to India with what was virtually the same offer as that of August 1940. In the meanwhile, the Muslim League, whose provincial governments had not resigned at the outbreak of war, had become totally estranged from Congress.

On August 8th, 1942, Congress called for a widespread return to mass civil disobedience. The government acted immediately by declaring Congress illegal and arresting its leaders. Riots and sabotage throughout India followed. Repression was again immediate. Over 60,000 people were arrested, 18,000 detained without trial, 940 killed, and 1,630 injured in clashes with police and troops.

In May 1944, Mahatma Gandhi was released from jail on grounds of ill health. His first act was to hold discussions with Jinnah, but they had no positive result. In March 1945, the viceroy, Lord Wavell, returned from London with the proposal that all members of his executive council (except the commander-in-chief) should be Indians drawn from among the leaders of the political parties, with equal Muslim and Hindu representation. A conference held at Simla in June 1945 broke down because there was no agreement between Congress and the Muslim League. Shortly afterwards, a Labour government came to power in Britain and decided to hold fresh elections in India. These were held at the beginning of 1946 and the result was an overwhelming victory for Congress in the general seats and for the Muslim League in those seats reserved for Muslims.

On February 19th, 1946, the British prime minister announced a mission to India of some members of his cabinet. The mission arrived in India in March. After a series of discussions with Congress and Muslim League leaders in which no area of agreement between the two parties could be found, the mission announced its own recommendations on May 16th.

These proposed (1) a federal government, to include the princely states; (2) the division of India into three provincial groups consisting of the North-West Frontier Province, Sind, Baluchistan and the Punjab; Bengal and Assam; and the rest; (3) a constitution to be framed by a constituent assembly elected on a communal basis by the provincial legislative assemblies; (4) the provinces could, if they wished, leave the new federation after the election of the assembly; and (5) a provisional national government should be established forthwith from the leaders of the different parties.

The proposals were accepted by the Muslim League on June 6th, but Congress rejected them, though offering to join a constituent assembly for the purpose of framing a new constitution. The British cabinet mission left India on June 29th. The Muslim League then demanded that the viceroy should go ahead and constitute a provisional government, even though Congress refused to take part. This, of course, was not acceptable, and the League withdrew its previous approval of the mission's proposals. The viceroy then reconstructed his executive council – but with Congress members only. The League's reaction to this was to declare August 16th as a day of 'direct action'. On that day, though most demonstrations were peaceful, Calcutta became the scene of the most brutal communal riots. A number of Hindus were killed and Hindu property was looted and destroyed; in self-defence, the Hindus, too, took to the streets. The Muslim League government of Bengal took no decisive action. Neither did the British governor, nor the central government.

Other outbreaks of communal violence followed when Congress nominees were sworn in to the viceroy's executive council. But the viceroy succeeded in bringing Muslim League members into his council and informed Congress that the League had agreed to join a constituent assembly. The council was not, however, notable for harmony, and the situation deteriorated even further when it transpired that the League had in fact no intention of joining in the assembly. Nevertheless, the assembly met on December 9th, 1946 and appointed committees to draft the provisions of the new constitution. The Muslim League did not participate.

On February 20th, 1947, the British government announced its intention of leaving India by June 1948 and appointed Lord Mountbatten as viceroy, to carry out the transfer of power. The Muslim League once more embarked on 'direct action'. Violence, murder and arson convulsed the Punjab and the North-West Frontier Province. Congress reluctantly accepted the fact that, if independence were to be achieved, India must be divided.

On June 3rd, the new viceroy broadcast a declaration of British government policy. Its substance was: (1) If Muslim-majority areas so desired, they should be permitted to form a separate dominion, and a new constituent assembly would be set up for the purpose. In that case, however, Bengal and the Punjab would have to be partitioned if the representatives of Hindu-majority districts in the legislatures of those provinces so demanded. (2) A referendum would be carried out in the North-West Frontier Province to ascertain whether or not it wished to join Pakistan. (3) The district of Sylhet would be joined to the Muslim area of Bengal after the people's views had been discovered by a referendum. (4) Boundary commissions would be set up to define the boundaries of the Hindu and Muslim provinces in Bengal and the Punjab. (5) Legislation would be introduced in the current session of parliament at Westminster to confer immediate dominion status on India (or on the two countries, if partition was decided upon), without any prejudice to the final decision of the constituent assembly (or assemblies) in this respect.

Both Congress and the Muslim League finally accepted the plan, and the India Independence Act passed through parliament on July 1st, 1947. The date set for the transfer of power

Troops at drill in front of Government House and the English church, Bombay 1767

Two British officers being entertained in an Indian house. One is smoking a hookah. c. 1800

A dinner party in the 1840s. The guests all have their own servants

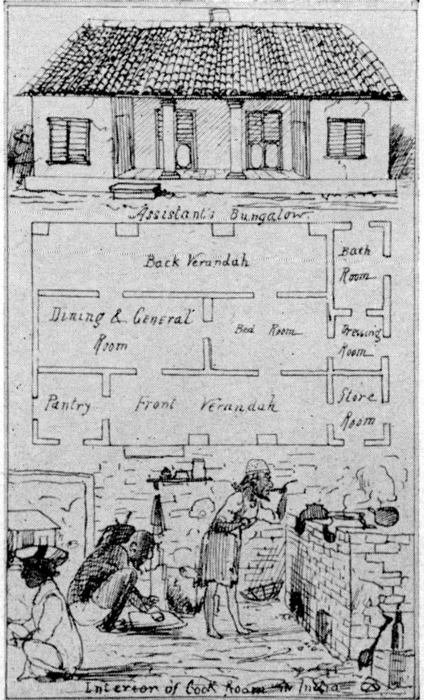


The simple bungalow designed for an assistant at an indigo plantation. c. 1880

A great classical mansion for the British representative in a native state. c.1813

The British conquered India with Indian soldiers

*Left:* Sepoys of the Company's army, c. 1806

*Below:* The British Resident's camp at the court of Sindia, the Maratha chief, in 1809

The Mughal emperor, Shah Alam, granting to Clive sovereign rights in Bengal. August 1765

T. B. Macaulay, who introduced English education into India

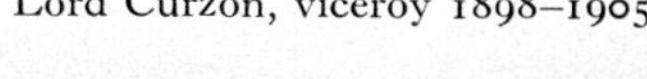

Lord Curzon, viceroy 1898–1905

A village school in early nineteenth-century Bengal

Oxen used for drawing water. This is an early nineteenth-century view, but the method persists in some parts of India today

*Above:* Jamsetji Tata (1839–1904). Industrialist

*Above right:* Ram Mohun Roy (1772–1833). Educational reformer

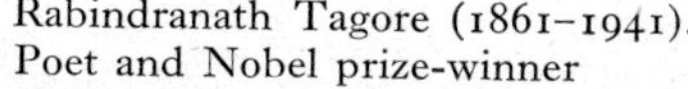

Rabindranath Tagore (1861–1941). Poet and Nobel prize-winner

M. A. Jinnah (1876–1948) and Mahatma Gandhi (1869–1948). Nationalist leaders

A Japanese leaflet issued on behalf of Subhas Chandra Bose's Indian National Army during the Second World War

to India and Pakistan had been advanced to August 15th, 1947. On that day, the constituent assembly in Delhi declared India a dominion within the British Commonwealth. Lord Mountbatten was to be its first governor-general. In Karachi, Mr Jinnah was chosen to be first governor-general of Pakistan. The British Indian empire was at an end.

# 1

# *The British in India*

## ATTITUDES

THE BRITISH community was taken by surprise in 1857 when the Bengal army began its rebellion. The British had assumed that all was quiet, that the reforming and progressive actions of government had spread only gratitude and affection. When reports came in of the massacre of British officers and their wives and children, they were horrified and called loudly for revenge. All elements gave way to hatred, but racial antagonism was strongest amongst the non-official merchant community and the planters. Though, when the Mutiny ended, the government was prepared to pursue a policy of conciliation, many of the British were not and the memory of the Mutiny remained as a constant reminder that it was unwise to trust the natives. It was a not unnatural reaction to the times when a trusted servant or a regimental soldier had suddenly changed, apparently without reason, into a murderer. In spite of the fact that many British came to realize, after the hot flush of the Mutiny had died down, that they and their government were not entirely blameless, the distrust never wholly disappeared.

After 1858, the numbers of the British, both official and non-official, increased steadily over the years. 'Anglo-Indian' society had its stratifications and was large enough to contain most of the activities of the British in India. Officials and soldiers were compelled – particularly outside the large towns – to have contact with Indians, but it was almost entirely *official* contact. Social relations were extremely rare, and the civil servant who was interested in Indian culture even rarer. The British became completely what they were already becoming in the last twenty years of Company rule – 'a separate caste, with several sub-castes, strictly preserving the usual characteristics of endogamy, commensality, and mutual control by members'.

The expansion of the railway network cut out that intimacy with the country which long-distance travelling overland had brought. As the century grew older, passages from India to Britain became faster. The pressures of disease, however, remained constant until the discovery of anti-malaria and anti-cholera protection late in the century.

The British community considered every attempt to allow Indians into the higher levels of government service and the judiciary as a direct threat to their position. The growth of middle-class nationalism was looked upon with disfavour and suspicion. Outbreaks of religion-inspired violence raised fears of another rebellion.

When, in 1883, a Liberal viceroy brought in a Bill by which Europeans could be tried by Indian magistrates, the non-official community reacted as it had done almost fifty years earlier at the time of the Black Act of 1837. The non-official community, already feeling menaced by the expansion of local government bodies to include Indians, was incensed at the viceroy's action. Most members of the community said that it was an insult, and some even went to the length of suggesting that Englishwomen would be in danger, as Indian judges would abuse their powers in order to fill their harems with white women! At a mass meeting held in Calcutta in February 1883 there were many wild speeches. A leading British lawyer warned his audience against 'the wily natives' who had poisoned the minds of the rulers against the British community. Even apparently 'advanced' members of the community considered the Bill an insult. Mrs Annette Beveridge, who had gone to India to help Indian women, claimed that the Bill would subject 'civilized women [i.e. Englishwomen] to the jurisdiction of men who have done little or nothing to redeem the women of their own race, and whose social ideas are still on the outer verge of civilization'. The agitation resulted in the founding of a European and Anglo-Indian Defence

Association. In the end, the British succeeded in winning the right to trial by a jury – of their own countrymen.

As political extremism grew in the last decade of the nineteenth century and burst into terrorism in the first decade of the twentieth, the British-owned press – which represented to a large extent the views of the non-official community – strongly attacked all nationalists, whether moderate or extremist. The Allahabad *Pioneer* of May 5th, 1908 suggested that the sort of vengeance might be meted out which had been given to mutineers in 1857. 'The wholesale arrest of the acknowledged terrorists in a city or district,' it wrote, 'coupled with an intimation that at any repetition of the offence ten of them would be shot for every life sacrificed, would soon put down the practice [of throwing bombs].'

The first world war brought changes in the composition of the non-official community. A great many new recruits to large European business undertakings arrived in India and altered the general balance of the community. These new arrivals, however, were no less xenophobic. General Dyer, who opened fire on an unarmed crowd of civilians at Amritsar in 1919, was widely supported by the British community and a large sum of money was subscribed for him after he had been forced to resign.

During the years after the war, as the British government yielded to nationalist pressures, the British community continued to fight in its own defence, but slowly began to realize that the tide was running irresistibly against the old order. Nevertheless, racial arrogance remained undiluted and racial sentiments were expressed no less vulgarly than they had been before. Some British still tried to break through the barriers between themselves and the Indians, but few had much success. There was a certain amount of public fraternization, but it was mainly with those Indians – princely rulers and businessmen – who had little identification with the reality of the nationalist struggle.

The texture of British life in India became, with the electric fan, the refrigerator and the motor-car, smoother and less irritating. The pioneering of air routes to India brought

'Home' within a few days' journey. The sense of dangerous exile which had given the British so much moral support began to disappear just at the time when British India was nearing its end. In the last twenty years of its life, the British in India had little influence upon events. Their prejudices remained to antagonize many Indians. In rapidly changing circumstances, they were still on occasion outspokenly offensive. But in the end, it was the government in London which made the decisions, and in the last years of British rule that government was less responsive to the demands of the British community in India than it had ever been before.

## CURIOSITY

In 1861, Alexander Cunningham sent a memorandum to the viceroy complaining that the government paid no attention to the antiquities of India. In response, Cunningham was appointed Director of Archaeology in 1862. The government anticipated that the appointment would only be temporary and that Cunningham would be able to complete all the necessary work of recording Indian antiquities in a few years! However, in 1871, Cunningham was given the title of Director-General of the Archaeological Survey of India. The title was impressive, but in fact Cunningham had no proper staff and in effect directed only himself. In 1874, the survey, which had been confined to northern India, was extended to the presidencies of Madras and Bombay. Dr James Burgess, who was given charge of the work, was nominally subordinate to Cunningham but in fact had a free hand.

Cunningham's main preoccupation was with Buddhist remains, a reflection of the contemporary interest in Buddhism in Europe. Between 1862 and 1884 he published twenty-three full volumes of reports on his tours. They contained a great mass of inadequately related material. Cunningham spent very little time at any of his sites, and much of the digging he carried out destroyed valuable archaeological evidence, but he did discover a wide range of objects of great importance to the history of Indian art. He was, indeed, an amateur. So, in fact, were most of the archaeologists of the time. James Burgess might condemn Cunningham's volumes as 'essentially the reports of unconnected tours ... not scientific or reliable', but he was not well acquainted with the latest scholarship himself though he was much more methodical in his work than Cunningham.

When Cunningham retired in 1885 Burgess took his place as head of the department and its work was extended, but with only a small increase in staff. There was still an aura of impermanency about the department, for the government anticipated that the survey would be completed in five years or so and that the department could then be disbanded, leaving the responsibility for the conservation of antiquities to local governments.

Conservation, in fact, was a new concept. It was not until 1881 that the central government had decided to appoint a Curator of Ancient Monuments, charged with preparing a list of such monuments and stating which should be kept in permanent good repair. The man appointed to the post had been an engineer officer, Major H. H. Cole, who produced a large number of reports including ten folio volumes published under the title *Preservation of National Monuments in India* (Calcutta 1881–5).

Cole's appointment, which had been for only three years, was not extended, and such impetus as he had been able to give to the work of conservation rapidly faded. After the retirement of Burgess in 1889, the work of the survey also suffered. The position of director-general was not filled, and the department almost came to a standstill. In 1895 the future of the survey was considered by the government. Though it was decided not to abolish it, the government decided that conservation was more important than research. In a reorganization that took place, conservation remained the responsibility of provincial governments. Where local officials were interested, conservation was carried out, but on the whole buildings of great historical and artistic value were allowed to decay.

The depressed state of government-sponsored archaeological work continued until the arrival in India of Lord Curzon in 1898. On a visit to India a few years before his appointment as viceroy, he had been particularly attracted by Mughal architecture. He had seen then the neglect of ancient monuments, and he was determined to do something about it. His reasons were complex but his actions were single-minded and he caused a tremendous shake-up among those nominally responsible for conservation. In a speech to the Asiatic Society in Calcutta, he stated his intention 'to assert more definitely during my time the Imperial responsibility of Government in respect of Indian antiquities to inaugurate or to persuade a more liberal attitude on the part of those with whom it rests to provide the means and to be a faithful guardian of the priceless treasure-house of art and learning that has, for a few years at any rate, been committed to my charge.'

Curzon's proposals for the reappointment of a director-general and the sanctioning of government funds for archaeological work were confirmed by the secretary of state in London in 1901. The man appointed, John Marshall, arrived in India in the following year. The revived department continued to be starved of both men and money. For a number of years, some of its workers held dual appointments – Aurel Stein, for example, was both Archaeological Superintendent and Inspector-General of Education in the North-West Frontier Province. The work of conservation and repair got under way. Huts were cleared from the approaches to palaces. The Taj Mahal had its squalid surroundings cleaned up. This work continued steadily until the end of British rule.

Scientific digging of sites at last began to bring current standards of professionalism into the work in India. Under Marshall's guidance many sites were scientifically investigated, including those of the pre-Aryan Indus valley civilization at Harappa and Mohenjodaro – one of the greatest archaeological discoveries of all time.

With the coming of scientific archaeology, the amateur ceased to be of much consequence, though there were still officials interested enough to investigate local painting and sculpture. James Fergusson produced his *History of Indian and Eastern Architecture* in 1875. But in the twentieth century, this sort of work became almost completely the monopoly of scholars in the West. The curiosity of the ordinary Englishman in India had to give place to the organized curiosity of government and universities.

## LITERATURE

After the Mutiny, administrators and soldiers continued the literary traditions of their predecessors. Many of their works were on history and administration, though they occasionally wrote light verse and novels. Among the historians, W. W. Hunter not only explored Indian history but something of the actual scene in the 1870s. The atmosphere of post-Mutiny India is contained in George Otto Trevelyan's *The Competition-Wallah* (1864). In the second half of the nineteenth century, many administrators wrote their memoirs. Few have literary value, but all are of historical and sociological interest. Of officials who could write about their work with style, there were few who could do as well as S. S. Thorburn whose *Mussulmans and Moneylenders* (1886), though concerned only with the Punjab, is one of the most revealing and humane documents on the state of the debt-ridden Indian peasant. Sir Alfred Lyall, who wrote poetry as well as history, was also a stylist writer.

Under the stimulus of Curzon, there was a revival of interest in the actual life of the British in India, and with his encouragement such works as E. J. Buck's *Simla: Past and Present* (1904) and H. E. Busteed's *Echoes from Old Calcutta* (1908) were written by government officials.

With the considerable growth in the size of the British community after 1860, British society in India took on a life of its own. The business element expanded, but new types of English residents – such as journalists and school-teachers – also appeared. After the opening of the Suez Canal (1869) the number of 'cold-weather' visitors increased. The English-reading public in India was now quite substantial and its needs could not be entirely supplied from Britain. There grew up a market for verse and fiction about the lives of the British in

India. There was also a growing market in Britain for tales about India and for descriptive works about life there. The expatriate community, though it occasionally believed itself menaced by growing Indian unrest, felt – at least till the end of the century – strong enough to laugh at itself. Novels such as H. S. Cunningham's *Chronicles of Dustypore* (1879) took a sly look at the life of the British in their ghetto (known in India as 'the station'). There was also a vague interest in the natives – as servants – as in 'EHA' *Behind the Bungalow* (1901). Most of this kind of work is still readable, and sometimes still amusing. G. Aberigh-Mackay's *Twenty-One Days in India*, first published anonymously in a Bombay newspaper in 1880, contains portraits of such pillars of 'Anglo-Indian' society as the commander-in-chief. 'At Simla and Calcutta the Government of India always sleeps with a revolver under its pillow – that revolver is the Commander-in-Chief. There is a tacit understanding that this revolver is not to be let off; indeed, sometimes it is believed that this revolver is not loaded.'

In this tradition is the Indian work of Rudyard Kipling, who became the laureate of Anglo-India for a larger audience than it could ever have considered possible. Kipling explored the shallow lives of the British in India and reflected some, but by no means all, of their prejudices. The few Indians who appear in such of his work as was written in India are either servants or 'incompetent' educated Bengalis. It was only after leaving India that Kipling was able to write, in *Kim*, what is undoubtedly the best work of fiction about India by an Englishman.

A number of other writers followed Kipling. Among the most interesting was Flora Annie Steel, whose *On the Face of the Waters* (1896) – a novel about the Mutiny – is again concerned with the British. Its Indian characters are merely symbols. No 'Anglo-Indian' writer was able to portray Indians with any sense of life. The journalist Edmund Candler made, perhaps, the first attempt in his *Shri Ram, Revolutionist* (1910).

In the last twenty-five years of British rule two outstanding novelists produced works dealing with British life in India.

One, E. M. Forster's *A Passage to India,* though hailed by Indians for its attack on 'Anglo-Indian' society and its prejudices, is just as offensive in its drawing of Indian character as its predecessors. Edward Thompson's novels, on the other hand, give an accurate feel of the disintegrating empire of the 1930s.

There were many writers of light verse, and Kipling's *Departmental Ditties* (1886) are very much in the tradition. Most of this sort of verse was published first (and sometimes only) in newspapers. Much of it was concerned with the 'in' jokes of British society. It is mainly humorous and deliberately imitative of well-known contemporary British poetry.

'O grim and ghastly Mussulman,
Why art thou wailing so?
Is there a pain within thy brain,
Or in thy little toe?
The twilight shades are shutting fast
The golden gates of day,
Then shut up, too, your hullabaloo –
Or what's the matter, say?'

That stern and sombre Mussulman,
He heeded not my speech,
But raised again his howl of pain, –
A most unearthly screech!
'He dies!' – I thought, and forthwith rushed
To aid the wretched man,
When, with a shout, he yell'd – '*Get out!*
*I'm singing the Koran!*'

*The Poet's Mistake*

For much of the nineteenth century, the sense of exile and of doing one's duty with suffering remained – it is everywhere in Kipling's Indian work – and it was sometimes expressed with almost pathological melancholy.

My fellow exiles, fill your glasses,
We'll sing one song before we die;

The tiger in the jungle-grasses
Has sucked the peasant's life-blood dry.

*The Song of Death*

For poets of some sensibility like Sir Alfred Lyall, India was the 'Land of Regrets' and the Englishman always a stranger. This attitude, however, did not survive the first world war, when the spread of communications removed the sense of exile, and the growth of nationalism and the constitutional changes lessened the sense of duty. Nevertheless, even as late as 1933, an anonymous poet could still write:

The wheeling months go round
And back I come again
To the baked and blistered ground
And the dust-encumbered plain
And the bare hot-weather trees
And the Trunk Road's aching white;
Oh, land of little ease!
Oh, land of strange delight!

*Back East*

## ART AND ARCHITECTURE

The men who went out to India after 1858 did not consider drawing and water-colour painting as manly accomplishments. They left those to the women. There was no longer an interest in the picturesque. India had ceased to be an unknown land, and there was no longer any need to illustrate letters home with drawings of exotic natives and their festivals. Even the professional artist had no particular interest in India – he was concerned, as were his clients, with narrative paintings demonstrating some unimpeachable and easily recognizable moral precept. One or two professional artists did visit India and one at least found himself appalled by the lack of any expression of good taste among the British in India. In any case, the camera had replaced the eye and the hand. By 1870, photography had triumphed over the paintbrush. Instead of illustrating books from paintings and drawings, it became fashionable to use photographs. As early as 1863, William Johnson of the Bombay Civil Service produced a volume on *Oriental Races and Tribes*, lavishly illustrated with photographs. In 1868, *The People of India: A Series of Photographic Illustrations with Descriptive Letterpress of the Races and Tribes of Hindustan* appeared with government approval. 'During the administration of Lord Canning,' wrote the editors, J. F. Watson and J. W. Kaye, 'the interest which had been created in Europe by the remarkable development of the Photographic Art, communicated itself to India and originated the desire to turn it to account in the illustration of the topography, architecture and ethnology of the country. There were none, perhaps, in whom this interest was awakened more strongly than in Lord and Lady Canning. It was their wish to carry home with them at the end of their sojourn in India, a collection, obtained by private means, of photographic illustrations, which might recall to their memory the peculiarities of Indian life. . . . When the pacification of India [after the Mutiny] had been accomplished, the officers of the Indian services, who had made themselves acquainted with the principles and practice of photography, encouraged and patronized by the Governor-General, went forth and traversed the land in search of interesting subjects.'

Even after the triumph of the camera, there still remained a small number of amateur artists in the Indian services. A number of minor professional artists such as Lionel Edwards painted routine pictures of British life in India – pig-sticking and polo – which at least have some vague documentary value.

*

The public architecture of the Indian empire in the late nineteenth century reflected the taste of Victorian England. The Public Works Department was its architect, and it produced a range of buildings embodying most of the fashionable features of Western architecture from neo-Gothic to pseudo-Italian Renaissance. As one artist who visited India in 1876 put it, as he gazed at the dais erected for the Great Durbar at

Delhi – at which Queen Victoria was to be proclaimed empress of India – 'Well, perhaps it is a type of the new Raj . . . cold, flaring and bare, without a rag of sentiment.' Yet today, for all the justifiable criticisms that can be levelled against the examples of '*dak* bungalow Gothic', as it has been called, they reflect in their demented Mughal motifs a pleasant zaniness which was not in the minds of their designers. It is significant that Lord Curzon, so much concerned with preserving India's past, should when he turned to public building have encouraged the pastiche of European styles. For him, as for many others, Indian art and architecture were really a matter of archaeology, something dead. The Victoria Memorial Hall in Calcutta, which Curzon initiated, is built of shimmering white marble, allegedly in the style of the Italian Renaissance, with the addition – according to the architect, Sir William Emerson – of 'a suggestion of Orientalism in the arrangement of the domes and minor details'.

When thc British decided to move their capital from Calcutta to Delhi in 1912, they employed two English architects, Sir Edwin Lutyens and Sir Herbert Baker, to design the major public buildings. The result was a series of grandiose barracks incorporating classical and Mughal motifs without synthesis or sympathy. The buildings were more a gesture of defiance to growing Indian assertions than anything else, for they were – and are – completely unsuited to the Indian climate. Yet New Delhi is perhaps the most fitting monument to the British in India. Many of the elegant eighteenth-century buildings have disappeared, though a few, such as Government House, Calcutta, still stand. The classical architecture of Calcutta and elsewhere was erected without defiance – it was a statement made, not to impress Indians, but to convince the British themselves of their new status as rulers. The Gothic railway stations and fake Renaissance *palazzi* of Victorian India were expressions of contempt, a kind of racial architecture. But when the British erected New Delhi, they intended it as a statement of their intention to remain in India. The result was it is a Eurasian architecture in which the European and Indian elements stand uneasily together.

# 2

# *The Nature of British Rule*

## GOVERNMENT: PRINCIPLES AND PRACTICE

THE MUTINY brought more than the end of the East India Company and a new relationship between the government of India and the Crown. It also brought a change in the spirit of government. In the words of Fitzjames Stephen it resulted in 'the breakdown of the old system; the renunciation of the attempt to effect an impossible compromise between the Asiatic and European view of things, legal, military and administrative. The effect of the Mutiny on the Statute-book was unmistakable.' The belief – the essential belief behind the Bentinck reforms – that cooperation between the British and Indian middle classes could produce sweeping reform, died. The legislation of the sixties and seventies, which included the enactment of civil and criminal law codes, was to be conceived in an aggressive no-nonsense manner, sword in hand.

On the surface, the new spirit seemed very little different from the stern-faced paternalism of the Punjab system. But the men who operated that system had done so with a genuine, though limited, affection for the people. The new spirit was cold, bureaucratic, optimistic, and racially arrogant. It was also cautious, though this may seem paradoxical. The caution was apparent in the government's continuing unwillingness to interfere directly in matters of religion and social custom. Such interference did take place, but not as part of conscious policy.

After the débâcle of the Mutiny, the aim was to impose a modern and efficient administration, operated by experts within the scaffolding of a codified law. The principles were to be English principles and *only* English principles. John Lawrence put the case in 1858 when he wrote: 'We have not been elected or placed in power by the people, but we are here through our moral superiority, by the force of circumstances, by the will of Providence. This alone constitutes our charter to govern India. In doing the best we can for the people, we are bound by our conscience, and not by theirs.' Lawrence, nevertheless, represented part of a dying system. As a good paternalist, he believed in simple personal rule. As viceroy (1864–9), he resisted the creation of an executive council for Bengal which had been removed from the governor-general's immediate authority in 1854. His opposition was based on the thesis that the best form of government emerged from a personal administration with a strong central authority. Dalhousie had already advocated the abolition of the governorships of Madras and Bombay in 1853. Lawrence reinforced this with his view that there was 'as strong a necessity as there possibly could be, for one central absolute authority in India, to which all other authorities in that country must entirely defer'.

There was, however, opposition in Britain to any form of centralization in India. There was, too, the fear that had been expressed at the end of the previous century by Edmund Burke that unchecked despotism would inevitably lead to corruption and oppression. In 1784, the government had set up a board of control in Britain, with a member of the British government at its head, to oversee the Company's rule. Even after 1858 – with the Company dead, and direct authority for the governing of India invested in a minister of the Crown – it was still thought necessary to hold on to some principle of control, some balance of authorities. To check the activities of the secretary of state for India, a Council of India was set up, consisting in the main of former directors and employees of the Company. The secretary of state was obliged to consult this council before sending instructions to India; in emergencies, however, he was empowered to act without it. Parliament also attempted to develop effective control over Indian affairs by requiring that an annual statement of finances and of moral and material progress should be submitted to the House of Commons.

Sir Charles Wood, who had been president of the board of control from 1853 to 1855, was secretary of state between 1859 and 1866. In this capacity, he favoured decentralization in India. The presidency governments were permitted to retain their quasi-independent state vis-à-vis the government of India. The government of India itself was made entirely subordinate to the home government.

All these assorted checks and balances did not permit any belief in the advisability – or even the possibility – of some form of representative institutions in India. The checks were regarded as a means of restraining concentration of power at the centre, not only because such concentration was considered morally indefensible but because it left too large a margin for error. One man's decision, if he had no guidance from the opinions of others, could lead to disastrous results in terms of human life. It was suggested, for example, that if the lieutenant-governor of Bengal had had an executive council to advise him the Bengal administration would have been less unprepared for the terrible famine which broke out in Orissa in 1866; the decision not to act had been taken by the lieutenant-governor alone. The complexities of the modern state could not permit decision to rest in the hands of one man. It was a question of efficiency, no more.

Parliament also expected the legislative council to play an important role – though not in limiting despotism. Its function was to be a 'public' forum for discussing the acts of the government. In the Central Legislative Assembly, Dalhousie had seen the germs of a representative institution, but when the Indian Councils Act of 1861 was passed any such possibility was explicitly denied. The new Act allowed for the nomination of 'non-official' Europeans and Indians to the legislative councils, but they were there to offer advice, not to represent any sector of popular opinion. The viceroy of the time, Lord Canning, who had been the last governor-general under Company rule, believed that Dalhousie had made a great mistake in implying that the central legislative council bore any resemblance to a parliament. Nevertheless, Canning was aware of the growing interest among educated Indians in the activities of government and believed that, in some way, it should be satisfied. Bartle Frere, an experienced British official, remarked that he himself knew 'few things more striking than the change which has come over the Natives in this respect. Twenty years ago they were remarkable for their general indifference to all public questions which had no immediate local bearing. But this indifference has given place among the more intelligent classes to a feverish curiosity which has of late years frequently struck me as one of the most noteworthy changes in the general characteristics of Native society.' It was essential, Frere believed, that the government should have some way of knowing whether or not the laws it passed were sensible without having to wait for a rebellion to prove it.

There was to be no confirmation, however, of Dalhousie's premise that the Central Legislative Assembly might develop a representative character. Sir Charles Wood expressed the matter with some precision in the House of Commons in June 1861. 'You cannot possibly,' he said, 'assemble at any one place in India persons who shall be the real representatives of the various classes of the Native population of that empire.'

The concept of Indian government enshrined in the Act of 1861 was one of despotism tempered, but not controlled, by discussion. As well as placing checks on personal authority, the Act did reflect certain political considerations. It was felt that some reward was necessary for those who had remained loyal to the British during the Mutiny. The first three Indians nominated to the central legislative council were therefore the Maharaja of Patiala, who had supplied a force to help the British; Raja Dinkar Rao Raghunath, *diwan* (prime minister) of the Maharaja of Gwalior; and Raja Deo Narain Singh, another supporter of British rule. In fact, all Indians appointed to the council before the reforms of 1892 seem to have been awarded the honour in payment for their own or their fathers' support during the Mutiny.

The existence of legislative councils did not affect either the functioning of the government or what might be termed the philosophical preoccupations of some of its members. Ever since the first Utilitarians, India had been treated as a kind of laboratory for political experiment. It did not cease to be so after the assumption of power by the Crown; the Utilitarian tradition was long-lived, even though it needed re-interpretation in the circumstances of post-Mutiny India. The outstanding problem was not new. It was the same as the problem to which Cornwallis and Munro had given rival answers. Was the administration of India to be government by law, or government by personal discretion?

A new interpretation was supplied by Sir James Fitzjames Stephen, law member from 1869 until 1872. According to Stephen, the problem was how to reconcile the rule of law with the energy of the man on the spot. 'The question is between one kind of law and legal administration and another, not between government by law and government without law. The question, indeed, lies much more between different forms of administration than different forms of law.' A modern state must, he argued, be an efficient and highly coordinated organization following precise rules and free from individual eccentricities. At the same time, the executive arm of the government should not be weakened by legal rigidity. 'The maintenance of the position of the District Officers is absolutely essential to the maintenance of British rule in India.' Stephen's solution was to leave the administration of criminal law with the executive, while allocating civil law to the judiciary. His reasons were not new; the man who ruled should be the man able to inflict punishment. 'In a few words, the administration of criminal justice is the indispensable condition of all government, and the means by which it is in the last resort carried on. But the District Officers are the local governors of the country; therefore the District Officers ought to administer criminal justice.' Stephen was, in fact, convinced that a strong and vigorous government was perfectly compatible with the rule of law. 'The notion,' he wrote, 'that there is an opposition in the nature of things between law and executive vigour, rests on a fundamental confusion of ideas and on traditions which are superannuated and ought to be forgotten.'

Stephen likened the administration of India to a highly-disciplined army with well-defined instructions and efficient organization. He continued the work of law codification, relating much that had previously come under administrative orders with the structure of formal law. His attitude was purely practical, and he was little concerned with theories. He found the general structure of law and administration good, and contented himself with suggesting remedies for specific defects. What was really needed, he thought, was better training for officials. 'Whatever may have been the defects of Indian government, want of interest in the work done, want of vigilance in superintending the manner in which it is done, want of energy and enterprise in improving the manner of doing it, are not amongst them.'

As law member, Stephen believed as strongly as his predecessors had done in the revolutionary effects of the rule of law. Indeed, he was convinced that the destruction of the Indian village community by means of English concepts of property rights and the rule of English law was an example of progress. 'The fact that the institutions of a village community throw light on the institutions of modern Europe, and the fact that village communities had altered but little for many centuries, prove only that society in India has remained for a great number of centuries in a stagnant condition, unfavourable to the growth of wealth, intelligence, political experience, and the moral and intellectual changes which are implied in these processes. The condition of India for centuries past shows what the village communities are really worth. Nothing that deserves the name of a political institution at all can be ruder or less satisfactory in its results. They are, in fact, a crude form of socialism, paralysing the growth of individual energy and all its consequences. The continuation of such a state of society is radically inconsistent with the fundamental principles of our rule both in theory and in practice.' Stephen also considered that there was no need to interfere in personal law relating to Hindus and Muslims. The actions of modern government would, in themselves, create such changes as were needed.

There was nothing paternalist about Stephen's views. The break-up of village communities and the transfer of land to moneylenders appeared to him a necessary part of the pains of progress. But neither did he contemplate associating the Indian middle classes with the administration. In this, his views made a distinct break with the liberalism of the 1830s, which had envisaged not only cooperation between the races but even ultimate self-government for India. Both Stephen and John Strachey – who became a member of the viceroy's executive council in 1868 and finance member in 1876 – accepted the fact that, for simple economic reasons, educated Indians should be given government appointments and even consulted on legislative questions. But both were convinced, as Strachey was to put it, that it would be the beginning of the end for the empire if major executive powers were entrusted 'to the hands of Natives, on the assumption that they will always be faithful and strong supporters of our government. In this there is nothing offensive or disparaging to the Natives of India. It simply means that we are foreigners, and that, not only in our own interests, but because it is our highest duty towards India itself, we intend to maintain our dominion. We cannot foresee the time in which the cessation of our rule would not be the signal for universal anarchy and ruin, and it is clear that the only hope for India is the long continuance of the benevolent but strong government of Englishmen. Let us give to the Natives the largest possible share in the administration. ... But let there be no hypocrisy about our intention to keep in the hands of our own people those executive posts – and there are not very many of them – on which, and on our political and military power, our actual hold of the country depends. Our Governors of provinces, the chief officers of our army, our magistrates of districts and their principal executive subordinates ought to be Englishmen under all circumstances that we can now foresee.'

This rejection of any major cooperation from the various sectors of Indian society soon came under attack in both India and Britain. Faced with a growing sense of Indian nationalism, a trade recession, famine, and agrarian rioting in the 1870s, Lord Lytton (viceroy 1876–80) concluded that it was foolish for the government not to seek support from at least one level of Indian society. As a Conservative, he favoured the claims of the Indian aristocracy. 'I am convinced,' he wrote in May 1877, 'that the fundamental mistake of able and experienced Indian officials is a belief that we can hold India securely by what they call good government; that is to say, by improving the condition of the *ryot*, strictly administering justice, spending immense sums on irrigation works, etc. Politically speaking, the Indian peasantry is an inert mass. If it ever moves at all, it will move in obedience, not to its British benefactors, but to its native chiefs and princes, however tyrannical they may be. The only political representatives of native opinion are the Baboos, whom we have educated to write semi-seditious articles in the native Press, and who really represent nothing but the social anomaly of their own position. ... To secure completely, and efficiently utilize, the Indian aristocracy is, I am convinced, the most important problem now before us.'

Although the British prime minister, Disraeli, responded in the same year by proclaiming Queen Victoria as empress of India, it made no difference to the character of the Indian administration. In fact, the government made it even more difficult for Indians to become candidates for the Indian Civil Service by reducing the examination age from twenty-one to nineteen. Nevertheless, it claimed to agree with Lytton when he attached 'great importance to the obvious political expediency of endeavouring to strengthen our administration by attracting to it that class of Natives whose social position or connexions give to them a commanding influence over their countrymen.' A special branch, known as the Statutory Civil Service, was formed in 1879 in which prominent Indians could be employed. The service was, however, abolished on the recommendation of the Indian Public Service Commission of 1886–7 and replaced in 1892 by new cadres of the provincial and subordinate civil service, reserved for Indians.

Between the years 1876 and 1880, the Liberal party – in opposition in Britain – indulged in a crusade against the government's India policy, attacking the Bill which made Queen Victoria empress of India as well as the restrictive legislation passed by the government of India in 1878 against native-language newspapers. In an article published in 1877, the Liberal leader, William Ewart Gladstone, argued that, morally, it was necessary that India should be governed for the good of Indians. Furthermore, he said, the British had actually created an Indian middle class, and they owed it to that class to govern in just such a manner. 'The question who shall have supreme rule in India is, by the laws of right, an Indian question; and those laws of right are from day to day growing into laws of fact. Our title to be there depends upon a first condition, that our being there is profitable to the Indian nations; and on a second condition, that we can make them see and understand it to be profitable. . . . It is high time that [these truths] pass from the chill elevation of political philosophy into the warmth of contact with daily life; that they take their place in the working rules, and that they limit the daily practice, of the agents of our power . . . for unless they do, we shall not be prepared to meet an inevitable future, we shall not be able to confront the growth of the Indian mind under the very active processes of education which we have ourselves introduced.'

The Liberals' opportunity came with their success in the elections of 1880, and during the viceroyalty of Lord Ripon (1880–84) a number of reforms took place – against considerable opposition from some quarters in India. The restrictive Press Act was repealed and steps were taken to breathe at least some life into organs of local self-government.

An attempt had been made during the viceroyalty of Lord Mayo (1869–72) to establish working municipal institutions. 'We must gradually associate with ourselves in the Government of this country,' wrote Mayo, 'more of the native element. We have neglected this too much. . . . I believe that we shall find the best assistance from natives in our administration, not by competitive examination or the sudden elevation of ill educated and incapable men, but by quietly entrusting as many as we can with local responsibility, and instructing them in the management of their own district affairs.' The experiment had not been successful.

When Ripon tried to give the municipal councils real power and initiative, he was resisted both by British officials and by the majority of the non-official British community. The opposition, complained Ripon, came from the type of man 'who regards India and her inhabitants as made for his advantage and for that alone, who never looks upon himself in any other light than that of a conqueror, and upon the natives otherwise than as "subject races".' In Britain, too, there was considerable opposition to Ripon's general policies. Fitzjames Stephen, in a letter to *The Times* on March 1st, 1883, attacked them on the grounds that Ripon and the government intended to shift 'the foundations on which the British Government of India rests'.

In fact, Gladstone's policies – not only in India – were producing a split amongst Liberals and alienating particularly those intellectuals who had seen Liberalism as the servant of great political causes and the symbol of a dynamic and positive individualism. All this appeared menaced by the rise of democracy. It was this and Gladstone's apparent willingness to dismantle the empire – the Irish Home Rule Bill seemed the first step – which put the great experiment of India in peril. Gladstone's actions and attitudes stimulated a variety of responses, not only defence of the 'ideology' of Indian government, but new statements of imperial purpose and responsibility.

Stephen, in his writing, had postulated the special role of the law. It was, he said, 'the gospel of the English . . . and a compulsory gospel which admits of no dissent and no disobedience.' The operation of the law depended on the state's coercive powers, which should not be eroded by any extension of representative institutions. The situation was, he suggested, bad enough in Britain now that the franchise was being extended. In India, if the authority of the government were once materially relaxed, 'if the essential character of the enterprise is misunderstood and the delusion that it can be carried out by assemblies representing the opinions of the natives is admitted, nothing but failure, anarchy and ruin can be the result.'

Reverence for the law implied a responsibility to uphold it

and a duty to expand its beneficent rule. The early Christian reformers in India had been conscious of the immanence of God and of the need to bring the heathen into his fold. Once inside, they believed, happiness was assured. This belief had been so strong that it had even distorted the application of the essentially non-religious ideas of the Utilitarians. By Stephen's time, however, it was becoming fashionable to dispute the existence of God and the supernatural world, and that fear of divine retribution which had lain behind the actions of the early reformers had lost its force. Substitutes had to be found which would inspire the new imperialism with a zeal similar to that which had formerly drawn its strength from Christianity.

Such substitutes already existed within the British intellectual tradition. Carlyle had fiercely defended the proposition that might was right and that the principal factor in man's religion was man's work. Other philosophers also propounded the new gospel in which worship was replaced by 'service' and God by 'country'. In this way, all the enthusiasm of religion was transferred to purely secular objects. The gospel of the new religion of patriotism was the gospel of duty, of work done without fear of criticism or expectation of gratitude. Its virtues were self-denial, law, order, and obedience.

The doctrines of the new religion of empire were military doctrines and were based upon the use of force, authority and direction. In Stephen's view, there was no widespread desire in India for representative institutions; if there had been, it probably could not have been resisted. But educated Indians were the tiniest of minorities, interested only in their own advantage and not in that of the mass of India's people.

Such an authoritarian view did not go unchallenged. There were those who thought that the best way to rule a dependent empire was to do so indirectly, by using indigenous institutions and manipulating the puppets of a native ruling class. This was the attitude favoured by Cromer in Egypt and other imperialists in Malaya and Nigeria. Cromer had acquired his colonial experience in India, as had Sir Alfred Lyall, who was the spokesman for many theorists of indirect rule. These men, and others who thought as they did, believed just as wholeheartedly as Stephen and Strachey in the moral approach to political power and its exercise. But they differed by refusing to accept force and military strength as the basis of that power. Nor did they believe in what has come to be called the Westernization of alien societies by imposing sophisticated political institutions which had no traditional roots. Lyall, for example, maintained that the effect of Western civilization on India was to dissolve the bonds of Indian society without putting anything in their place. Concentration of power in the hands of the British, who were indifferent to the traditional demands and pressures of Indian society, was producing, said Lyall, 'that condition of over-centralized isolation with shallow foundations and inadequate support, which renders an empire as topheavy as an over-built tower.' Lyall and Cromer were both convinced that there had to be some compromise between the 'civilizing' acts of the British and the feelings of the people, and that the British must therefore develop some genuine respect for the traditional beliefs and institutions of their subjects. If this were not forthcoming, discontent would surely polarize and lead to an attack upon the alien rulers as the only remaining symbol of authority. According to Lyall and others, legitimate scope for expression should be given to India's princes and educated classes.

On the surface, the theorists of indirect rule appeared to be advocating a policy which was designed to permit competing elements to cancel each other out. It was certainly not, however, conceived for that purpose.

But Lyall did propose a quieter administration and the abandonment of aggressive legislation. In fact, after 1885, there developed a period of inertia in Indian administration.

The growth of Indian nationalism after the founding of the Indian National Congress in 1885 brought pressure on the government of India to reform the councils. The government's own feeling was that some reform was not only necessary but sensible, and that if something were not done Britain would, in the words of the viceroy, Lord Dufferin, 'soon have something like a Home Rule organization established in India, on

Irish lines, and under the patronage of Irish and Radical Members of Parliament'.

In 1892 a new Councils Act was passed by the Conservative government in Britain, with the full support of the Liberal opposition. It was intended as a sop to nationalist demands. Under the new Act, the provincial councils – though not the viceroy's central council – were to be permitted to discuss questions relating to administration and the budget, and the majority of non-official seats were to be filled on the 'recommendation' of such groups as municipalities, chambers of commerce, and religious communities. This amounted in practice to a system of elections. The Act was a triumph of practical politics. Nothing essential had been given away, but some concessions had been seen to have been made. The co-operation between Conservatives and Liberals in the passing of the Act showed that the Liberals were accepting what might be called the necessities of empire – the fact that the possession of overseas dominions might dictate policy rather than respond to abstract theories.

All this activity, however, did not touch the actual administration of India. Even the matter of local self-government lay in an area almost insulated from the realities of everyday life. The trend of administration towards simple efficiency and more Western-type institutions was no more than a trend. Stephen might conceive the Indian state as a sort of leviathan, but it was nothing of the sort. Adaptations of practice were constantly taking place, and on other grounds than economy – though economy did limit the size of the administration. In tribal areas, a much simpler system operated, using indigenous institutions. The authoritarian spirit certainly existed in the administration, but as an ideal rather than a reality. By the time the last exponent of dynamic purpose arrived in India in the person of Lord Curzon (viceroy 1898–1905), the administration had become ponderous, like an elephant – 'very stately, very powerful, with a high standard of intelligence, but with a regal slowness in its gait'.

Curzon sought to bring to India a new sense of purpose or, rather, a sense of the old purpose writ large and expressed in the vocabulary of the new century. Like his mentors, Stephen and Strachey, he was convinced that India was the keystone in the arch of British power. He was, in fact, the epitome of intellectual imperialism. His aim was to overhaul the machine so that it might push India into the modern world. He believed in looking to the future. It was, he claimed, the fundamental duty of his administration 'everywhere to look ahead; to scrutinize not merely the passing requirements of the hour, but the abiding needs of the country; and to build not for the present but for the future.' With this as the firm foundation of his policy, he tried to restore to British rule in India the creative energy of the first era of reform; he tried, too, to purge it of that contempt for even the best of Indian civilization and culture which had corroded and helped to destroy the reformist purpose. Curzon believed that the destiny of the Indian people had been entrusted by Providence to the British. This was the lesson of the past, and a lesson which he believed was being confirmed by the present.

The British had created – and how else but with the assistance of Providence? – the greatest empire the world had ever seen. They had been granted the secret of the machine, the power with which to dominate not only men, but the forces of Nature as well. It is difficult for us today, with our different view of the historical process, to accept Curzon's idea of history as anything other than humbug, a cynical *realpolitik* explained as the work of God's invisible hand. But in the nineteenth and early twentieth centuries, awed by the majesty, by the very physical extent of their dominions, it was hardly surprising that the British should turn to divine interpretations. The God whose hand they saw in all their deeds was, of course, a very British god, imbued with British virtues, speaking – as it were – their own language. Formal Christianity may have played little part in the religion of the imperialists, but they anthropomorphized a god who embodied the ideal of their empire.

This view was peculiarly sophisticated – and eminently satisfying. It raised the British empire from a mere conquest and a continuing tyranny to the status of a dynamic crusade, pledged to the greatest happiness for the greatest number. Its motivating force was duty, and its purpose to construct the promised land. 'If I thought it were all for nothing,' said Curzon at a banquet in February 1903, 'and that you and I, Englishmen, Scotchmen and Irishmen in this country, were simply writing inscriptions on the sand to be washed out by the next tide; if I felt that we were not working here for the good of India in obedience to a higher law and a nobler aim, then I would see the link that holds England and India together severed with a sigh. But it is because I believe in the future of this country and the capacity of our own race to guide it to goals that it has never hitherto attained, that I keep courage and press forward.'

With such a creed, Curzon could admit no meaningful place for Indians themselves except as recipients of British beneficence. Indian intellectuals, Indian nationalists who claimed the right to lead the masses, had to be brushed aside as grit in the great machine. The Indian princes had to be acknowledged; their subjects could not be denied the benefits of English rule merely because archaic treaties gave the princes at least some measure of independence. But the peasants were the main target of reform; from improvement in their condition would come the justification of British rule. 'While I have sought,' Curzon declared in his farewell speech at the Byculla Club, 'to understand the needs and to espouse the interests of each [of India's various races and creeds] – my eye has always rested on a larger canvas crowded with untold numbers, the real people of India.'

The difference between Curzon and Dalhousie, the last great reforming governor-general among his predecessors, was not merely a half-century of conservatism. The philosophers and theorists whose executive arm Dalhousie was, had believed that India could be changed into a simulacrum of the West by opening her doors and allowing English education, English morals, and English conception of justice to flood in. Curzon, observing at the end of the nineteenth century the effects of the invasion of Western liberal ideas, felt something of the disintegration it was bringing about. He saw that a minority of

Indians had derived from English education a political vocabulary with which they could question and dispute British rule, but that their learning contributed nothing to help the mass of the people. He sought, by diverting a new generation of Indians into technical education, to convert them from talkers into doers. The ideal of early reformers had been to make Indians into liberal Englishmen; Curzon wanted to make them into scientists and technicians. He believed that, if he managed to inspire them with the same enthusiasm as impelled the younger generation in Britain, they could transform India.

Curzon's was a vision of startling modernity, and one which today underlies the whole philosophy of economic planning in the underdeveloped countries of the world. In this sense, he came to India too soon, but in the political sense he had arrived too late. It was no longer possible to ignore the demands of educated Indians or those of revivalist nationalism. The partition of Bengal (1905) – a sensible measure, considered in abstract and as part of a general movement towards increased administrative efficiency – awakened the fears of educated Indians that the government intended to ignore their views completely. During Curzon's viceroyalty, at least, this was a perfectly reasonable supposition. 'We felt,' wrote Surendranath Banerjea, 'that the whole of our future was at stake and that it was a deliberate blow aimed at the growing solidarity and self-consciousness of the Bengalee-speaking population.'

But Curzon's administration produced more than political disorders. It had positive and lasting effect. His creation of a directorate-general of archaeology, and the policy of protecting and repairing ancient monuments, demonstrated a new respect for Indian culture.

There were also significant and lasting changes in land-revenue policy. Here, Curzon's rule represented the swan song of the Utilitarian ideal in India. In 1900, Romesh Chandra Dutt – a former civil servant who was current president of the Indian National Congress – addressed a series of open letters to the viceroy on matters of land assessment. He sought to prove that rural poverty and the incidence of famine were largely the result of British land policies. There is some evidence that Curzon himself encouraged Dutt to make these criticisms so that he should be able to reply. Curzon was fully aware that the assessments system was by no means ideal but he believed that British rule, far from inflicting new hardships on the Indian peasant, had on the whole protected him from them. Nothing could have pleased Curzon more than a good opportunity to point this out.

The British had always maintained that they were trustees for 'the Indian poor, the Indian peasant, the patient, humble, silent millions'. Certainly, the same could not be said of educated Indians and members of Congress at that time. Before 1905, the educated classes and those Indians who were members of Congress and of the legislative councils tended, for the most part, to be landed proprietors and men from the higher castes. They were strongly opposed to agricultural reforms and particularly to the reform of tenant rights. Congress, nevertheless, had frequently expressed its sorrow at the growing poverty of the Indian people and had suggested that the only remedy was an extension of representative institutions, which would, Congress was convinced, 'prove one of the most important practical steps towards the amelioration of the condition of the people'.

The government preferred more immediate action, attacking the landlord and the moneylender, both of whom had influence in Congress and the legislative councils. It was determined to gain support from the mass of the people by carrying out reforms, and had earlier opposed expansion of the legislative councils, on the grounds that more representatives from the educated classes would mean a block to progressive legislation. Much reformist legislation had, in fact, been manoeuvred through the councils only by means of the official (i.e. nominated) majority vote. But the Councils Act of 1892 had abolished the official majority.

Curzon welcomed the opportunity to reply to Dutt's charges and, in effect, to justify British rule in India – not so much to Indians as to public opinion in Britain. There, he was convinced, growing preoccupation with matters in Europe was diverting the government's attention from the great work in India.

Curzon had another reason for wanting to bring public pressure to bear upon the home government. Though he himself had piloted the Indian Councils Act of 1892 through the British parliament, he had thought of it only as a means by which the government of India might tap opinion to which no Englishman had access by birth. In practice, however, the Act had created a body of representatives whose views were inimical to the progressive designs of Curzon's administration. He suspected that the British parliament, in its ignorance, might be contemplating a further extension of the representative principle in India. Himself a natural autocrat with no faith in democracy, a man who implicitly believed that benevolent despotism was the one form of government calculated to protect and promote the interests of the illiterate masses, Curzon knew that it was up to him to demonstrate the danger that lay in representative institutions for India.

The correspondence with Dutt supplied an opportunity to demonstrate to the British public that only an administration unhampered by quasi-legislative institutions could achieve what every right-thinking Englishman wanted – namely, to protect the interests of those who had no one to turn to but the British. Curzon brought in an expert, Bampfylde Fuller, to draft the great state paper with which he proposed to demolish Dutt and proclaim the superior nature of British rule. Unfortunately, Fuller thought he was writing an inter-office memorandum, and when he submitted it to the viceroy, Curzon found the document 'very long, very complex, very learned . . . and thoroughly confusing'. He did not want a scholarly and closely reasoned treatise on land revenue in India. He wanted a propaganda document, a paper which, in the words of the secretary of state, would lay down 'comprehensive principles intelligible to anyone who reads them'. That, he said, was what was needed to satisfy public and press opinion in Britain.

Curzon therefore decided to rewrite the paper himself and, thanks to his immense facility for absorbing and regurgitating facts, he produced a document which, with the most minor of alterations, satisfied the experts. *Papers regarding the Land Revenue System of British India* was finally presented to parliament at Westminster in January 1902. It was a remarkable document which had – and continues to have – considerable effect on the life of the Indian peasant. Hailed at the time as 'a landmark in the history of the land revenue policy of India under British rule', it signalized a fundamental change in the economic thinking which had dominated revenue policy for nearly a century. The basis of that thinking in relation to land revenue was the doctrine of rent (see page 78f).

In 1900, the revenue which the government of India derived from the land amounted to two-fifths of its total income, and the census of 1901 recorded that some 196,000,000 people in India derived their living from agriculture or cattle-rearing. Though there were many different forms of land tenure in British India, the 'land tax' was not in fact a tax in the European sense, but a rent paid by the tenant for the use of land in which he had proprietary rights, subject to paying the assessed amount. The amount of rent was fixed according to the actual area of land on which rent had to be paid. This did not take into consideration infertile or unworkable land, or even land which, for various good reasons, was not under cultivation. Unlike tax, rent is not a variable sum. It had to be paid whether the land was used productively or not. Generally speaking, the revenue officials who most sincerely believed in the Utilitarian doctrine were also convinced that high revenue demands, unsentimentally enforced, did not create rural poverty or indebtedness. On the contrary, they believed that low demands encouraged improvidence and inefficient farming, which in turn led to debt and low resistance to famine.

But the basis of Dutt's charges against the government's land policies was not that they hurt the peasant, but that they discriminated against the landlord class and its satellites. Dutt claimed that a permanent settlement of the land revenue, such as had been made in Bengal, gave protection against famine and should be extended. In this he had the backing of some revenue officials, but Curzon was easily able to demolish the

though accepting the liberal premise that 'one day' (i.e. not in the speaker's lifetime) Indians would demand self-government and should not be denied it – did not believe in transplanting English *institutions* to India.

The Morley-Minto reforms proposed an enlargement of the councils. They accepted the principle of election to the Governor-General's Legislative Council (called, for convenience, the Centre) and in the provinces. The electoral 'constituencies,' however, were still to be communities and groups. At the Centre there was to be an official majority, but elsewhere the non-officials were to predominate. The powers of the councils were to be enhanced, though they were still to have no executive authority. Nevertheless, the area of discussion was now much wider and the representative principle – however restricted – now entrenched. But the reforms also incorporated the invidious principle of separate electorates for under-privileged minorities, though in 1909 only the Muslims were recognized as such. The principle was not then regarded, at least by Morley, as a device for separating the two main Indian communities. It was fundamentally part of the policy of balancing interests, and attempting to unite moderate and conservative elements against extremist nationalists. The idea of a separate electorate for Muslims – a highly traditionalist and backward community – also appealed to Morley on paternalist grounds. It was still, in the early years of the twentieth century, a firm principle that the function of the British government in India was to protect those who could not protect themselves. The only difference in 1909 – and it was a difference which underlined the very real decline in British authority in India – was that it was now necessary for the government to make Indians into allies, however powerless those allies might be.

The Morley-Minto reforms were the first example of Lyallist doctrines applied in India. Apparent self-government was to be tolerated as long as it was not allowed to interfere with good government. In its executive capacity, however, and in spite of what had appeared to be concessions, the government of India acted as if no change had taken place. When there was an upsurge of violence after the partition of Bengal, the government was repressive. This mixture of reform and repression appealed neither to Morley nor to India's educated youth. Furthermore, the working of the reformed councils forced moderate nationalists to be associated in the passing of repressive legislation. By 1911, the moderate leader, G. K. Gokhale, was demanding that the British government should declare its intention of helping India to develop genuinely democratic institutions.

The government, however, was much more concerned with a series of devices aimed at disarming moderate opposition and, at the same time, suppressing violent nationalism. It was first decided that the partition of Bengal should be revoked and that the imperial capital should be moved from Calcutta to Delhi. Lord Hardinge, now the viceroy, believed that the reunification of Bengal would remove the source of extremist agitation, while the movement of the capital to Delhi would not only disguise the concession in Bengal but would remove the government from a centre of extremist activity. It would also, by reviving the old Mughal imperial capital, unequivocally restate Britain's intention of remaining in India. Finally, it would symbolize the government of India's isolation from the governments of the provinces and permit the devolution of apparent power to those governments without in any way impairing the ultimate authority of the government of India.

Time was passing. The Morley-Minto reforms had created the shadow of responsible government – though it is hard to see why the British government should have thought that nationalists would be satisfied with a shadow. Nevertheless, the reforms did appear to have had some effect on certain of the extremist leaders, particularly upon Tilak (see page 324ff.). When he was released from prison in 1914, he acclaimed the reforms and condemned acts of violence. Curiously enough, instead of isolating the extremists the reforms seemed to have sent them back into organizations and areas formerly dominated by the moderates. Though acts of terrorism continued, the moderate and extremist nationalist leaders were apparently united and prepared to accept progressive rather than revolutionary change.

The war that broke out in Europe in August 1914 brought about a truce in nationalist agitation against the British. There was, in fact, an outburst of pro-British enthusiasm which in the light of subsequent events seems almost incomprehensible today. Many nationalists thought that by helping Britain towards victory they might reap some tangible reward. This belief was encouraged by the allied statesmen's insistence that the war was being fought to make the world safe for democracy. Self-determination for all peoples was the battle cry. Unfortunately, the Indian nationalists were naïve enough to believe that 'all peoples' included Indians. At the time, nationalist demands were directed towards achieving self-government within the British empire, and this, they thought, was comparatively little to ask. Indian recruits flocked to the army – about 1,200,000 volunteered – and there were spontaneous contributions to war loans and the like. The British reduced their garrison in India to fifteen thousand men, and many British administrators went off to fight, handing their jobs over to Indian subordinates. In this way, two of the nationalists' demands – a reduction in the 'army of occupation' and more, higher posts for Indians – were coincidentally granted.

Indians, like everyone else, had believed the war would soon be over. When it dragged on, however, enthusiasm waned. This was partly a result of the government's inability to make use of its newly found popularity; intent only upon governing, whether Indians liked it or not, it was unable to channel enthusiasm into productive endeavour. Recruiting declined, and money was no longer freely lent. In 1916, the Easter Rebellion in Ireland helped to stir the imagination of Indian nationalists.

Before 1914 there had been a number of serious administrative breakdowns. The requirements of war intensified inefficiency, and soon the Indian army in Mesopotamia found its supply lines from India in hopeless chaos. The government was compelled to impose pressures and restrictions on Indian businessmen which soon convinced them that they should – in the interests of their own businesses – support the nationalist movement.

The war against Turkey, whose ruler was the Caliph of Islam, seriously disturbed Indian Muslims, and in 1916, Tilak, who had modified his more revivalist views, was able to persuade the Muslim League to join Congress in the 'Lucknow Pact'. The pact resulted in considerable nationalist activity throughout India, and the government in London – worried about the course of the war in Europe, as Russia seemed about to collapse – decided that some holding action must be taken. Obviously, repression was out of the question; there were not enough British troops available for the task. A carrot had to be substituted for the stick.

In December 1916, a new and preponderantly Conservative government under a Liberal prime minister, Lloyd George, took office, and in July of the following year Edwin Montagu, a Liberal, was appointed secretary of state for India. On August 20th he declared in the House of Commons that 'the policy of His Majesty's Government, with which the Government of India are in complete accord, is that of the increasing association of Indians in every branch of the administration, and the gradual development of self-governing institutions with a view to the progressive realization of responsible government in India as an integral part of the British Empire. They have decided that substantial steps in this direction should be taken as soon as possible.' Montagu also announced that he intended to go to India for discussions with officials and representative Indians.

When Montagu arrived in India in October 1917, he was received by some nationalists almost as a liberator. It was the first time that any member of the British government had actually gone to India to find out the opinions of Indians themselves. The result of the secretary of state's inquiries was published in the summer of 1918 under the title of *Report on Indian Constitutional Reforms*. The contents of the document have been overshadowed by the failure of the reforms it advocated, but it enshrined a new and quite revolutionary idea – that, in the words of Gladstone, it is 'liberty alone which fits men for liberty'. For the first time, a declaration of faith in the ability of the Indian people to operate responsible self-government was explicitly stated. The report, in fact, rejected the strictures Morley had made at the time of the 1909 reforms, and expressed a belief that parliamentary government *could* work in India.

This idea stemmed, firstly, from the natural belief that liberal democracy as practised in Britain was the best of all forms of government (and it had already proved impossible to convince Indian nationalists that there might be a better), and secondly from the fact that parliamentary government was what the nationalists were asking for. If a carrot was to be offered, there was no doubt that it had to be a real one.

Unfortunately, fine phrases do not of themselves create a workable system. The problem of minorities still remained, bedevilled by Muslim fears that representative government would mean Hindu domination. In India itself, these fears had been to some extent allayed by the Lucknow Pact – which had necessitated concessions from both sides – in which Congress had acquiesced in the establishment of separate electorates for Muslims. In Britain, however, many statesmen believed that in spite of the pact a Hindu majority *would* discriminate against smaller groups if it had the opportunity. They therefore sought to give constitutional protection to such groups.

In his report, Montagu felt himself justified in maintaining separate electorates, though only for the largest minorities – the Muslims and the Sikhs. When his Act was passed through parliament in 1919, however, separate representation was extended to Indian Christians, Anglo-Indians (Eurasians), and Europeans. This was almost certainly the work of Indian civil servants who lobbied powerful interests in Britain. By continuing the principle of separate electorates, the administration hoped to keep the nationalist movement divided and to support its own assertion that the Indian National Congress was *not* representative of all the Indian people. When the final Act was promulgated, the government of India was able to relax in the knowledge that the actual effect of the reforms would be to leave authority where it had always been – in the hands of the British.

The major change brought in by these reforms was embodied

in the principle of 'dyarchy', the division of powers, encumbered rather than assisted by a delicate system of checks and balances. The central executive remained responsible to no one but the secretary of state in London. Legislation was, theoretically, to be the function of a new central assembly and a council of state, both with elected majorities but also with an official or nominated, bloc. Any legislative authority which these bodies might have, however, was rendered nugatory by the fact that such legislation as they might refuse to pass could still become law by being 'certified' by the viceroy.

The provinces were also to have legislative councils, and certain responsibilities were to be assigned from the Centre to provincial control. This devolution covered both finance and administration and the provinces became to some extent self-governing, though real power – through revenue legislation and control of the armed forces – remained with the Centre. Administration at the provincial level was divided into two areas. 'Reserved' subjects, including finance, justice and the police, remained under the control of the governor, while 'transferred' subjects such as education and public health were entrusted to ministers responsible to the legislative councils.

The franchise was restricted by a sliding scale of property qualifications, which meant that the number who could vote in provincial council elections was something over five millions, in elections for the Central Legislative Assembly nearly one million, and in elections for the Council of State a select group of some seventeen thousand. The population of India at the time was over 300,000,000.

The period between Montagu's visit and the actual passing of the Act had witnessed events in India which were only paralleled in the after-effects of the Mutiny of 1857. The government of India had begun to feel itself actively menaced by revolutionary activity, though in fact this illusion was only the product of nationalist propaganda. Nevertheless, the government felt itself handicapped by the existing security regulations and set up a committee under Mr Justice Rowlatt to inquire into what it called 'criminal conspiracies' – i.e.

terrorist activities. The Rowlatt report was published shortly after the report of Edwin Montagu, and together they made rather odd reading. On the one hand, the British at Westminster were envisaging some delegation of powers, while on the other, the British in Delhi were reinforcing their authority with all the apparatus of a police state – trial of political cases without jury, and the weapon of summary internment. Indians saw the British giving with one hand and slapping down with the other.

The end of the war had brought back the old administrators, gloomy at the prospect of slow promotion after the excitements of war. To Indians, no longer convinced of their inferior position, it seemed that they brought the worst features of the British occupation back with them, and that the Sedition Acts which followed the Rowlatt report were ushering in a new period of repression.

The time taken in enacting the Montagu-Chelmsford reforms had crippled the moderate nationalists. Even before the proposed reforms were published, their leadership of Congress had been undermined. In 1918, the moderate leaders broke away from Congress and, in the following year, formed the National Liberal Federation of India. Thereafter, they ceased to be of influence in the nationalist movement. The possibility of cooperative reform was gone forever. So was the possibility of government by force.

In 1919, serious rioting broke out in the Punjab. At Amritsar on April 10th, two nationalist leaders were arrested and deported. A large crowd attempted to enter the European cantonment. They were turned away and began rioting in the city. Order was restored by the military, under one General Dyer, and all public meetings and assemblies were declared illegal. Nevertheless, on April 13th a meeting gathered in a large, enclosed space known as the Jallianwalla Bagh. When he heard of this, General Dyer went personally to the spot with ninety Gurkhas and Baluchi soldiers and two armoured cars with which he blocked the only exit. Then, without warning, he ordered his men to open fire on the densely packed crowd. On his own admission, they fired 1,605 rounds before he withdrew, ordering the armoured cars to remain and prevent anyone from entering or leaving the Bagh. Official figures gave 379 dead and 1,200 wounded. Dyer's action was approved by the provincial government.

The following day, a mob rioting and burning at another spot was bombed and machine-gunned from the air. On April 15th martial law was declared and not lifted until June 9th. During this period, Indians were forced to crawl on all fours past the spot where a woman missionary had been attacked, and, according to the report of the Hunter commission which inquired into the disturbances, public floggings were ordered for such offences as 'the contravention of the curfew order, failure to salaam to a commissioned officer, for disrespect to a European, for taking a commandeered car without leave, or refusal to sell milk, and for similar contraventions'.

The Hunter commission of inquiry was set up in October 1919 with four British and four Indian members. Three of the British were members of the civil service, and the Indians were men of moderate opinion. All criticized the actions of General Dyer – but in such mild phrases as 'unfortunate' and 'injudicious'. The Indian belief that the old repressive attitude was being revived was reinforced by General Dyer's own testimony to the commission, for he made it clear that he had gone down to the Jallianwalla Bagh with the intention of setting a ferocious example to the rest of India. 'I fired,' he said, 'and continued to fire until the crowd dispersed, and I consider this is the least amount of firing which would produce the necessary moral and widespread effect it was my duty to produce if I was to justify my action. If more troops had been at hand, the casualties would have been greater in proportion. It was no longer a question of merely dispersing the crowd, but one of producing a sufficient moral effect from a military point of view not only on those who were present, but more especially throughout the Punjab.'

Though the government of India vehemently dissociated itself from such a policy of intimidation, Dyer was expressing the general attitude of many of the civil and military in India. Dyer was removed from his command, but his actions (and presumably his motives) were supported by a large section of the British press as well as by members of parliament and others. A sum of £26,000 was subscribed as a testimonial for this gallant British soldier.

It is not difficult to understand the very special place that the massacre of Amritsar has in the minds of Indians. In British-Indian relations, it was a turning point even more decisive than the Mutiny. Henceforth, the struggle was to permit of little compromise, and the good faith of British concessions was always to be held in doubt.

Events after 1920 were no longer under Britain's control. Conservative administrations in Britain made reluctant concessions, not in response to quiet and reasoned demands but to nationalist agitation – whose aim was not now self-government, but independence. Both authoritarian and liberal views continued to receive expression, in Britain and in India.

The Act of 1919 had provided for a commission of inquiry to review the working of the Act after ten years. In November 1927 the commission arrived in India. The date had been brought forward primarily because it seemed possible that, by 1929, a Labour government might be in power in Britain, and at least one member of the Conservative cabinet actually believed that the Labour party meant what it said about India's right to self-government. Far better, thought Lord Birkenhead, the secretary of state for India, to set up the commission early and give the impression that the Conservatives, too, were interested in India – so interested as to be prepared to bring the date forward by nearly two years. It was this same Birkenhead who had been the only member of the cabinet to oppose the reforms of 1919; he was determined that there would be no more if he could help it. To ensure that the commission should be kept as much on his side as possible, it had to consist of members of parliament. The Labour party cooperated by choosing only obscure back-benchers as their representatives. The commission's chairman was Sir John Simon, a lawyer wrapped in the passionless cloak of legal precedent. He was an ideal choice, for it was unlikely that even the vaguest suggestion of radicalism would ever cross his mind.

The commission's report was not published until 1930, and the new Labour government which had taken office in the summer of 1929, under the leadership of Ramsay MacDonald, dissociated itself from the commission's findings. Shortly before taking office, the new prime minister had declared: 'I hope that within a period of months rather than years there will be a new dominion added to the Commonwealth of our Nations, a dominion which will find self-respect as an equal within the Commonwealth. I refer to India.' Everything seemed set for Indian self-government. Labour leaders had actually spoken of it. In October 1929, the viceroy, Lord Irwin, reiterated in a rather vaguely worded announcement that dominion status was indeed the goal. Unfortunately, these were only words. Nationalist leaders were not particularly interested in them and continued their agitation.

The British government still clung to the principle of slow constitutional reform. A Round Table conference was held in London in November 1930, but no representatives of the Indian National Congress were present – although the carefully chosen Indian delegates represented every other special interest from the princes onwards. Obviously, the conference could be of little value, and in fact it brought about nothing except a new stage in the relationship between the princes and British India. But one thing the conference made clear, that all the delegates (even including the princes) wanted responsible government in India. Congress, it seemed, was not alone.

Lord Irwin persuaded the Congress leader, Mahatma Gandhi – who had been arrested in May 1930 – to call a halt to agitation and go to London. In return, repressive ordinances were to be withdrawn. By the time Gandhi reached the conference, however, the Labour government in Britain had fallen and been replaced by a so-called 'National' government under the former Labour prime minister, Ramsay Macdonald. In reality, the new government was dominated by Conservatives.

At the conference, Gandhi offered no constructive suggestions or solutions. He did, however, make clear his opposition to the perpetuation of separate electorates for minorities. The government in London decided that, as it could not win cooperation, it must make its own decisions. The government in India continued to act decisively against terrorism and civil disobedience.

The conclusions of the government in London were given expression in the Government of India Act of 1935. This Act incorporated all the stages of constitutional development up to that date and added two new principles – that a federal structure should be organized, and that popular responsible government should be set up in the provinces. Under the terms of the Act, new provinces were to be formed, and Burma was to be separated from India and given a new constitution following the lines laid down in the Act of 1919. In India, dyarchy – with its 'reserved' subjects – was to be maintained at the Centre, and the overall authority of the British parliament was to be sustained. In the provinces, however, dyarchy was abandoned, and an almost completely responsible parliamentary government based upon a much wider franchise was established.

The federal provisions of the Act had been designed to incorporate the princely states into the new system of government. But the princes would not cooperate, and nationalists viewed the federal proposals as an attempt to perpetuate British rule by playing on the nationwide divisions between special-interest groups. That part of the Act which incorporated the federal provisions never, in fact, came into force.

The 1935 Act came into force two years later. It was the last positive achievement of British rule in India.

Essentially, the power of the government remained unaltered. The steel frame of the administrative and judicial system continued to dictate state action until the end of British rule. But the political struggle could hardly be said to have taken place in isolation, for it affected several levels of Indian life. One of the aims of Indian non-cooperation was to make the administration unworkable. It did not succeed until the last two years before independence, and then only in certain parts of India. The administration was, however, being frayed in other ways. The District Officer, for example, had early seen his authority diminished by the various quasi-democratic boards and councils. The peasant, who had looked to the District Officer for impartiality, had done so precisely because he was not an Indian and because there were other Englishmen higher up to whom the peasant could appeal if the District Officer failed him. But, as changes took place, he observed that the District Officer was being subjected to outside pressures; the new district board might include among its members the brother of the peasant's landlord or the second cousin of the moneylender. It seemed to the peasant that a board consisting of men such as these – and the sectional interests they represented – would make a fair hearing of his own case impossible. The District Officer's impartiality seemed diminished, and the peasant concluded that he could probably be bypassed by influential men. Nevertheless, even with these qualifications, the district level of government in India still displayed echoes of the Utilitarian ideal.

Though power still remained unalloyed at the Centre, and – generally speaking, in practice – at district level, the 1935 Act was a tremendous advance towards ultimate self-government. In the willingness of Indian nationalists to work the new constitution (even while they condemned it), there seemed a chance that cooperation might still be possible. Whether such cooperation could have been achieved is very much a matter of opinion, for the actual pattern of events prevented the reforms from being worked out. The 1935 Act, however, formed the basis of the constitution as well as of the parliamentary institutions of independent India and, on these grounds alone, can be said to have had considerable and lasting influence.

The Act was also influential in another direction. By embodying the democratic concept of rule by the majority, it rejected the longstanding belief that India was a plural society. The government of India had always been reluctant to interfere in social, cultural and religious matters, especially after the Mutiny, a rebellion based on the fear that Britain intended to use her absolute power to change Indian society. The 1935 constitution now guaranteed to the majority the power to use its will on any minority. The Muslims saw in this a dangerous threat posed by the Hindu majority to their cultural and religious integrity. Such a threat could not be tolerated, and led ultimately to the partition of India in 1947.

The outbreak of war in 1939 demonstrated for the last time that the real centre of power in India remained in Delhi, with the British – for the viceroy unilaterally declared that India, like Britain, was at war with Germany. Two months later, by November 15th, 1939, all the Congress provincial governments had resigned in protest, not at the declaration of war, but at Britain's refusal to make an immediate grant of independence. The record of the war years is one of attempted compromise with nationalist elements, when Britain stood alone in Europe after the collapse of France, and again when the Japanese threatened to invade India. When the latter threat receded, the government of India was still not prepared to jeopardize the war effort and preferred to keep the principal nationalist leaders in jail.

The end of the war, however, brought two important revelations. One was that the British Labour government – which had won an overwhelming victory in the 1945 elections – was unwilling to hold on to India by force. The other was that it was impossible to do so anyway. Just as Curzon's imperialism had been unacceptable to a Britain concerned with major social and political reform, so any desire to hold on to India was repugnant to a Labour administration similarly intent on massive domestic change. Attempts to maintain the unity of India so that power could be transferred without partition were unsuccessful. The effects of Western ideas and Western institutions were not to be reversed.

On August 15th, 1947, in Karachi, the capital of the new dominion of Pakistan, and in New Delhi, the capital of the new and truncated India, the words of the last emperor of undivided India were read out by the new governors-general. 'On this historic day when [India/Pakistan] takes her place as a free and independent Dominion in the British Commonwealth of Nations I send you all my greetings and heartfelt wishes. With this transfer of power by consent comes the fulfilment of a great democratic ideal, to which the British and [Indian/Pakistani] peoples alike are firmly dedicated.'

## LAW

Macaulay's great hopes for a radical reform in the law of British India withered away in the lukewarm attitude of the men who succeeded him as law member and in the uncertainty of the years preceding the Mutiny. His vision of justice had not been restricted to legal frameworks and court administration. In December 1835, for example, he had proposed the establishment of a committee to inquire into the matter of prisons and prison discipline. His argument was that 'the best Criminal Code can be of very little use to the community unless there be a good machinery for the infliction of punishment'. The committee was set up and its report – which was sternly Benthamite in tone – was issued in 1838. The home authorities, however, rejected its recommendations on grounds of cost.

It was generally accepted that criminal law reform was badly needed. Under the terms of the Charter Act of 1853, a Law Commission was established, not in Calcutta but in London. One of its tasks was to draft a code of criminal procedure. Lacking any indication of the kind of criminal law the code would be expected to administer, the commission could hardly carry out its task satisfactorily. It asked the government of India for an opinion. Finally, a select committee of the legislative council declared in favour of Macaulay's draft of 1835. 'We have come to the conclusion to recommend to the Council that the Penal Code, as originally prepared by the Indian Law Commissioners when Mr Macaulay was the president of that body, should form the basis of the system of penal law to be enacted for India.' Though the select committee thought that various revisions and amendments were desirable, they did not intend to recommend 'any substantial alteration in the framework or phraseology of the original code'.

Modifications were made, but when the penal code was actually enacted in 1860 it retained the characteristic philosophical overtones which had marked Macaulay's draft. It was distinguished, too, by a new and original method of legislative expression. In the words of Fitzjames Stephen: 'In the first place the leading idea to be laid down is stated in the most explicit and pointed form which can be devised. Then such expressions in it as are not regarded as being sufficiently explicit are made the subject of definite explanations. This is followed by equally definite exceptions, to which if necessary, explanations are added, and in order to set the whole in the clearest light the matter thus stated explained and qualified is illustrated by a number of concrete cases.' This clarity – and it was the pattern for later Indian codes – was one of the enduring Utilitarian legacies. It brought to Indian criminal law a precision and lucidity which were not to be found in the law of England.

What was absent was the spirit which had envisaged total change in the entire pattern of law, criminal, civil and domestic. This revolutionary concept would have implied such intensive interference in the social structure that it could not have been expected to appeal to the policy-makers of post-Mutiny India, with the experience of 1857 behind them. Indeed, the Law Commission had already recommended the advisability of leaving Hindu and Muslim law outside the legislative scope of the government of India.

A general system of law applying to all classes of persons in India was welcomed, not least by the men who had to administer it. In the words of Sir George Trevelyan, it earned 'the gratitude of Indian civilians [i.e. members of the civil service], the younger of whom carry it in their saddlebags and the older in their head'. Its effect upon the majority of Indians is less easy to define. Certainly, the code made allowance for particular Indian circumstances. For example, the section relating to the sale of obscene books or pictures was modified to permit of such items being kept or used for religious purposes. The section concerning bigamy allowed customary law to prevail. Originally, there was no legislation against child marriage, nor against incest.

The scale of punishment, too, displayed in the original draft a humanitarian attitude far in advance of its time. Even the death sentence, which really applied to only two offences –

treason and murder – was not generally speaking mandatory, it being open to the court to inflict a sentence of transportation for life to a penal settlement. Corporal punishment did not feature in the original draft, but it was introduced in 1864 by a special Act which was followed by later amendments. In general, little change was made in the sentences which had been prescribed in the first enactment. In the later stages of British rule they were frequently attacked as being uncivilized, out of touch with modern standards. The attacks were at least partially based on the assumption that the sentences stipulated in the code were mandatory, whereas in fact they were simply the maximum for particular offences. Courts were not compelled to pass the maximum sentences – only such punishment as they thought fit.

*

As has been outlined in Part One (page 90 ff.), the problems of civil law and its administration resisted codification. Nevertheless, a body of substantive civil law was essential in the circumstances of post-Mutiny India. In December 1861, a commission was established to propose such a body of law, and to do so in the terms of the Law Commission's report of 1855 (published 1856). This laid down that English law should form the foundations, but that the superstructure should be prepared 'with a constant regard to the conditions and institutions of India, and the character, religions, and usages of the population'. The commission's first conclusion was that an urgent need existed for legislation on the disposal of property after death by persons other than Hindus and Muslims, who were already covered by their own domestic law. The Indian Succession Act was passed in 1865, and this was followed by a law of contracts and of evidence in 1872 and other enactments in succeeding years. By 1882, the process of codification could be said to have come to an end.

The need for procedural codes was finally recognized in Acts of 1859 and 1861, the first dealing with civil and the second with criminal procedures. These considerably simplified the administration of justice. Perhaps the most important provision of the codes was the abolition of written pleadings, an extremely tedious process by which the very simplest cases had demanded a lawyer and had taken at least three months to reach a decision. Theoretically, at least, the abolition satisfied Utilitarian requirements that justice should be swift. 'Under the proposed code of [civil] procedure', wrote the secretary of state in May 1859, 'the plaint is to be limited to certain specified particulars; and when the suit has been instituted, no written pleadings in the technical sense of the term are to be admitted. The parties are to be orally examined, and they will be at liberty to tender, at the first hearing of the suit, written statements, confined, as much as possible, to a simple narrative of facts. In this way the question at issue between the litigants will be ascertained by a process much more simple and expeditious, and better calculated to a satisfactory result than which now prevails.'

Unfortunately, the code made no change in the system of appeal, which remained complicated, slow, and expensive. One interesting survival was the stamp duty on the institution of suits, which was retained partly because of the revenue it brought, but also because there was a well-founded belief that it discouraged irresponsible litigation. Unfortunately, by discriminating against the poor, it also discouraged responsible litigation.

The High Courts Act of 1861 ended the situation by which two courts of appeal (the *sadr* and the Supreme Court) had existed in the kind of competition which did not assist justice. In the lower courts, however, there was little fundamental reform. The movement towards uniform administration of justice took some time, and though by 1882 the North-West Provinces, Madras, and Bombay were mainly operating on the Bengal principle, judicial and executive functions remained united in the Central Provinces, the Punjab, Sind, Oudh, Assam – and in British Burma. In civil cases, the jurisdiction of the courts remained tied to a monetary qualification, a system which encouraged problems and the need for lawyers. There was even a special brand of justice confined to the small cause courts, from whose decisions there was no appeal. There were a number of high courts responsible to no superior authority. Their application of the codes was, not infrequently, eccentric and almost invariably lacking in uniformity. There was, however, what might be called a 'discipline of justice' which, according to Fitzjames Stephen, welded the men who operated it into an 'organized half-military body'.

But justice could be distorted. An alien system, based as it was on alien moral concepts, was bound to suffer in a society which gave general acceptance to very few of those concepts. Perjury, for example, was not thought to be particularly reprehensible. It was not too difficult for a clever lawyer to manipulate the law, to his and his client's advantage. Even the comparative speed of decision – normally a virtue – had profound social consequences, particularly in matters of debt.

Nevertheless, law was essential to the structure of a modern state, and indigenous systems offered no satisfactory basis. The rule of law is an indissoluble part of the function of government; it is, in fact, the foundation of the state. The British had no choice but to impose some pattern of law on India. Indeed, the rising Indian middle classes demanded the protection – as well as the more personal advantages – of Western law. The codes themselves, especially those of procedure, offered a measure of protection in a society which was primarily illiterate. Certainly, there were evils, some of them a product of the restrictions which were placed on judges' decisions. There were, however, sound reasons for such restrictions. Indian judges were very different from British judges. They were not recruited from among practising lawyers. They had never argued the law, only administered it. In such circumstances, to permit discretion could lead to illegality.

The growth of a Western-based system of law reflected the extension of a Western-based polity, and the British supplied the legal framework for a developing society. The range of judicial legislation grew ever wider, covering everything from prisons to company law, from customs duties to the protection of industrial labourers. Most of it was concerned with creating the infrastructure of a modern industrial state. Very rarely indeed did the British enact laws which ran counter to traditional Indian ideas. Those which did are dealt with in the context of social policy (see pages 116 ff. and 263ff.). In the light of independent India's experience, the British attitude may well appear to have been misguided; but in terms of alien domination, it was sensible enough.

### *The Law relating to Land*

Basic law relating to property and property rights remained, generally speaking, untouched by the transfer of power from the Company to the Crown. Nevertheless, new motives – both economic and political – brought about certain changes in land tenure. These applied almost exclusively to land not in cultivation. In December 1858, the secretary of state for India instructed the government of India to look favourably on applications from people 'desirous of obtaining grants of unoccupied land for the purpose of carrying on the cultivation of Cotton and of other exportable products for the supply of manufactures to this Country [Britain]'. Most of the land finally granted was used for plantation industry. The secretary of state's despatch made it quite clear that the authorities in India were not to restrict grants of land to Europeans, who customarily had the major interest in plantation industry. This was an extremely important qualification, for, when the government of India drew up rules in 1871 for the disposal of waste land, they included an option permitting the people who were granted such land to pay a lump sum which would permanently free them from revenue demands. In other words, they were to be enabled to acquire absolute proprietorial rights.

This had a political purpose, for it was also proposed that the right of redemption should be extended to lands already settled. Sir Charles Wood put the matter precisely in 1862. The security of fixed property, he wrote 'and comparative freedom from the interference of the fiscal officers of the Government will tend to create that class which although composed of various races and creeds will be peculiarly bound to the British rule; whilst under proper regulations, the measure will conduce to the improvement of the general resources of the empire'. In fact, after the experience of the Mutiny, the governments of both Britain and India believed that British rule must rely on the affection – or, at the very least, on the self-interest – of the agricultural classes. The growth of a landed middle class appeared to be desirable development.

Utilitarian principles, however, were strongly opposed to any redemption of land revenue. If the government gave up its revenue from rent, it would be necessary to impose other taxes instead. This, according to the Utilitarians, would tend to check trade and diminish consumption. But the proposal was killed, not by theories, but by the financial strain of suppressing the Mutiny and the subsequent effects on the Indian economy. The financial requirements of the government of India dictated that the existing system be maintained.

It became increasingly obvious, however, that where a *zamindari* settlement had been made, the government must act to protect the peasant, and to limit rack-renting and eviction. A beginning was made in Bengal in 1859 with an Act which sought to identify and protect tenancy rights. The burden of proof lay upon the tenant, who had to supply evidence that he had continuously occupied his holding for twelve years. Unfortunately, landlords tried in the eleventh year to induce tenants to change their holdings, so as to prevent them from acquiring tenancy rights. The report of the Famine Commission of 1871 blamed local officials for many of the injustices which ensued. 'The administration in Bihar [then part of Bengal] stands in the discreditable position of countenancing, and so abetting, notorious abuses for fear of the commotion which would ensue if the people knew their rights and were encouraged to assert them.' The commission's strictures also applied to landholders, including Europeans, whose methods of indigo cultivation 'involved an amount of lawlessness and oppression, in the shape of illegal seizure and retention of land, and to a minor degree, in the shape of extorted agreements to cultivate, and of seizure of ploughs and cattle'. A modification of the 1859 Act was promulgated in 1885. The narrow twelve-year rule was abandoned and a wider definition substituted, by which occupation of land in the same village would qualify.

The Bengal Act of 1859 – in its unmodified form – was applied in parts of the United Provinces until 1901. In 1926, the twelve-year rule was abandoned. In other parts of India, various tenancy protection acts were passed in areas where *zamindari* settlements existed.

In an endeavour to protect the cultivator from the moneylender, a number of laws were passed. Rural indebtedness resulted primarily from the establishment of proprietorial rights and the transfer of such rights, by due process of law, in repayment of debt. An early measure which did not prove particularly successful was the Deccan Agriculturalists Relief Act of 1879, which was passed after peasant rioting in 1873. By the end of the century, it was recognized that the land was being transferred from the hands of cultivators to those of the moneylenders by the simple operation of the civil law, and that the passing of protective legislation had had little or no effect. Even the authorization of provincial governments to grant agricultural loans had made little difference to rural indebtedness.

In 1899 an experimental measure, the Punjab Land Alienation Bill, was introduced into the Central Legislative Council. The object of the Bill was to restrict the sale and mortgage of land so that moneylenders could not claim land in repayment of debts. Hitherto, the peasant who borrowed money had had to pledge either his harvest or his land, and the moneylender's position had been strengthened by laws concerning the rapid recovery of debts. Litigation was common, and the pleader, or professional advocate, profited by his knowledge of the law and the peasant's ignorance of it. The proposed Bill threatened the profits of both the pleader and the moneylender by prohibiting a man from selling land to anyone except a resident of the same village or a relative in the male line. Mortgages were to be limited to a term of fifteen years. The Bill was bitterly attacked, but nevertheless passed into law.

In the 1930s, legislation intended to reduce the burden of outstanding debt was passed by provincial governments, but it too, in practice, met with little or no success.

*Hindu and Muslim Domestic Law*

Virtually no changes took place in Islamic personal law during the period of Crown government, because of the Muslim belief that legislation is the prerogative of God.

The British interfered little in matters of Hindu personal law, partly for the usual reasons of security, and partly because of the formidable problems involved in any attempt at codification. Changes did, however, take place, not through the enactment of specific laws – except in a very few cases – but by the application after 1864 of British methods of interpretation to customary law, after Hindu law officers attached to the courts had been dispensed with.

In general, the British sought to protect customary law – even, in some cases, to extend its application. In 1935, for example, an Act was passed in the North-West Frontier Province which was designed to impose orthodox Muslim law on customary law, and in 1937 the Act was extended to cover the rest of British India. Various laws were also passed to give statutory definition to the customary laws of such other Indian communities as the Parsees.

During the last twenty-five years of British rule, there was a variety of pressures in favour of reform which led to the enactment of such laws as the Hindu Law of Inheritance (Amendment) Act of 1929, the Gains of Learning Act (1930), the Hindu Woman's Right to Property Act (1937), and the (Bombay) Hindu Married Woman's Right to Separate Residence and Maintenance Act (1946). Though such legislation did affect that fundamental Hindu institution, the joint family, it did not affect the main body of customary Hindu law.

The government of India remained, until the end of British rule, reluctant to interfere in the question of child marriage, though the penal code of 1861 had declared that the consummation of a marriage in which the wife was under ten years old constituted rape. It was extremely difficult to make such a protective measure effective. In 1884, the government stated its attitude – and the statement was to be valid for the remaining years of British rule – in reply to a memorandum on widow remarriage and the age of consent submitted to it by a Hindu reformer, B. M. Malabari. 'When caste or custom enjoins a practice which involves a breach of the ordinary criminal law the State would enforce the law. When caste or custom lays down a rule which in its nature is enforceable in civil court, but is clearly opposed to morality or public policy, the State will decline to enforce it. When caste or custom lays down a rule which deals with such matters as are usually left to the option of citizens, and which does not need the aid of civil or criminal courts for its enforcement, State interference is not considered either desirable or expedient. In this matter His Excellency in Council considered interference by the State undesirable and hence this social reform must be left to the improving influence of time and to the gradual operation of the mental and moral development of the people by the spread of education. The Government of India do not desire to interfere ... until sufficient proof is forthcoming that legislation is required to meet a serious practical evil and that such legislation has been asked for by a section important in influence or in number of the Hindu community itself.' Even when legislation was finally enacted, the government preferred the initiative to come from Indian members of the legislative assembly.

# 3

# *Indian India: Areas of Impact*

## ECONOMIC LIFE

### *Agriculture*

AFTER THE assumption of power by the Crown, the government's attitude towards the peasant tended, generally speaking, to be protective. Land legislation was biased against the land-owning classes.

The government's attitude was partly an expression of the continuing paternalist sense of responsibility; partly political (at least towards the end of the nineteenth century, in response to the growth of middle-class nationalism); but principally, until other forms of revenue surpassed that derived from land, for reasons of finance. The government's view was precisely stated in a dispatch from Lord Mayo (viceroy 1869–72). 'For generations to come the progress of India in wealth and civilization must be directly dependent on her progress in agriculture. . . . There is perhaps no country in the world in which the State has so immediate and direct an interest in agriculture. The Government of India is not only a Government but the chief landlord. The land revenue is derived from that portion of the rent which belongs to the State, and not to individual proprietors. Throughout the greater part of India, every measure for the improvement of the land enhances the value of the property of the State. The duties which in England are performed by a good landlord fall in India in a great measure upon the Government. Speaking generally, the only Indian landlord who can command the requisite capital and knowledge is the State.'

Government action to improve agricultural production began as early as 1866 with a suggestion by the Famine Commission of that year that there should be a separate department of agriculture. In 1869, under the combined pressures of the Manchester Chamber of Commerce – which wanted better quality control in cotton production – and the newly-arrived Lord Mayo, a definite scheme was formulated. In 1870, a Department of Agriculture, Revenue and Commerce was created. Unfortunately, the attitude of the government in London was not favourable and ten years later the department ceased to exist, its work during its short life having been almost entirely concerned with revenue matters. The Famine Commission of 1880 recommended that the government pay attention to a general improvement in agriculture, in the interests of increasing food production. In the following year, the central Department of Agriculture was resurrected and provincial departments were established, but the emphasis of its actions was once more almost entirely confined to the collection of statistics for revenue purposes.

There was, however, a genuine and growing opinion among the British in India that the government should take positive action to improve agricultural output. It was a Famine Commission report, that of 1901, which was once again to provide the impetus for action. It suggested the general need for 'improved agricultural teaching to the better classes; the promotion of Mutual Associations; agricultural research and experiment; inquiries regarding tillage and manure; the investigation of crop diseases and their remedies; the provision of improved seed; the experimental introduction of new staples; the improvement of cattle breeding; the investigation of cattle diseases; and the development of the fodder supply. To some of these subjects', the report went on, 'more or less attention has, we know, been already given; but they all claim greater and more systematic attention. To this end, the employment of a stronger expert staff in every province is necessary. The steady application to agricultural problems of expert research is the crying necessity of the time.' The 'more or less attention' paid to some of these subjects had consisted of the rather ineffectual appointment of an agricultural chemist and the establishment of four agricultural institutions which operated experimental farms on the most unscientific lines.

An Inspector-General of Agriculture was appointed in 1901. The first holder of the office was a Canadian who gathered around him a staff of scientific experts. The main need of these experts was for an institute fitted with laboratories and scientific equipment, and here the government ran into financial difficulties. But money was to come from a totally unexpected source. An American millionaire named Henry Phipps, touring India in the winter of 1902–3, was so impressed by the viceroy's efforts to help the peasants that he offered £20,000 (to which he later added a further £10,000) to be spent on any project that the viceroy considered would help the welfare of the people of India. The viceroy, Lord Curzon, proposed a scheme for an agricultural institute which met with Phipps's immediate approval. Plans were formulated, and in April 1905 the foundation-stone of the new institute was laid at Pusa in Bihar. The buildings were destroyed by an earthquake in 1934 and the institute re-established at Delhi.

The expansion of the agricultural service was impeded by the outbreak of the 1914–18 war, but under the Montagu-Chelmsford reforms of 1919 (see pages 232–3), agriculture became a 'transferred' subject, and in 1920 re-staffing began.

For a while, there was some neglect of agricultural matters by the elected governments in the provinces, partly because nationalist effort was concentrated more on acquiring political power than improving the condition of the peasant. But the overall absence of major improvement – despite propaganda, research, better seed, legal enactments, and so on – was not entirely due to the demands of nationalism. (It is, of course, not unreasonable for a movement pledged to remove alien rule to prefer to perpetuate bad conditions, which may be used to attack the government.) The experience of independence has shown that certain factors in India, of which the British were well aware, persistently resist agricultural change. The innate traditionalism of the Indian peasant is difficult even for a government of Indians to influence. It could hardly have been expected that the British – who never lost their wariness of interfering in the traditional system, whether for economic or humanitarian reasons – could have achieved more. Though a considerable amount was attempted, there were very real limits on governmental action. Lord Mayo, whose commonsense attitude still has pertinence today, remarked in 1870: 'In connexion with agriculture we must be careful of two things. First, we must not ostentatiously tell native husbandmen to do things that they have been doing for centuries. Second, we must not tell them to do things which they can't do, and have no means of doing. In either case, they will laugh at us, and they will learn to disregard really useful advice when it is given.' There was no point, Mayo insisted, in preaching to the Indian cultivator about such new ideas as steam ploughs and ammoniac fertilizers. 'I do not know,' he wrote, 'what is precisely meant by ammoniac manure. If it means guano, superphosphate or any other artificial product of that kind, we might as well ask the people of India to manure their ground with champagne.'

Not everything the government attempted to do was resisted. There was a measure of success in certain areas with the supply of new varieties of seed. But despite some progress, every official inquiry produced a general picture of continuing waste and inefficiency. The reasons for this were summed up in 1939 in a work originally prepared for the guidance of candidates for the Indian Civil Service:

> *Natural environment.* – The farmer's disabilities that are due to his natural conditions are five in number:
>
> (1) The uncertainty of the harvest, due partly to the vagaries of the monsoon, which become all the more serious when artificial supplies of water are not available, and partly to frequent attacks of insect pests and fungoid disease.
>
> (2) The cultivation of crops which are poor either in respect of their yield, their market value, or their susceptibility to disease.
>
> (3) The lack of sufficient manure, resulting in low fertility.
>
> (4) The use of dead stock (tools and implements) which, though adequate when each village was self-contained and each farm self-sufficient, are ineffective now that Indian farmers are growing crops which compete in the world's markets.

(5) The use of ineffective livestock, their low productive value, and the heavy losses of livestock due to epidemics.

Of these disabilities, the first, in so far as it is due to lack of water, is the special concern of the irrigation department. The fifth is the special concern of the veterinary department. The rest are the concern of the department of agriculture.

*Social and personal disabilities.* – Amongst the farmer's disabilities which are due to his social environment and personal characteristics are the following:

(1) His attachment to his land, his home, and his family, which make him unwilling to leave them except under severe economic pressure – and even then only temporarily.

(2) The congestion of the rural population in closely packed and insanitary villages – originally due to the need for mutual protection and a common water-supply, and incurable except by extensive replacement, at a great cost, of old by model villages.

(3) The absence of alternative methods of earning a living and of subsidiary occupations.

(4) A general tendency to improvidence, due partly to the difficulty of making profitable use of surplus stocks in the absence of adequate transport facilities, partly to the risk of possessing savings in the absence of any safe place to keep them. These inconveniences of rural life in India, however, have been greatly reduced under British rule, which has greatly improved communications, has increased security, and introduced post-office savings banks. But the peasant's safe is still generally a hole in the wall or floor of his house or in the corner of a field; and there are still dacoits [bandits] abroad to compel him to disclose it.

(5) The unproductive expenditure which is imposed on the peasant by caste custom in such matters as social and religious ceremonies, the repayment of ancestral debt, and the maintenance of his social prestige; and also by his litigiousness.

(6) The small value of his assets, which make it difficult for him to borrow money, even for productive pur-

poses, at a reasonable rate of interest. The tenant's assets consist of his crops, his cattle, his agricultural implements, his women's jewellery, his trees, and his *jajmani* [fixed circle of clients], if he has one; to which a landlord or other person with a transferable right in his holding can add his land. But of these the first three make adequate security only for short-term loans, since he can spare neither his live nor his dead stock for any length of time. The fourth he will keep intact till he is at his last financial gasp; extensive pawning of jewellery is a sure sign of great distress. Trees and *jajmanis* make better securities for loans, but not all tenants have them. There remains the land, a good security, but overloaded with debt.

*Disabilities due to modern progress.*– The establishment of British rule, whilst freeing the peasant of some difficulties, has helped to create others. It has put an end to the internal disorders and extortionate revenue demands which once put the farmer's harvest in jeopardy. It has made possible the disposal of surplus stocks and the cultivation of money crops. The recognition of rights in land has converted it from a liability to an appreciating asset. But other developments have reacted adversely on the rural population:

(1) Internal security and the expansion of cultivation that followed it have led to an enormous increase in the population, a difference of nearly 100 millions between 1881 and 1931 [excluding Burma, about 90 millions]. This has led to serious pressure of population on the soil and to the overcrowding of agriculture as an occupation.

(2) By reason of increased facilities in the disposal of his produce and the increased value of land as security, the cultivator has become more prosperous, and being naturally improvident has been led both to spending and to borrowing more.

(3) The establishment of civil courts has assisted the moneylender to tighten his hold on the peasantry, and has led to a great increase of litigation, frequently needless and always costly.

(4) The moneylending and banking class has taken over the business of marketing the crops, to the cultivator's great disadvantage.

The government's activities in all three areas of disability were limited, partly by finance and partly, in the twentieth century, by the growth of nationalist movements. In the case of 'natural disabilities', water was the great problem; under Crown government, irrigation works were greatly extended, and by the end of British rule nearly fifty million acres – one-quarter of the land under cultivation in British India – were supplied with water from canals, reservoirs and wells which had been constructed by the government. In social matters the government sought to protect the cultivator by means of a series of legal enactments. But though these did have some effect, they did not alter what might be called the psychological climate, which consisted – and consists today – of a balance of prejudices, customs, family and caste pressures, reinforced by illiteracy.

Attempts to reduce the immense burden of rural debt (estimated in 1930 to be over £675,000,000) by breaking the peasant's dependence on the moneylender were not particularly successful. The experience of agricultural cooperative credit societies in Germany and Italy was thought to hold out some hope for India, and such societies were introduced by an Act of 1904. The government, however, was basically unwilling to do more than give guidance and assistance *when it was asked for* – a survival of the old principle that self-help was the best. Where the initiative was taken by officials, credit societies did catch on, and by the end of British rule the principle of cooperation had been greatly expanded, in other areas as well as the provision of credit. In 1947, there were over a hundred thousand societies, with about four million members. Unfortunately, the original purpose of reducing rural indebtedness was not achieved, primarily because the majority of debts were incurred for social rather than economic reasons. The world economic depression of 1930 had its effect in India, and a large number of credit societies failed. Recovery was slow, but the development of cooperative

The mixture of state and private enterprise worked tolerably well, but it had major disadvantages, particularly in matters of control. After 1905, therefore, the state slowly began to acquire private lines, and by 1940 nearly three-quarters of British India's railway system was owned by the government and nearly half operated directly by it. Track mileage had by then reached 43,000.

Of vital importance to the expansion of the railway system was a supply of coal with which to fire the engines. Some coal extraction had been begun under Company rule, and in 1846 about 90,000 tons were being produced by coalfields in Bengal. Increasing demand led to the opening up of new coalfields in Bengal, Bihar and Orissa. Production passed the million-ton mark in 1880, and reached six millions in 1900, twelve millions in 1917, and over thirty millions by 1940. The growth of factory industry in India benefited from the extension of railways, and it benefited, too, from the increased production of coal which could be used to drive steam-powered machinery.

As was to be expected, the railways increased the flow of trade. By 1908, overseas trade had increased to five times the volume of 1858. Prices, too, tended to become equalized throughout the country. Railways contributed to the decay of indigenous industry, but they were a stimulus to modernization, making the distribution of imported products easy, encouraging the establishment of industry beyond the immediate vicinity of the ports, stimulating the production of cash crops, and the growth of a money rather than a barter economy. But the railways also brought India into the vortex of world trade. The consequences of economic depressions many miles away from India were to have their effect until, in the inter-war years of 1919–39, prosperity and depression in India were closely related to the general cycle of world trade.

The earliest important economic effect of the extension of communicatons was felt in the cotton-mill industry. Expansion was comparatively slow until 1887 when a mill was opened at Nagpur by the Parsee entrepreneur, J. N. Tata, and progress became extremely rapid. The industry continued to ex-

societies had at least introduced a basis for change ir rural situation, a basis which has been taken advantag though not with any conspicuous success – since inc dence.

During British rule, no solution was found for the ess problems facing Indian agriculture. Indeed, it would been surprising if one had been. Food production cont to lag behind the minimal requirements of a growing pc tion. Attempts to remove the burden of debt were unsu ful, as no attempt was made to attack the causes, whic in the social system itself, an area regarded as being ou the scope of sensible government interference. That the duce of the soil could be increased by efficient manage and modern methods was shown in the developme European-owned plantation industry. But in the field of sistence agriculture, there was no profitable role for European entrepreneur and no inclination in the small In commercial class to invest, or participate, in the manage and improvement of estates. There were, however, a few very few – enlightened landlords.

### *Trade, Industry and Transport*

The expansion of industry in India depended on the a sition of capital and the extension of railways. The fo tions of a railway system had been laid before 1858 expansion was very considerable immediately afte Mutiny. By 1869, four thousand miles of track were in tion. All of it had been laid with private capital, tho government guaranteed rates of investment interest 5 per cent in order to attract capital to the venture. I for its guarantee, the government had the right to co penditure and operation, and to have mail and troo free of charge. It also had an option to purchase the twenty-five years. This arrangement had its defe the 1870s the government itself began to construc when another and more effective system of gu evolved in 1880, private companies took up th construction once more.

pand until, by 1914, India ranked fourth in the world's cotton-manufacturing hierarchy. The jute industry, too, benefited from the railway, as it did from steam-driven machinery, and in the early twentieth century India held a virtual monopoly of the world's jute production. The iron and steel industry was founded on a sound commercial basis in 1911 by the sons of J. N. Tata, at Jamshedpur in Bihar, and by 1940 India had the largest single steel plant complex in the world. There are other examples in other modern industries.

Basically, the expansion of Indian industry was a twentieth-century phenomenon. A report relating to 1902–3 showed that expansion at that time was mainly limited to the cotton and jute industries. 'Nothing illustrates better the present state of industrial development in India than the fact, that after the cotton and jute industries ... there was only one of the manufacturing industries ... namely the iron and brass foundries, in which as many as twenty thousand persons are returned as having been employed during the year. In the preparation of agricultural staples for the market, employment is found for larger numbers; indigo factories ... employed over 81,000 workers; cotton ginning, cleaning and pressing mills over 65,000; jute presses, 22,000. But of manufacturing industries, properly so-called ... the most important after cotton and jute mills, are the iron and brass foundries (20,674), silk filatures (10,652), tanneries (8,626) and others of still less importance.'

The government's role in industrial expansion before 1914 was confined to encouraging private capital and enterprise, particularly European. A Department of Commerce had been established in 1905, but its effects were not felt until very much later. The first Industrial Commission was appointed in 1916, and presented its report two years later. India, it said, was still predominantly a producer of raw materials rather than manufactured goods. The war of 1914–18 did, at least, have the effect of directing the government's attention towards the need for some measure of Indian self-sufficiency in fields other than the production of armaments. Towards this end, the Fiscal Commission of 1921 recommended a policy of tariff protection and government stimulation for local industry.

Growing political unrest after 1921, however, diverted the government from such measures. It can truthfully be said that the activities of the Indian National Congress delayed economic development. During the 1930s, there was a substantial withdrawal of British capital from India, and the Congress party's general tendency towards socialism – at least in its public statements – made some Indian capitalists unwilling to expand the level of their investments. Nevertheless, expansion there was, particularly in the number of Indian-owned banks and investment trusts. The second world war helped to expand industrial production, particularly in materials previously unknown in India – hydrogenated oil, machine tools, basic chemicals, power alcohol, synthetic resins, and plastics. Although the withdrawal of foreign capital continued after independence, it still represented 44.7 per cent of India's total capital investment in 1949.

Despite political conditions, industrial interest on the part of Indian nationals continued to grow after 1911. Before that date, except in Bombay, the British had played the major investment role. They had almost a monopoly in tea, jute and coal, although Indians dominated the cotton industry. Generally speaking, before 1914, those Indians who became interested in factory industry were the Bengalis of eastern India and the Parsees of the west. But the general policy of protection after 1923 and the repatriation of British capital during the 1930s encouraged certain commercial and banking castes to move into industry. Indeed, in the 1930s the traditional banking community of Marwaris began to dominate the cotton and sugar industries. One of their number, G. D. Birla, was one of the principal financial supporters of the Indian National Congress prior to independence.

Although the involvement of Indian capitalists increased, the number of Indians in the higher echelons of Indian industry did not. This was mainly a result of the system of managing agencies. These institutions, which emerged after the collapse of the agency houses (see page 107 ff.), began as traders but later became the organizers and managers of industry. The managing agency system supplied a pattern of industrial organization by exercising overall financial and administrative control over the various businesses managed by the agencies. Each agency also put up capital and floated new concerns. Consequently, though the number of industrial undertakings might be large, the number of directors was small. In fact, Indian industry was under the control of a very few individuals. The managing agency system was economical, supplying central administration and an easy channel for investment. By encouraging industrial expansion, it increased the scope of industrial employment at supervisory and clerical levels, though not at the level of the boardroom. Even so, most of the higher positions in Indian industry – whether it was European- or Indian-owned – were held by Europeans and Anglo-Indians, and Indians were almost entirely confined to subordinate and clerical grades. This was particularly obvious in technology-based industries. Such a situation resulted partly from a bias in favour of foreign experts and lack of properly trained Indians, but the primary reason was one of economy. In both the short and the long run, it was cheaper to use a European than it was to train an Indian for the same job.

Uneven and fragmentary though it was, the industrial expansion of the last quarter-century of British rule did furnish the infrastructure of a modern industrial state. It also, however, created a serious imbalance in the economy. Individual enterprises might often be extremely profitable, especially after protective tariffs were imposed. But protection increased consumer costs, forcing the mass of India's people to pay more for what they bought. Increased industrial output failed to absorb more workers from the growing population. The tendency was towards labour-saving techniques and the destruction of labour-intensive indigenous industry. The dominance of Europeans at managerial and technical levels left independent India unprepared for development, while the government's feeble attempts to increase rural consumer capacity were almost totally ineffectual.

Though the government of India in the first half of the twentieth century engaged in such economic activities as irrigation and railways in a manner unprecedented in the nineteenth, it did so only because private enterprise would not take on the task. The history of British India has often been presented as a history of great and powerful administrators, but after 1858 the government of India was fundamentally weak. When British private enterprise felt itself discriminated against by the Indian government, it was able to exert pressure on the secretary of state in London who, in turn, was constitutionally in a position to dictate to India. Strong viceroys might be able to impress their will in certain areas of Indian administration – even, on occasion, on the secretary of state himself – but there were other areas where they had no influence whatever. Among the most important of these were discriminatory tariffs which, until 1923, operated for the most part against Indian industry. There were also the financial demands of imperial defence, and the high cost of maintaining security forces in India – which represented a considerable proportion of the Indian budget.

In the years between 1919 and 1939, the government gave assistance to industrial enterprise in various ways. One outstanding example – the erection of hydroelectric installations in the Bombay presidency – a product of private Indian enterprise, was made possible by the passing of a Land Acquisition Act. But this action was permissive, not imitating. The government of India could probably have raised money for *state* industrial enterprise by increasing taxation which, by many standards, was extremely low. Politically, however, this might have presented a threat to internal security, and the government refrained. Among legislators in Britain and administrators in India there was, too, a distinct distaste for state capitalism.

One of the most enduring criticisms of Britain's rule in India (and in other parts of her empire) is that she exploited the colonial economy to her own advantage. It would be more truthful to say that exploitation was far too limited. There is no doubt that substantial private profit was made from economic activity, and that it brought some real benefit to Britain. But really productive exploitation – productive, that is, in a nation-building sense – would have required immense public investment and close planning control. For financial and political reasons, neither of these was possible.

## SOCIAL POLICY

The government of India, believing as it did that the large-scale reforms of Lord William Bentinck had been one of the causes of the Mutiny, could hardly have been expected to look favourably on proposals for more. It preferred to pin its faith on the long-term effects of British law, and only accepted, with reluctance, legislation initiated by Indian reformers – in the firm belief that most of it could not be enforced anyway. One typical example was the progression of laws relating to the age of consent, the last of which was passed in British India in 1929. Laws there were, but the laws were ineffective – primarily because most Indians never heard of them. Such legislation only touched the fringes of Indian practice. There was no way of enforcing it except through propaganda. It was demonstrative legislation, no more, for its effectiveness depended not on the police but on private welfare initiative and the growth of public opinion.

The government was well aware of these factors and it preferred, when it acted on its own initiative, to do so only in matters which, in the first place, did not apparently affect the social order or interfere with custom, and, in the second, where positive results could be achieved.

This attitude can be seen in the development of famine policy as well as in labour legislation. Before 1858, there had been frequent famines in British India which had been tackled on purely local lines and with makeshift arrangements. After a famine in northern India in 1837, the local government had laid down the principle that the state should find work for the able-bodied – but nothing was done for those who were too old or too weak to work.

In 1860, a small-scale famine in the North-West Provinces

was mitigated by the irrigation works which had been constructed over the years, as well as by the railway, which had advanced far enough to be used for carrying grain to points reasonably near the distressed areas. But the government, while willing to provide work, left those who could not work to private charity. Private charity was insufficient, and the local government was forced to take on the whole burden of relief. It did so with some reluctance, not because it lacked humanitarian principles, but because it believed that self-help was more dignified than charity – as if dignity mattered to a man dying of starvation. The government also relied on the law of supply and demand to produce food.

An inquiry was held into the causes of this famine, but no famine policy was framed as a result. In 1866–7 another and much more terrible famine struck eastern India and, in particular, Orissa. The lieutenant-governor of Bengal discounted warning reports from local officials. The law of supply and demand once again failed to function – the demand was certainly there, and so was the supply, but merchants preferred to hoard their stocks in order to take advantage of rapidly spiralling prices. When the seriousness of the famine was finally recognized, supplies from outside Orissa could not be moved in because the monsoon rains had sealed off the area by flooding such roads as did exist. Although there was no adequate statistical machinery, it was estimated that one-third of the population had died of starvation and disease. After the rains, the government poured grain into the area, but it was largely wasted as new crops were by then being harvested.

The report of the committee of inquiry did produce a change of outlook, particularly on the part of the viceroy, Lord Lawrence. When famine appeared again in 1868, he stated categorically that it was the function of government and its officials to save life. Loans were raised to increase irrigation works and to finance extra railway construction, but relief projects were inefficiently operated. In some areas, relief was on too high a scale; indeed, it was reported that people were living far better on relief than they did in ordinary times. Though such reports were undoubtedly exaggerated, they offended the Victorian principle that charity was in itself demoralizing. The Famine Commission established in 1880 reported that, though the state indeed had an obligation to save life, relief should be given in such a way as 'not to check the growth of thrift and self-reliance among the people. . . . The great object of saving life and giving protection from extreme suffering may not only be as well secured, but in fact will be far better secured, if proper care be taken to prevent the abuse and demoralization which all experience shows to be the consequence of ill-directed and excessive distribution of charitable relief.' On this basis, a Famine Code was framed.

The code was extremely elaborate, but a great deal was actually done following its promulgation in 1883. 'Protective railways' were constructed, lines of little commercial profit which could be used to carry food to places of shortage. Before they existed, the only means of transportation had been unwieldy wooden carts pulled by slow-moving bullocks. And since famine does not only affect man, the draught animals usually could not be fed either, and many people had starved because food could not be transported from the nearest railway station. By 1897, however, things were different. The railways had been built. Plans existed for relief works at which wages would be fixed according to need, and food was to be sold at special shops at prices fixed by the government. At work sites, there were to be hospitals and doctors as well as places for the workers and their families to live. The code also made provision for remitting land taxes and for the free distribution of seed.

The procedure laid down in the code provided for detection of the symptoms of a forthcoming food shortage, and for the declaration of, firstly, a state of scarcity, and then a state of famine. The code laid down a progressive series of steps to be taken at each stage.

In 1896–7, a serious famine occurred in northern India, affecting some 30,000,000 people. The relief system worked reasonably well, and a subsequent commission of inquiry was generally satisfied with its operation. In 1899, however, the rains failed again, compounding the tragedy of the earlier years. Though the government still feared the effects of too much charity, an immense relief operation was mounted. The viceroy, Lord Curzon, who found indiscriminate charity positively dangerous, did, however, issue a warning in January 1900. 'In my judgement,' he told the legislative council in Calcutta, 'any government which imperilled the financial position of India in the interests of a prodigal philanthropy would be open to serious criticism. But any government which, by indiscriminate almsgiving, weakened the fibre and demoralized the self-reliance of the population would be guilty of a public crime.'

A new Famine Commission, which reported in 1901, suggested various changes in the code in order to increase efficiency. It was recognized that the code could not prevent famine but that there were resources available to a modern government which could mitigate its effects. Optimism about the future was summed up by Curzon in 1905. 'We may compete and struggle with Nature, we may prepare for her worst assaults, and we may reduce her violence when delivered. Some day perhaps when our railway system has overspread the entire Indian continent, when water storage and irrigation are even further developed, when we have raised the general level of social comfort and prosperity, and when advancing civilization has diffused the lessons of thrift in domestic expenditure and greater self-denial and control we shall obtain the mastery. But that will not be yet. In the meantime the duty of the government has been to profit to the full by the lessons of the latest calamity and to take such precautionary steps over the whole field of possible action as to prepare ourselves to combat the next.'

Although famines continued – the last under British rule was that in Bengal in 1943 – the Famine Code remains the earliest and, despite all qualifications, one of the greatest examples of the acceptance by the state of responsibility for the welfare of those it rules.

*

As the economic organization of India became more complex,

the government of India passed a wide variety of laws which included labour laws designed to protect the growing industrial proletariat. The inspiration for such legislation came from Britain. The question of child labour in India, for example, was first raised in the House of Lords in 1877 by the reformer, Lord Shaftesbury – though the provincial governments of Bombay and Bengal were already contemplating such legislation before he raised the matter.

On the rather inadequate grounds that no complaint had been received by the government, it was generally thought that protection of labour was unnecessary. Indian industrialists resisted such legislation, insisting that it would hamper the expansion of indigenous industry and that, as the Indian worker was poor, he worked as long hours as he could. Limitation of those hours, it was argued, would bring real hardship. This view had powerful support among British officials. When Lord Ripon decided that there must be compulsory legislation controlling the hours of work, one of the reasons advanced against it was that Indian houses were dirty and squalid while the factories were clean, well ventilated, and conducive to health. In the case of child labour, it was said that India should not be compared with Britain. 'A child of eight in Europe is a helpless baby; in India he is almost a man', wrote Ashley Eden, lieutenant-governor of Bengal, to the viceroy in March 1881.

Despite opposition, a law was passed which came into force in July 1881 by which no child under seven could be employed in a factory. Children under twelve were not to be employed for more than nine hours a day. One of the other provisions concerned the fencing of dangerous machinery. Further and more progressive Acts were passed in 1891, 1911, 1922 and 1934. There were later amendments to the 1934 Act which limited working hours to fifty-four a week and raised the age of employment to twelve. No one under the age of seventeen was to be employed unless medically certified as fit to work. Similar protection was awarded to female labour.

One of the particular problems facing the government of

India was that of women's employment in the mines. In 1928, nearly 30 per cent of the labour force employed underground was female. By 1936, however, no women at all were employed underground.

One of the difficulties of imposing protective labour legislation in India was that workers were unwilling to accept what was, in effect, a reduction of their earnings. Even the passing of welfare legislation could not compensate.

The growth of industry in India coincided with acceptance in Britain of the workers' need for state protection. But sophisticated legislation designed to protect part of an essentially illiterate and extremely poor society left an immense gap between the legislation itself and the effectiveness of the legislation. In 1939, it was said that 'taking all labour legislation into account, affecting factories, mines, plantations, docks, railways, harbours, etc., it is doubtful whether more than seven or eight millions at the outside come within its protecting influence. The rest who constitute by far the greater majority of the industrial workers are engaged in small or what is known as unregulated industries.'

Modern industry, if it is to operate properly, depends on at least some degree of worker education. This did not exist in India. In Britain, the trades union movement carried out some worker-education activity. In India, however, the combining factor is caste, i.e. a system of relationships based primarily on function. The growth of organizations representing *industrial* functions was extremely slow, and the initiative was to come mainly from members of the educated classes who worked in positions below managerial and supervisory levels and who believed that their own positions could be bettered by alliance with the workers.

Though an association of Bombay mill hands was formed as early as 1890, it was not until after the first world war that any real success was achieved in forming genuine trade unions. The changed situation was described in the report of a Royal Commission in 1931. 'Prior to the winter of 1918–19 a strike was a rare occurrence in Indian industry. . . . Lacking leadership and organization, and deeply imbued with a passive outlook on life, the vast majority of industrial workers regarded the return to the village as the only alternative to the endurance of the hard conditions in industry. The end of the war saw an immediate change. There were some important strikes in the cold weather of 1918–19; they were more numerous in the following winter, and in the winter of 1920–21, industrial strikes became almost general in organized industry. The main cause was the realization of the potentialities of the strike in the existing situation, and this was assisted by the emergence of the trade union organizers, by the education which the war had given to the masses, and by the scarcity of labour arising from the expansion of industry, and aggravated by the great epidemics of influenza.'

The existence of labour organization was recognized by the Trade Union Act of 1926. Many of the unions were merely temporary combinations formed for some definite and immediate object, and there was a tendency to form unions by factory rather than by occupation. There was virtually no collective bargaining in the sense of negotiations taking place between worker organizations and employer organizations. The Act of 1926 did not specify compulsory registration of unions, and very few took advantage of the protection it offered union members against civil and criminal proceedings in return for properly audited accounts and the provision that half the union executive should be workers.

In 1920, an All-India Trades Union Congress was founded, but it was almost entirely an administrative fiction and had an extremely small membership. It was subject to a series of splits in the 1930s, and in 1942 had only 337,695 members out of some six million workers covered by the government's protective legislation.

### *Public Health*

The movement towards government responsibility for the health of the people in India originated in similar legislation in Britain. In its first stages, the movement was concerned with the health of the British themselves and, in particular, of the army. Mortality was extremely high among British troops. After the experience of the Crimea, when Florence Nightingale had forced the British government to make an inquiry into the sanitary state of the army, it was decided to carry out a similar investigation in India.

The royal warrant establishing a Statutory Commission on the Health of the Army in India was issued in May 1859. The commission sat in London, and no official survey of actual conditions in India was made until 1872. Nevertheless, the commission's report was horrifying. Florence Nightingale was invited to make observations on it. The British government made what seemed to be an attempt to suppress the report. Miss Nightingale thereupon published her observations. They were expressed with rather sharp humour. 'When asked about Drains,' she commented, 'the army in India was like the London woman who replied, "No, thank God, we have none of them foul, stinking things here!"' Of actual conditions in India, she wrote: 'Bombay, it is true, has a better water supply but it has no drainage. Calcutta is being drained but it has no water supply. Two of the seats of Government have thus each one half of a sanitary improvement, which halves ought never to be separated. Madras has neither... At Agra it is a proof of *respectability* to have cess-pools. The inhabitants (152,000) generally resort to fields.'

John Lawrence was much impressed by Miss Nightingale, and established a Sanitary Commission in Bengal. But its reports were filed rather than implemented. Lawrence found that the local population resented, as an interference in their religion, a law banning the throwing of dead bodies into the river Hugli, on which Calcutta stands. He was a timid viceroy and, at this, seems to have lost interest in sanitary reform and allowed sanitary administration to become a department of the inspectorate-general of prisons! Dr John Sutherland, a member of the Sanitary Commission in London, remarked in 1866 that Lawrence was 'our worst enemy'. Certainly, nothing was done in India – not even for the army, on which, in the final analysis, British power depended.

The first Sanitary Commissions in the provinces were appointed in 1880, and some attempt was made to bring modern public health practices to India, though not with conspicuous success. The government of India preferred to believe that educating the people of India in matters of public health was almost, if not quite, of more importance than positive government action.

The reforms of 1919 made public health a transferred subject in the provinces. In 1937, a central Advisory Board of Health was established. Most active medical work, however, was carried out by missionaries. Even in 1947, over half the municipalities and three-quarters of the administrative districts lacked medical officers of health. At least a third of towns with over thirty thousand inhabitants had no proper water supply. Villages were virtually untouched by sanitary legislation. Some four thousand hospitals and dispensaries had been established in rural areas, but each of these had to serve a population of about 62,000 people.

Considerable progress was, however, made in the development of prophylactic inoculation against cholera and bubonic plague, and the second world war brought campaigns against malaria – though these were primarily designed to protect British and American troops.

As in every other sector of government activity in British India, finance was utterly inadequate for the needs of a medical service. The majority of Indians continued to live and die without the benefits of Western medical science. The old systems flourished still. Sympathetic medicine was widely practised, the goddesses of smallpox and other diseases continued to receive sacrifices, and the evil spirits of disease were exorcized by methods common in the European Middle Ages. Mahatma Gandhi, as always, lucidly expressed the reactionary element in the freedom movement when he attacked Western medicine. 'Doctors are injurious to mankind,' he wrote in *Hind Swaraj*, 'but European doctors are the worst of all. They violate the religious instinct, for many of their medical preparations contain either animal fat or spirituous liquor, which are taboo to Hindus and Muslims. Medical treatment fosters self-indulgence, so that men are deprived of self-control and become effeminate. Hospitals are institutions for propagating sin.... To study European medicine is to deepen our slavery.'

Fortunately, these views were not to be accepted by the government of independent India.

## EDUCATION

Sir Charles Wood's Educational Dispatch of 1854 (see page 144) had introduced a new principle into government policy – that the state had a responsibility for educating those who could not afford to educate themselves. This did not mean that there was to be a system of compulsory education, and for two very sound reasons. The first, crucial one was that there was simply not enough money to provide even the most primitive education for millions of Indians. Furthermore, even if resources had been available, any attempt at compulsion would have offered a threat to security. The Mutiny was to make clear, once and for all, what would result from any apparent government attempt to interfere in religious matters; and religion permeated education, as it did every other aspect of Hindu society. Queen Victoria's proclamation in 1858, announcing the assumption of the government of India by the British Crown, specifically stated that: 'firmly relying ourselves on the truth of Christianity ... we disclaim alike the right and desire to impose our convictions'. Wood's dispatch had been a challenge to the whole traditional order, for its avowed purpose was to change it, and there were many people who, in spite of the Mutiny, thought it was still the government's duty to attempt to do so. But they were in a minority, and it was the Indian upper and middle classes who continued to enjoy the almost exclusive privilege of education; the government's limited financial resources were sufficient to satisfy their demands.

Not a great deal of progress took place between the date of the dispatch and the outbreak of the Mutiny, although universities were established at Calcutta, Madras and Bombay. These were not teaching institutions, but examining bodies on the model of what London University was at the time. By

1859, Calcutta had eleven affiliated colleges, Bombay two, and Madras one. Though statistics were by no means accurate for all schools, they show that there were thirteen government colleges with 1,909 students and four aided colleges with 878 students; seventy-four superior government schools with 10,989 students, and 209 aided schools of the same or somewhat lower grade, with 16,956 students; twenty-five normal schools with 2,241 scholars; and sixteen colleges for special subjects, with 1,154 scholars. These numbers were small in relation to the population, but showed a substantial increase over the figures for 1845 (see pages 142–3). The missionary schools, which numbered 193 in 1860–61, had 23,963 pupils. In the context of the time, the government's achievement was considerable. In Britain, less than half the children of school age actually went to school, and there was no plan for introducing a national system for education until 1870. Education, indeed, was only one of the fields in which Indian state activity was ahead of British.

Though there could be some satisfaction over the state of English education in India, the same could not be said for vernacular schooling. In Bengal, it was almost totally ignored – for the sound reason that 'educational gentlemen from England, themselves little familiar with the natives and their vernaculars, were quite unable to comprehend and appreciate the indigenous native education . . . consequently they ignored and neglected the indigenous schools'. Vernacular schools did exist in Bengal, but the government acted as if they did not.

Again, voices were raised in opposition to the diffusionist, or filtration, theory of education. Lord Mayo (viceroy 1869–72) wrote in a private letter to Sir W. W. Hunter: 'I dislike this filtration theory. In Bengal, we are educating in English a few hundred Babus at great expense to the State. Many of them are well able to pay for themselves and have no other object in learning than to qualify for government employ. In the meantime we have done nothing towards extending knowledge to the million. The Babus will never do it. The more education you give them, the more they will keep to themselves and make their increased knowledge a means of tyranny.

If you wait till the bad English, which the four hundred Babus learn in Calcutta, filters down into the forty millions of Bengal, you will ultimately be a Silurian rock instead of a retired judge. Let the Babus learn English by all means. But let us try to do something towards teaching the three R's to Rural Bengal.'

In 1874, Sir George Campbell – lieutenant-governor of Bengal – made a report on a new policy he had instituted. 'Village communities and individuals', he wrote, 'are invited to set up schools with Government assistance. The plan is to grant to village schoolmasters who maintain tolerably efficient schools in the native fashion and submit to a certain amount of inspection and control, a subsidy or grant-in-aid far short of an adequate salary, but which, eked out by fees and customary emoluments, may enable them to live. The grant is usually no more than from 2 to 3 or 4 rupees per month . . . and at this rate a little money goes a long way.' The final paragraph of Campbell's report revealed something of the great social and political consequences of the Bengal government's new educational policy. 'A very satisfactory feature of the new scheme is that the Mahomedans take to it just as kindly as the Hindoos. For instance, we find that of 36,993 pupils in the primary schools of the Rajshahye Division, regarding whom returns have been received, there are 18,380 Mahomedans to 18,613 Hindoos. The higher education of the upper classes of Mahomedans in Bengal is a subject beset with very great difficulties, but there seems to be no special difficulty regarding the education of the Mahomedan masses.'

Indian Muslims had not taken to the advantages of higher education in the same way as Hindus. When English was adopted (in place of Persian) as the official language of India in 1837, they had lost their principal qualification for government employ. Generally speaking, they retired into communal isolation. The government had tried to expand English education facilities for Muslims, but had met with considerable resistance. Nevertheless, some Muslim leaders were aware that, if the Muslim community continued to repudiate the new education and the English language, they were likely to find themselves an underprivileged minority at the mercy of those who, by means of the new learning, were entering government service in ever-increasing numbers. In Bengal, which was always in the van of progress in British India, a Muslim leader, Abdul Latif, made a vigorous plea for English education for his co-religionists, suggesting that it might well be in the British interest to do something about it – which was perhaps a little harsh, considering the government's previous efforts and the Muslim community's resistance to them. 'Mohammedan education can never cease', he said, 'to have a strongly marked feature of political interest, which will force itself on the notice of all who desire to make the enlightenment of the Indian races the handmaid of loyalty and devotion to the British power. I beg you', Abdul Latif continued significantly, 'to bear in mind that it is no longer open to debate whether respectable Mohammedans are willing to have their children imbued with the principles of a sound healthy English education'. It was not until 1873, however, when a trust fund was established from the estate of Haji Muhammad Moisin, that Muslim students received active encouragement. The fund was administered by the government and paid two-thirds of the fees at any English school for Muslim students.

The incentive towards establishing English-style educational institutions which would cater exclusively for Muslims came not from Bengal, however, but from the North-West Provinces. In association with a number of Muslim intellectuals and British well-wishers, a Muslim reformer, Syed Ahmed Khan (see page 302), founded the Aligarh Movement, so called after the Muhammadan Anglo-Oriental College established there in 1875. The aim at Aligarh was to give a sense of community, not necessarily in religious terms – for Aligarh was to be open to non-Muslims – but in social and academic terms. At this period, such a concept was only possible for non-Hindus. Communal dining, for example, was out of the question in mixed institutions which included Hindus, because of caste, which insisted on rigid food customs. More important to the founders of Aligarh, however, was the question of religious instruction. Government schools gave none, for obvious reasons. Missionary institutions were concerned with Christian teaching. One of the problems confronting Syed Ahmed and his associates was that Indian Islam had become orthodox and unyielding, partly in self-defence against the incursion of Western ideas. Should a modern theology be taught at Aligarh – which would offend the orthodox – or a traditionalist theology, which was inconsistent with the reformist ideas of the college's founder? The decision was in favour of orthodoxy, which would win and maintain the support of the Muslim community in general. But no definite syllabus of studies was laid down.

The government's general attitude to rural education was changing, and the changes were reflected by Sir George Campbell's policy in Bengal. In 1870, the home government issued instructions that 'Government [of India] expenditure should be mainly directed to the provision of elementary education for the mass of the people'. The responsibility for such education was thereupon shifted from the central government to local authorities. Some Indian historians have suggested that this change of heart was inspired by the fact that, in 1869, four Indians had been successful in the Indian Civil Service examinations. If higher education was to lead to more Indian applicants winning posts in the higher reaches of the civil service, they argue, this would undoubtedly have constituted a threat to the privileged position of the British in that service. The diversion of funds from higher education to rural schooling, on the other hand, would still make it possible to control the number of Indians applying – as they had a right to – for appointments in the ICS. The fact that four Indians had succeeded in entering a service previously dominated by the British had no influence at all on the decision of the home government. The 1870 changes were made in an attempt to move a stage further towards the complete educational system envisaged in the dispatch of 1854. If proof were needed that the home government's decision was not motivated by fears that the ICS would be swamped by Indians, it could be found in the education budget for 1879–80. 68 lakhs (1 lakh = 100,000) of rupees were allotted thus – 11.5 lakhs for 1,606,216 primary school pupils, and 56.5 lakhs for 303,868 students in high schools and colleges.

The disproportionate expenditure seemed a complete contradiction of the aims expressed in the 1854 dispatch. There were, however, serious problems involved in any attempt to correct the bias. Educated Indian opinion was strongly opposed to reducing the extent of the government's support for higher education, and the government could not rid itself of the old wariness of interfering in the social structure by expanding mass education, especially if it meant increasing aid to missionary schools. Nevertheless, Lord Ripon (viceroy 1880–84), a Liberal with liberal views on education, was determined to extend the range of government-supported education as far as possible. In 1870, education had been made the responsibility of provincial administrations and the government of India retained very little residual control. Available reports provided very little information about the state of elementary education in the provinces, so a commission was established to review the working of the whole system and make recommendations on expanding elementary education without reducing the outlay on higher education. This, of course, was the crux of the matter. A national education system was beyond the financial resources available to the government; the commission was expected to suggest the best way of using an educational appropriation which could not be increased. It was also instructed to inquire into women's education, the municipal management of schools, scholarships, and the training of teachers.

Eighteen months later (in October 1883), the commission submitted its report. It found that little had been achieved in elementary education, although there had been substantial growth on higher levels. It recommended that the cheapest way of extending education might be by encouraging private enterprise. Certain government schools and colleges could be handed over 'to bodies of Native gentlemen who will undertake to manage them satisfactorily as aided schools'. This was, in fact, a throwback to the ideas of the first educational reformers, who had proposed using a Western-educated minority to pass on education to their less fortunate compatriots. Under the new system, it was intended that the government should retain control of institutions of higher learning but that it should offer no more than guidance on the lower levels; 'having shown the way, it recognizes no responsibility to do for the people what the people can and ought to do for themselves'. When the new policy came into operation, however, elementary education in rural areas suffered for the almost total lack of government control and direction, and failed to expand in the way the framers of the policy had anticipated. The new policy merely accelerated the growth of higher education, for it was at this level that demand was greatest.

In one sense only, the commission's recommendations actually worked in practice. There was a substantial increase in the number of educational institutions and therefore in the number of students. The expansion was almost entirely urban, and in the area of higher education, because the urban classes had both wealth and incentive where the rural classes had not. The standard of education, however, declined as a result of inadequate facilities, lack of textbooks, and – even more important – badly-trained teachers. Government schools were unsatisfactory enough, but aided institutions were frequently worse.

In all educational establishments, there was an emphasis on the purely literary type of syllabus. The 1882 commission had noted the dangers of such an impractical attitude, and had suggested that courses in commercial, engineering and agricultural subjects should be offered by selected schools. These proved mainly unsuccessful because, again, this was not what most Indians wanted. It was also an unpalatable fact that English education was creating a large number of unemployables – people who could find no jobs suited to their qualifications. In India's industrially backward economy, it was believed that any real effort to train technicians would (as a government resolution of June 18th, 1888 phrased it) merely 'aggravate the present difficulties by adding to the educated unemployed a new class of professional men for whom there is no commercial demand'.

As ever, there were political threats to be faced when the government contemplated changes in education. The educated classes, who had at first regarded English education as an instrument which they might use to achieve a share in the profits of British rule (through appointments in government service, commerce, or the professions) early became conscious that their education should fit them to participate in the decision-making apparatus of government. Any apparent attempt by the British to limit higher education seemed to them to be a deliberate act of discrimination. This attitude was to come to a head in the response to the educational reforms of Lord Curzon (viceroy 1899–1905).

In September 1901, Curzon called a conference 'to consider the system of education in India'. It met in private, and its deliberations were not publicized. The conference was attended by education officials and members of the central government, the viceroy himself presiding. All but one of its members were government officials, and no Indians were present. In his opening speech, which was of great length, the viceroy examined the trends of government policy over the preceding seventy years. His main criticisms were directed against the emphasis on an English literary education, and the fact that plans for establishing technical schools had not been implemented. Part of the reason for this, Curzon insisted, lay in the lack of enthusiasm displayed by the middle and upper classes, but the British government had also been at fault. It had been unwilling to expand technical education because it feared that this might only increase unemployment. Such technical schools as did exist, taught only subjects of little practical value. The government had vacillated, and had spent its energies on proliferating schemes of doubtful utility. 'The autumnal leaves are not more thickly strewn in Vallombrosa,' exclaimed Curzon, 'than the pigeon-holes of our Departments are filled with Resolutions on the subject, inculcating the most specious and unimpeachable maxims in the most beautiful language.' He came to the conclusion that 'if technical education is to open a real field for the youth of India, it is obvious that it must be conducted on much more businesslike principles'.

On the subject of general education, Curzon maintained that the 'too slavish imitation of English models' had sprung from an ignorant contempt for the vernacular literatures of India. 'Ever since the cold breath of Macaulay's rhetoric passed over the field of the Indian languages and textbooks,' he said, 'the elementary education of the people in their own tongues has shrivelled and pined.' He believed that something definite must therefore be done to organize elementary education in Indian languages.

As for the universities, Curzon was astonished by the complete absence of 'a history, a tradition, a *genus loci*, a tutorial staff of their own'. They were, he implied, not universities at all – and it was the government's fault. By making an English education the key to government employ, it had made examinations the sole criterion of worth. All that was expected of students was an accurate memory. 'We go on,' said Curzon, 'sharpening the memory of our students, encouraging them to the application of purely mnemonic tests, stuffing their brains with the abracadabra of geometry and physics and algebra and logic, until after hundreds, nay thousands, have perished by the way, the residuum who have survived these successive tests emerge in the Elysian fields of the BA degree.'

Curzon disclaimed any desire to 'fetter colleges and schools with bureaucratic handcuffs', but he insisted that there must be central control. He denied any inclination to create an Imperial Education Department 'packed with pedagogues and crusted with officialism', but suggested that a director-general of education should be appointed to help the various educational bodies attain 'that community of principle and of aim without which they went drifting about like a deserted hulk on choppy seas'. Curzon's orotund disclaimers threw a smokescreen around his basically simple plans. He proposed to extend vernacular education in order to help counteract what he regarded as excessive anglicization. His establishment of a

Department of Archaeology and his desire to preserve ancient monuments were part of the same policy. He hoped to revive and encourage the study of Indian culture, which gave sanction to order and authority and, at the same time, inhibited the political speculation which was a natural product of an English liberal education.

Curzon declared his aims in his opening speech, though – like so much of it – they were couched in the form of a disclaimer. 'There exists a powerful school of opinion,' he said, 'which does not hide its conviction that the experiment of English education was a mistake, and that its result has been disaster. When Erasmus was reproached for having laid the egg from which came forth the Reformation, "Yes," he replied, "but I laid a hen's egg, and Luther has hatched a fighting cock." This, I believe, is pretty much the view of a good many of the critics of English education in India. They think that it has given birth to a tone of mind and to a type of character that is ill-regulated, averse from discipline, discontented, and in some cases actually disloyal.' It was this belief which formed the basis of Curzon's desire for reform.

In pursuit of his aim to encourage the vernaculars, Curzon placed great emphasis on the importance of elementary education. The English language was all very well for universities, he said, 'but for the vast bulk it is a foreign tongue which they do not speak and rarely hear'. The need to extend government influence over the masses seemed essential to Curzon. The activities of political extremists had convinced him that an educated minority would be able, when it so desired, to manipulate the illiterate majority for political purposes, just because that majority was ignorant and uneducated. The consequences of seditious activity would, he believed, be lessened if the government could inhibit the growth of the English-educated minority while, at the same time, educating the masses. 'What,' he demanded, 'is the greatest danger in India? What is the source of suspicion, superstition, outbreaks, crimes – yes, and also of agrarian discontent and suffering among the masses? It is ignorance. And what is the only antidote to ignorance? Knowledge. In proportion as we teach the masses, so we should make their lot happier, and in proportion as they are happier, so they will become useful members of the body politic.'

Curzon also sought to insert strictly Indian studies into the curriculum of higher education by making them compulsory subjects. He hoped, too, to divert Indian students from a purely literary education by establishing faculties of science. He emphasized the importance of teacher training, hoping to create a separate and specialized profession through which the government could exercise control and discipline. Training colleges were, in fact, established, but the number of properly qualified teachers did not increase at the expected rate. The profession of teaching had no great appeal for young Indians, since the rewards were generally very low and the profession had no social status to offset this disadvantage.

Some years earlier, the government had evolved a technique – designed primarily to prevent Indianization at the higher levels of the civil service – of creating other types of government employment. One of these had been the engineering branch of the Public Works Department. As far back as 1876, the home government had advised the viceroy of the time that such engineering colleges as existed in India should be reserved for the 'wants of natives of India' rather than for the 'persons of European parentage' who then formed the majority of students attending such colleges. The word 'native' had always been somewhat ambiguously defined, and the government of India had chosen to take it as including Eurasians – largely because Eurasians already filled most Public Works Department posts, and the government was anxious to preserve for them some form of privileged status. Unfortunately, in 1882, the secretary of state sabotaged the government of India by announcing that 'natives' meant 'persons of pure Asiatic origin'. The original principle of creating new types of government employment, however, seemed to Curzon to be a rational idea and he tried to put it into practice.

By expanding technical education, Curzon hoped to encourage private enterprise to employ Indians at technical levels. Almost all manufacturing industry in India at that time was managed by Europeans who, in the words of the Madras Chamber of Commerce, 'when requiring men with expert knowledge for responsible posts . . . would almost certainly prefer to employ a European, whose capacity and general reliability they could better form an opinion of'. In a partial attempt to overcome this, Curzon instituted state scholarships so that Indians could study abroad for higher technical qualifications than could be achieved in India. Aware, too, that any expansion of technical education would only increase unemployment unless it was coordinated with real industrial development, he set about promoting the improvement of existing native industries and encouraging the development of new industries wherever possible. Curzon's efforts to promote technical education were, however, productive of little tangible result, and it was to be left to Indian industrial and political leaders (such as the Parsee iron and steel firm of Tata) to take the real initiative in advancing the study of science and technology.

The Simla education conference finally broke up, after agreeing to 150 resolutions – each of which had been drafted by the viceroy himself. Though the deliberations had not been made public, Curzon's opening speech had been reported and, on the whole, the majority of educated Indians welcomed the viceroy's proposals for education reform.

During the conference, Curzon had decided that the problem of the universities should be given separate and public consideration. A University Commission was therefore set up in January 1902 and given the widest powers of inquiry into all aspects of university administration. It was instructed to recommend such measures as might tend to 'elevate the standard of university teaching and to promote the advancement of learning'. The commission was presided over by Thomas Raleigh, then Legal Member of the viceroy's executive council. The members of the commission included a Muslim who was Director of Public Instruction in the princely state of Hyderabad, and a Hindu judge of the Calcutta High Court was later appointed when Hindus complained that their community was not represented.

The commission's report was presented in June 1902, and the Indian educated classes suddenly became aware that their status was in danger. 'The Town Hall and the Senate Hall of the University [of Calcutta] have been packed with shouting and perspiring graduates,' wrote Curzon to the secretary of state, 'and my name has been loudly hissed as the author of the doom of higher education in India.' But when, towards the end of 1903, the precise nature of Curzon's proposals for university reform became known, the opposition of educated Indians – particularly those in Bengal – almost reached the stage of hysteria.

The main accusation levelled against the proposals was that they would make the universities into a department of state, placing them – according to G. K. Gokhale, one of the nationalist leaders – under 'the narrow, bigoted ... rule of experts'. This charge was not altogether unfounded. But the real fear of the educated classes was that they might lose their own predominant influence in the institutions of higher education. They were convinced that the government intended to restrict the opportunities for higher education open to young Indians. Contemporary apologists for Curzon denied this, maintaining that the sole purpose of the reforms was to improve the universities by making them places of learning rather than of examination. Certainly, this *was* one of Curzon's aims.

Before the Curzon reforms, university organization had left a great deal to be desired. The senates of these institutions were mainly composed of people with personal or official influence. They were also excessively large. In Calcutta, the senate consisted of 180 members, most of them with extremely dubious academic qualifications. Bombay was even worse; there, the senate numbered 310. Nor did the award of fellowships bear much relation to scholarship. In Bombay, for example, there were fellows of the university who could not sign their own names. But the most serious complaint was that the universities were not teaching institutions at all. They were merely places where students from affiliated colleges sat examinations. The standard of the students themselves –

and, possibly, the Olympian detachment of the examiners who set the papers – can be judged by the fact that, in one year at Madras, four-fifths of the students who had been certified by their teachers as of university standard failed to pass the entrance examination. The Universities Bill was designed, according to Curzon, 'to stop the sacrifice of everything in the colleges which constitute our University system to cramming, to bring about better teaching by a superior class of teachers, to provide for closer inspection of colleges and institutions which are now left practically alone, to place the government of the Universities in competent, expert, and enthusiastic hands, to reconstitute the Senates, to define and regulate the powers of the Syndicates, to give statutory recognition to the Fellows, who are now only appointed on sufferance ... to show the way by which our Universities, which are now merely examining Boards, can ultimately be converted into teaching institutions; in fact, to convert higher education in India into a reality instead of a sham'.

In pursuit of these aims, the senates were to be reformed, the number of fellows fixed at one hundred and their period of tenure restricted to five years. But what really enraged educated Indians was the provision which vested in the government the right of ultimate decision on the recognition of schools and the affiliation, or disaffiliation, of colleges. The colleges were thus to be subject to government inspection and would have to comply with government conditions in respect of their governing bodies, the qualifications of their teaching staff, their financial situation, the standard of their buildings and accommodation, the adequacy of their libraries, and their facilities for practical instruction in science.

Educated Indians claimed that, by these means, the government proposed to restrict the number of students receiving higher education. They were, in fact, right. The university reforms represented an attempt to reduce – by legislative action – the output of Western-educated Indians, and, in consequence, the number of unemployed. The attempt was not successful; the number of students was not reduced, nor was the number who failed their examinations.

Nevertheless, Curzon's reforms did have important consequences. They prepared the way for converting Indian universities into teaching institutions. In 1917, the Sadler Commission tried formally to implement Curzon's proposals, recommending that students should receive instruction from university staffs. It proved impossible in practice to do away with the system of affiliated colleges, but an attempt was made to reduce them to manageable proportions by founding new universities. Curzon, too, was responsible for the innovation of science as a separate subject with a separate degree, although the movement towards science subjects was slow in India – as, indeed, it was in Britain. In the first decade of the present century in India, 85 per cent of students graduating did so in arts, 9 per cent in medicine, 4 per cent in engineering, and only 2 per cent in science. Teacher training, too, failed to produce anything like the number of teachers required. The number of college students, however, continued to increase – from 17,356 in 1907 to 61,200 in 1917. In secondary schools, the number of pupils rose from 47,000 to 1,107,000.

This growth resulted principally from the increased social and economic pressure on the Hindu middle classes. Population increase played an important part. The openings for employment had grown, but so had the competition, and the competition came not only from members of the Hindu middle classes, but also from Muslims and lower-caste Hindus. The number of students grew, and the number of educated unemployed grew. Most of them had hoped for jobs in the professions, but few could be absorbed and the type of education they had chosen rarely provided them with qualifications for other more technical appointments. The government was aware of this and tried to divert the flow of students into technical colleges. Their attempts were not successful, however, for such institutions did not have the social *cachet* of universities. Criticisms that the government did not do enough for technical education were valid, but the government was hamstrung by limited resources. Although independent schools were established to give instruction – much of it very inadequate – in a variety of technical and semi-technical subjects, the whole educational system was clearly out of control. Lines had undoubtedly been laid down, but very little ran along them.

The government and its finances were only partially to blame. What might be called the subterranean results of British rule were, in the twentieth century, beginning to come to the surface. Political change in India had come about at speed, but social and economic change lagged perceptibly behind. In effect, two civilizations were rubbing together, producing areas of inflammation.

In the case of education, the effects can best be seen in the conditions which followed the implementation of the Montagu-Chelmsford reforms in 1921. These reforms were designed to create a measure of self-government in India, by means of the system known as 'dyarchy'. It was based on a division of responsibilities between the provincial governors (the executive authority) and elected assemblies; a number of 'subjects' were 'transferred' to popularly elected ministers. One of the 'transferred' subjects was education. At the time, there was economic recession following the end of the first world war. There was, too, grave political disorder, for the principal nationalist movement, Congress, was determined to prevent the new constitution from working efficiently. One of its tactics was to boycott government schools and to establish in their place 'national' schools in which Hindi was the language of instruction. Certainly, Congress succeeded in draining students away from government institutions, but it was unable to supply any constructive alternative. The boycott lasted for two or three years, and was followed by a massive return to orthodox educational institutions – with the result that an already inadequate system became quite unfitted to fulfil even its minimal purpose. The transfer of responsibility for education to the provincial assemblies only increased the confusion and chaos.

As early as 1924, a conference of Indian universities set up an inter-university board to establish, among other things, standardization of academic qualifications; it also discussed the exchange of professors, and general coordination of the work of universities. All these matters undoubtedly needed attention, but very little was in fact done.

In 1935, the government of India created a Central Advisory Board of Education, whose primary purpose was to evolve an integrated educational policy covering all levels and having at least some relevance to graduate employment. In the course of its researches, the board carried out an inquiry into vocational education. Its report was issued in 1937 and greatly influenced the deliberations of a committee set up soon after by the Indian National Congress to examine the question of education. The committee's conclusions were put into practice by Congress governments in the provinces, but the result of attempts to mix vocational with general education was that both types suffered.

During the last years of British rule in India, educational facilities continued to expand. The number of colleges offering higher education increased from 425 in 1940–41 to 593 in 1945–6. But, principally because of the chronic shortage of money, general education still lagged behind. A really adequate system would have demanded compulsory attendance – which was in fact tried experimentally in some areas – and it had been calculated in 1936 that compulsory education for India's 53,000,000 children would have cost between five and six times as much as the total revenue of the government of India. Although this calculation was based on the current education costs of England and Wales (and it could be assumed that expenditure would be much lower per head in India), the sum involved remained financially impossible.

Finance was always the rock on which any plan for extending education foundered. Idealism, a genuine desire to impart the benefits of some sort of purposeful education, always figured in the plans of the government. Unfortunately, the realities of alien rule permitted only the most partial expression of such ideas. There were any number of grand designs, inspired by both moral and political motives, but they were all vitiated by lack of money and by the fact that, in the late nineteenth and early twentieth centuries, the British were no longer sure of what they wanted to do in India. The immense self-confidence of the early educational reformers had evaporated, not so much because of the Indian experience as because of the wider threat being posed to Britain by new and more virile imperialist nations. Nevertheless, although her purpose was being eroded by doubt, Britain's attitude had become almost irrelevant in the context of the cumulative effects of English education in India.

What were these effects? If one of the primary functions of education is the expansion of literacy, then very little had apparently been achieved by the end of British rule. In 1947, about 90 per cent of the population was still unable to read or write. Although reasonably accurate, this figure needs clarification. Between 1881 and 1931, for example, the population increased by nearly 100,000,000; at the same time, the number of literates also increased significantly. Yet the total percentage of literates remained roughly constant, because the spread of education only just managed to keep up with the increase in population. More was not achieved because of the dead hand of finance and the active fear that compulsion might lead to civil disorder. Even in those areas where experiments were made with compulsory elementary education in the last twenty years of British rule, the results were unsatisfactory. In rural areas, the Indian child plays an important ancillary role in the work of the family. Compulsory attendance at school deprived the family of part of its labour and the simple education the child received bore no relevance to the economic realities of rural life. Fundamentally, the direct effects of British educational policy on the rural masses were negligible.

The effect upon the middle classes – themselves partly created by English education – was very different. In the first place, the lack of caste discrimination at government-controlled, English-style educational institutions finally broke the intellectual monopoly of the Brahmin castes, creating a professional class of lawyers, doctors, engineers, and so on, for whom caste had no particular relevance and who generally supported Western-style political reforms. English education also encouraged a certain amount of occupational mobility which helped to shake established social customs. English education did not *create* nationalism – which would, in any case, have emerged as part of the general response to alien domination – but it did stimulate it and give it Western definitions and Western aims.

The English language was the sole medium of higher education in India, and it gave a sense of identity to those who used it. But it also petrified native languages, which remained unmodernized, their vocabulary detached from the needs of the contemporary world. During British rule, the only attempt made to bring an Indian language up to date was made, not in British India, but at the Osmania university in the princely state of Hyderabad, where the language of instruction was Urdu. It was found necessary to invent over forty thousand technical words. The demands of learning English often proved a real handicap to the assimilation of ideas, forcing students to understand and express themselves in a language they did not use in everyday life. The educated classes found themselves at odds with the reality of their environment. In matters of politics and commerce, they thought in English; in their domestic lives, in their native language. The inevitable results were conflict, anxiety, and – to use a psychiatric word – alienation.

The British did not censor the materials of education, and the government of India rarely made any attempt to control the dissemination of liberal ideas. Indeed, in the early years of educational reform, it deliberately encouraged them. Except for Curzon's unsuccessful attempt to change course, there was no real alteration even in the face of an aggressive nationalism. One of the results was that, when India became independent of Britain, her political ideas were what can only be described as those of a Victorian radical – ideas essentially ill-adapted to the needs of an independent India, and to the times. The emphasis on an almost exclusively literary education – for which Indians must share the blame – left India without any scientifically-biased educated class capable of playing a vital role when the time came, after 1947, to begin the modernization of the country. After independence, even, much of the substructure of a vastly (and over-hurriedly) expanded system of higher education remained British in inspiration. In spite of increasingly wider opportunities in industry and commerce and the growth of technical education, the slant is still towards arts subjects.

English education multiplied the sources of individual discontent, creating a ruthlessness which found one outlet in extremism. During British rule, that extremism could be given a nationalist purpose and directed into channels which could, at least, be called patriotic. But the pressures of unemployment and social alienation today have produced outbursts of violence among students which pose very much the same kind of threat to an independent Indian government as they did to that of the British.

## *Appendix*

### The Education of Women

William Adam, who prepared a series of reports for the government on the state of education in Bengal and Bihar, said in 1835 that the standard of instruction for women 'cannot be said to be low, for with a very few individual exceptions there is no instruction at all. Absolute and hopeless ignorance is, in general, their lot.' Adam maintained that there was a belief amongst Hindu women that a girl who had been taught to read and write would be widowed soon after marriage – a belief, he recorded, 'not discouraged by men'. Fundamentally, most men believed that a woman's place was in the home (a belief shared by many Englishmen, then and later), and that the only education she needed – in domestic economy – should be acquired in the home.

The early educational reformers, accepting this view and being unwilling to interfere in the established social pattern, ignored the problem of women's education. But Christian missionaries did not. The first missionary attempt at female education seems to have taken place in 1818, at the London Missionary Society's school at Chinsurah in Bengal. It was not particularly successful. In the following year, a number of Englishwomen founded the Calcutta Female Juvenile Society; by 1823, the society had six schools with 160 pupils.

The Calcutta School Society discovered – by what statistical method is not revealed – that only four hundred women out of approximately forty million could read and write. This inspired the British and Foreign School Society in London to send out a woman teacher in 1821. This lady – a Miss Cooke, who is better known in the history of women's education in India by her married name of Wilson – succeeded in organizing twenty-three girls' schools in Calcutta and its vicinity within two years of her arrival. Reginald Heber, the first Bishop of Calcutta, described a visit to one of Mrs Wilson's schools in December 1824, when Lady Amherst, wife of the governor-general, attended an examination of the pupils. 'It was very pretty to see the little swarthy children come forward to repeat their lessons, and show their work to Lady Amherst, blushing even through their dark complexions, their slim half-naked figures, their black hair plaited, their foreheads specked with white or red paint, and their heads, necks, wrists and ankles loaded with all the little finery they could beg or borrow for the occasion. Their parents make no objection', the Bishop went on, 'to their learning the catechism, or being taught to read the Bible, provided nothing is done which can make them lose caste. And many of the Brahmins themselves, either finding the current of popular opinion too strongly in favour of the measures pursued for them to struggle with, or really influenced by the beauty of the lessons taught in Scripture, and the advantage of giving useful knowledge, and something like a moral sense to the lower ranks of their countrymen and countrywomen, appear to approve of Mrs Wilson's plan, and attend the examination of her scholars.' Surprisingly enough, the Bishop's conclusions seem to have been at least partially right, and a large sum of money was actually given to Mrs Wilson to build a school by a leading member of the Calcutta Hindu community. Generally speaking, however, only the lower Hindu castes would permit their daughters to attend missionary schools.

The first successful attempt to establish a secular school for girls was made in 1849. This institution – set up by Drinkwater Bethune, Law Member of the governor-general's council – was intended for girls of 'wealth and rank'. The girls were to be under the charge of an Englishwoman, and were to study Bengali and English and 'a thousand feminine works and accomplishments in embroidery and fancy work, in drawing, and in many other things that would give them the means of adorning their own homes and of supplying themselves with harmless and elegant employment'. The school, however did not receive much support, and after Bethune's death in 1851 it had to be privately financed by the governor-general, Lord Dalhousie, until 1856 when it was taken over by the government and became the first institution in India dedicated to the higher education of women. Under Dalhousie's direction, the Bengal Council of Education was instructed to encourage female education, but only where a demand for it existed. The Education Despatch of 1854 accepted that female education was of importance, but failed to suggest that the government should do anything about it.

Elsewhere in India, female education before 1858 was very much the concern of missionary societies. In Bombay, the American Missionary Society opened a school in 1824, and this example was followed by other missionary organizations. In 1851, one private school for girls was opened at Poona and two at Ahmedabad. In 1854, there were sixty-five schools for girls in the Bombay presidency and about 3,500 pupils; 593 girls attended co-educational establishments. In Madras, the story was much the same, but there – as with male education in missionary schools – female education was by far the most advanced in India. In 1854, about eight thousand girls were attending missionary schools in the Madras presidency.

After the assumption of power by the Crown, the government still hesitated over its attitude to female education. Indians might be demanding education for boys, but there was still positive opposition to education for girls. Any government attempt to establish and staff schools for girls might, if not handled delicately, outrage not only conservative opinion but the so-called 'enlightened' classes – who were curiously unenlightened as far as women were concerned. Nevertheless, by 1875 the government had established nearly a thousand girls' schools with about seventy thousand pupils. Progress was never swift – there were less than a million girls at school in 1911–12, and approximately three millions in 1939, which represented about 2 per cent of the then female population.

It was obvious to the planners that providing education for girls was fundamentally a matter of social attitudes and that these could better be changed from within the Hindu and Muslim communities. Such customs as the seclusion of women, particularly in the north, did have an effect on education, though there were purdah schools. In Madras, where purdah did not exist, there was a particularly large increase in the number of girls attending school from 1927 onwards. The real incentive towards change was to come from Indian reformers who regarded female education as part of their general campaign to raise the status of women. One of the most influential of these was a Brahmin widow who had been converted to Christianity, Pandita Ramabhai (1858–1922). At Poona in the Bombay presidency she built a home for Hindu widows which was also a centre of Sanskrit learning. The Western conception of equality for women was implicit in Ramabhai's ideas and her views on education were dedicated to the same premise. Naturally, her activities aroused considerable opposition, but her home at Poona flourished – at one time there were as many as two thousand Hindu widows there.

A rather different view of the position of Indian women was taken by Dr Karve, who also founded a school for Hindu widows at Poona. In 1916, this became the Indian Women's University. Dr Karve believed that woman's role in life was fundamentally different from man's, and that her education should be different. Dr Karve therefore insisted that native languages should be the media of instruction. Karve's views were, in fact, opposed to the spirit of the time; conservative thinkers opposed him because they were opposed to any kind of education for women; the progressive element opposed him because he sought to Indianize women's education. By 1939 the number of undergraduates in the four colleges of the Indian Women's University had increased to 170; it had been six, twenty years earlier.

The movement towards extension of education for both Hindu and Muslim women undoubtedly owed its principal impetus to the nationalist movement. Egalitarian political ideas had some effect on the social position of women and, generally speaking, nationalists were in favour of female education. Nevertheless, the number of girls at school increased very slowly. In the field of higher education, however, the picture was more satisfactory. In 1935, for example, about five thousand women were studying for university degrees. In 1892, there had been only eighty-six, and even as late as 1929 only 1,800. But the educational standard of the candidates left much to be desired. Of the five thousand students of 1935, only 460 actually graduated. These figures are not unsatisfactory when they are compared with those for men students.

At the elementary level, most girls did not go to school after the age of eight or nine – the normal age for marriage before the Child Marriage Restraint Act was passed in 1929, making fourteen the minimum age at which a girl could be married. This generally kept the level of literacy among females extremely low. In rural areas, where even the minimal education for boys was accepted only if it had some economic utility, education for girls – which quite obviously had none – was usually disapproved of.

In urban areas, the educated classes slowly began to realize that their sons might well be happier with educated wives, and the possession of some educational qualifications began to appear as an important part of a bride's dowry. But the government did very little to expand female education, in spite of such hopeful statements as that of the Indian Statutory Commission of 1929, which recommended that, 'in the interests of the advance of Indian education as a whole, priority should now be given to the claims of girls' education in every scheme of expansion'. Whatever the government did or did not do, however, the infiltration of Western ideas was having its effect.

Progress in women's education was slow, because of the institutional timidity of British rule, its fear of social upheaval and, in the twentieth century, of mass political violence. The government's attitude also reflected that of articulate Indians, of whom only a small minority actively wanted education for women. In the last years of British India, self-government and, later, independence were the overriding aims. To these, education for women was irrelevant – however much was said about it in conferences and manifestoes.

## CULTURAL AND RELIGIOUS LIFE

### *Religion and Philosophy*

The tendencies which had emerged in the years before the Mutiny were to develop and receive new expression after 1858.

Many educated Indians began to demand a more positive programme of social reform, not from the government – which was obviously unwilling to take action – but from Indians themselves. Social reform had been one of Ram Mohun Roy's purposes in founding the Brahmo Samaj, and it was therefore not unnatural that increased pressures in favour of reformist activity should come from within that movement. It was to cause conflict and, in the end, a split in the Samaj. Debendranath Tagore, its leader, was essentially inward-looking, concerned more with contemplation than with action. Because of this, he favoured a gradual process of social reform. 'We [the Brahmos] are in and of the great Hindu community', he wrote in 1867, 'and it devolves upon us by example and precept to hold up as a beacon the highest truths of the Hindu shastras. In their light must we purify our heritage of customs, usages, rites and ceremonies and adapt them to the needs of our conscience and our community. But we must beware of proceeding too fast in matters of social change, lest we be separated from the greater body whom we would guide and uplift.'

This attitude failed to satisfy many of the younger Brahmos. The most important, Keshub Chunder Sen, had joined the movement in 1857. He founded many discussion groups, advocated widow remarriage, and organized famine relief. His fiery sermons, delivered in English, excited educated audiences throughout India, and branches of the Samaj were founded in cities outside Bengal, giving the movement a much wider area of contact. Keshub came into conflict with Debendranath when he insisted that Brahmos, most of whom were of the Brahmin caste, should give up wearing the sacred thread, the sign of that caste. They parted company and Keshub set up a separate organization called the Brahmo Samaj of India. Like Debendranath, he too came to rely more and more on personal intuition. In 1878, this fervent opponent of child marriage – who had been instrumental in persuading the government to pass a special marriage Act for Brahmos – allowed his thirteen-year-old daughter to marry a Hindu prince. Many of his followers broke away from him and formed yet another group, the Sandharan (general) Brahmo Samaj.

In his later years, Keshub attempted to create a synthesis between Hinduism, Islam and Christianity. He was particularly influenced by the spirit of Christianity. By assimilating the best of other religions, he envisaged that a new communion would emerge. 'Cultivate this communion, my brethren', he said in 1879, 'and continually absorb all that is good and noble in each other. Do not hate, do not exclude others, as the sectarians do, but include and absorb all humanity and all truth. Let there be no antagonism, no exclusion. Let the embankment which each sect, each nation, has raised, be swept away by the flood of cosmopolitan truth, and let all the barriers and partitions which separate man from man be pulled down, so that truth and love and purity may flow freely through millions of hearts and through hundreds of successive generations, from country to country, from age to age. Thus shall the deficiencies of individual and national character be complemented, and humanity shall attain a fuller and more perfect standard of religious and moral life.' Keshub called the product of his desire for synthesis the New Dispensation, which he believed he had received a divine commission to teach. The symbol of his new religion consisted of a Hindu trident, a Christian cross, and a crescent of Islam, but the main influence was Christian. He summed up the faith of his New Dispensation in these words: 'My creed is the science of God which enlighteneth all. My gospel is the love of God, which saveth all. My heaven is life in God which is accessible to all. My church is that invisible kingdom of God in which is all truth, all love, all holiness'.

Little remained of Keshub's work after his death in 1884, but he was one of the first to state the proposition that, though Britain had much to offer India in terms of science and industry, India had something to offer in return – the wisdom of the spirit. It was a proposition taken up by others after him, and it was one which offered inspiration to many in the Hindu nationalist movement.

Keshub Chunder Sen had played a valuable role in publicizing the ideas of Ramakrishna Paramahamsa (1836–86) and there were signs of Ramakrishna's influence in the New Dispensation. Ramakrishna was a man who had had no formal education and knew very little English. He was an ecstatic, and in his mystical experiences saw God in many forms, including those of Muhammad and Christ. Worshipping each manifestation, he matched his clothes, his food and his prayers to whichever religious condition was uppermost at the time. Ramakrishna's contention was that *all* religions were true, and that there was therefore no need for synthesis. The individual should follow his own chosen path. 'A truly religious man,' he said, 'should think that other religions also are paths leading to the truth. . . . Every man should follow his own religion. A Christian should follow Christianity, a Mohammedan should follow Mohammedanism, and so on. For the Hindus the ancient path, the path of the Aryan Rishis, is best.'

Ramakrishna's teaching and the way he presented it – not in completely thought-out works, but in a series of sayings which were full of sometimes rather broad humour and always good sense – was immensely appealing. 'A man,' he once said, 'after fourteen years of hard asceticism in a lonely forest, obtained at last the power of walking over the waters. Overjoyed at this acquisition, he went to his guru, and told him of his grand feat. At this the master replied: "My poor boy, what thou hast accomplished after fourteen years' arduous labour, ordinary men do the same by paying a penny to the boatman".' Ramakrishna used short alliterative phrases to express his principal ideas, for his method of teaching was through conversation. '*Naham naham*', he said. '*Tuhu tuhu*' (Not I, not I. Thou, thou). He preached a gospel of service. It was this particular aspect which inspired Ramakrishna's disciples, many of them young men from educated middle-class backgrounds.

One of the most important of Ramakrishna's disciples was Vivekananda (1863–1902), who propagated his master's teaching not only in India but in the West. In direct contrast with the Brahmos, Vivekananda regarded such things as idolatry and the caste system as good. Idols were necessary to men who could not envisage God without them. 'Those reformers', he wrote, 'who preach against image-worship, or what they denounce as idolatry – to them I say: "Brothers! If you are fit to worship God-without-Form discarding any external help, do so, but why do you condemn others who cannot do the same? A beautiful large edifice, the glorious relic of a hoary antiquity has, out of neglect or disuse, fallen into a dilapidated condition; accumulations of dirt and dust may be lying everywhere within it; may be, some portions are tumbling down to the ground. What will you do to it? Will you take in hand the necessary cleansing and repair and thus restore the old, or will you pull the whole edifice down to the ground and seek to build another in its place, after a sordid modern plan whose performance has yet to be established? We have to reform it, which truly means to make ready or perfect by necessary cleansing and repairs, not by demolishing the whole thing. There the function of reform ends".'

Vivekananda developed Keshub Chunder Sen's thesis that India could learn material things from the West but that the West should understand that, in spiritual matters, India had much to offer. He emphasized, for Indians, his master's teaching that all religions were equally good and that it was the duty of Hindus to preserve and cherish their own. Vivekananda, however, went further and suggested that Hindu thought had more to offer than other religions, thus helping to create among modern Hindus a sense of pride in being Hindu. Whether he would have approved of the extent to which such pride was to be taken by religious nationalists after his death is doubtful.

Despite his emphasis on social service, Vivekananda's thought had chauvinistic overtones which helped to create what can only be described as mystical patriotism. Aurobindo Ghose (1872–1950) – who came to be known as Sri Aurobindo – turned, after a Western education, to Ramakrishna and Vivekananda for inspiration. Aurobindo became an active extremist, though he left politics completely in 1910 and retired to the French enclave of Pondicherry where he remained until his death. During his active political life, which lasted for only four years, he gave to extremism a passionate sense of country and of religion, maintaining that nationalism was the work of God – not a political programme, but a religion and a creed.

Ramakrishna had accepted the separate validity of all religions. Dayananda Saraswati (1824–83) rejected them all. Nevertheless, his rejection led him to reform. Like the Brahmos, Dayananda looked to the past for justification and for criticism of the Hindu present. He found it in the *Vedas*. He, too, professed theism. Everything after the *Vedas*, he maintained, was superstition. Caste and untouchability were aberrations.

Dayananda had recognized the importance of Western science and proceeded to discover, if not the science itself, at least the seed of it in the *Vedas*. He found – not, perhaps, very convincingly – allusions to steam engines, railways and steamships. In 1875, Dayananda formed the Arya Samaj to publicize his views. Its official creed was theistic. Orthodox Hinduism restricts the castes permitted to read the *Vedas*. The Samaj invited all men to do so. It was strongly opposed to idolatry and animal sacrifice. While Aryas accepted the doctrine of transmigration of souls, they maintained that there was no ultimate union with God. Dayananda's views offended the orthodox and many attempts were made on his life. Finally, after he had accused a princely ruler of loose living, the woman involved had him poisoned – by means of ground glass in his milk.

Keshub Chunder Sen, Vivekananda, Christianity (particularly the Sermon on the Mount), Tolstoy, Thoreau and Ruskin all influenced the ideas of Mohandas Karamchand Gandhi (1869–1948), who is more widely known as a nationalist leader than as a religious thinker. In spite of his admitted liking for popular Christian hymns and his statements on the ethical value of Christianity, Gandhi's fundamental ideas were derived from Hindu tradition. His doctrine of non-violence – though he claimed to have been given it by Tolstoy – was more probably derived from the Jains, a Hindu sect of considerable influence in his birthplace of Gujarat, who will kill or maim no living thing. Even his belief that the British could be blackmailed into giving India her freedom (see page 331) has a sound Hindu precedent in the practice of sitting *dharna* (see page 89). Gandhi's real purpose was to reform Hinduism from within.

Gandhi was not a systematic thinker. Most of what he said had only some immediate purpose, for he was a politician by necessity. In spite of attempts by both Western and Indian admirers to make him a great religious thinker and philosopher, his ideas have little application outside the unique circumstances of the struggle for freedom. The respect in which he was held by millions of ordinary Hindus was a tribute not to what he said but to what he was – a man who had dedicated himself to their service. 'My life,' he said, 'is my message.' In his *Autobiography*, Gandhi stated his belief that Truth is God. 'To see the universal and all-pervading Spirit of Truth face to face one must be able to love the meanest of creation as oneself. And a man who aspires after that cannot afford to keep out of any field of life. That is why my devotion to Truth has drawn me into the field of politics; and I can say without the slightest hesitation, and yet in all humility, that those who say that religion has nothing to do with politics do not know what religion means. Identification with everything that lives is impossible without self-purification; without self-purification the observance of the law of ahimsa [non-violence] must remain an empty dream; God can never be realized by one who is not pure of heart. Self-purification therefore must mean purification in all the walks of life. And purification being highly infectious, purification of oneself necessarily leads to the purification of one's surroundings.' It was his justification for political action.

*

The sudden recognition after the Mutiny – in which traditional India had played an important part – that Muslims would not only suffer for the Mutiny but also for their lack of Western education, led to what is known as the Aligarh Movement, which was mainly responsible for bringing Western knowledge to Muslims (see page 275). The *animateur* of the movement was Sir Syed Ahmed Khan, who was the Muslim counterpart of Ram Mohun Roy, anxious to accept Western science but without damaging the fabric of Islam. Syed Ahmed's problem was that there existed only one sacred text, the *Koran*, which was universally accepted as the only authority. He was forced, therefore, to take the *Koran* and try to interpret it in the light of modern scientific knowledge.

Syed Ahmed was strongly opposed to superstition, and placed his hope in reason. He and his followers were called *nacheris*, a corruption of *naturis*, as they believed in natural religion, in interpreting the word of God by the work of God. Though his attempts to cleanse Islam of its belief in miracles and the irrational were hotly attacked by orthodox theologians, his basic idea that the best in Western thought could be assimilated into Muslim culture without endangering Islam was generally accepted among Muslim intellectuals in the twentieth century.

Syed Ahmed was followed by others, some of whom went much further than he had. Syed Amir Ali (1849–1928), whose book *The Spirit of Islam* (1891) was influential sought to defend Islam against the attacks of both Hinduism and Christianity. His method, like that of Syed Ahmed, was to reinterpret the *Koran* and to find in it authority for attacking such practices as polygamy. Not surprisingly, orthodox

Muslims founded their own self-defence organization to protect orthodox theology. Attacks on 'westernism' continued until the end of British rule, and after. But the progress of political Islam in India, instead of reinforcing orthodox theology, tended to support the modernist approach.

The poet, Muhammad Iqbal (1873–1958) was profoundly influenced by the German philosopher, Nietzche, and the French philosopher, Henri Bergson, though his main source of inspiration remained the Islamic tradition. He was also indebted to the Turkish mystic, Rumi. From Nietzche, he produced a sense of destiny for Indian Islam. In the Islamic community, he saw a real democracy but he believed, with all the modernists, that it was necessary 'to examine in an independent spirit, what Europe has thought and how far the conclusions reached by her can help us in the revision and, if necessary, reconstruction, of theological thought in Islam'.

Generally speaking, the Muslim masses – like the Hindu masses – remained untouched by the modernists, whose only effect was on the educated. Popular Muslim movements, like the Khilafat and the Khaksar, were political in purpose, though their appeal lay in religious slogans. The partition of India in 1947 entrenched the acceptance of Western nationalist ideas. It also entrenched certain elements of traditional Islam.

At least one attempt was made to create a synthesis of Muslim and Christian ideas. Mirza Ghulam Ahmad of Qadian (*c.* 1838–1908), largely in reaction to the activities of Christian missionaries and of the Arya Samaj in the Punjab, founded a new movement (the Ahmadiya) about 1879 by declaring himself to be the Christian Messiah, the Muhammadan Mahdi (the apocalyptic saviour), and the 'final incarnation' of the Hindus. He was, however, primarily concerned with proclaiming the unity of Islam and Christianity. He claimed that Jesus had not risen from the dead and ascended into heaven, but that he had recovered from his wounds of the Cross, journeyed to India, and died in Kashmir. After Mirza Ghulam Ahmad's death, the movement split into a liberal and a conservative wing, the former indistinguishable from the rest of the liberal middle-class Muslims and the latter from the orthodox. Ahmadiyas did, however, keep themselves exclusive from other Muslims, though in a social rather than a theological sense.

The activities of Christian missionaries increased after 1858, with the covert approval of the government. Though their energies pressed most heavily on the Hindu community, others also felt it necessary to defend themselves. The Sikhs, a reformist Hindu sect, had been established in the sixteenth century. Though they accepted practically all Hindu ideas, they rejected idolatry. Idol worship had, however, crept into ordinary religious practice, and by the middle of the nineteenth century a drift back to Hinduism was in progress. About 1890, a body of reformers emerged, who established a college for Sikhs and a number of local associations called Singh Sabhas. In response to the threats of both Christian and Hindu proselytizing, attempts to refurbish the old Sikh traditions were increased, as were social reform activities within the community. Theologically, there was very little effect, the tendency being to move towards a purer orthodoxy.

On the whole, Indians reacted to Western secularism in government and in law – as well as to the, at times intense, propaganda of Christian missionaries – by moving towards a defence of the old religions rather than attempts at synthesis. The defence took the form either of reaction, a solidification of the past, or of modernization and an attempt to reconcile religion with the concept of social and material progress implicit in Western ideas, secular and religious.

### *Art and Architecture*

The men who ruled the Company's dominions in the first half century of the British connexion had little or no dislike for Indian life and religion. They accepted the situation as it was and were anxious to have the life around them preserved in paintings. But the growth of a sense of moral superiority created a gap between the British and the Indians they ruled. After 1858, too, India had lost much of its novelty for Europeans. The extension of the railway reduced the vast treks across country which had been commonplace before its coming and banished for ever the closer acquaintance which such treks had brought. The Mutiny, too, increased British isolation, and it was isolation by choice. The camera displaced the artist. By the 1890s, Indian painting for British patrons had almost ended.

Without patronage from either the British or the Indian middle classes – who took their aesthetic as well as other standards from them – traditional art survived only in some of the native states. But even there it had become imitative and lacking in inspiration. At least one Indian artist (Ravi Varma) even began to paint in oils and in Western style, producing a large number of portraits of princes and officials, including (in 1879) the governor of Bombay.

Though the British now had little interest in traditional painting, many of them did admire traditional crafts which, in the third quarter of the nineteenth century, were falling into decline as the volume of cheap Western imports increased. Instead of taking the obvious way of saving them – by imposing protective tariffs – the government sponsored art schools. These institutions were not notably successful in the craft fields, and disastrous in that of painting. Indians were trained to draw in European style, and left the schools without any chance of making a living.

A change came when an Englishman, E. B. Havell, was appointed principal of the Calcutta School of Art in 1896. Havell believed, with some justification, that the schools had been valueless and, indeed, pernicious because of the emphasis on European techniques and European aesthetic values. He began to turn Indians in the direction of their own artistic traditions. Under his influence, young Indians – of whom the most noteworthy was Abanindranath Tagore, of the great Bengali family – began to experiment with styles based upon Mughal paintings. The results were feeble, sentimental and as detached from Indian reality as the boardroom portraits of Ravi Varma. Critics who disliked Abanindranath's work saw in its anaemic colouring Western influences without any compensating 'Indianness' other than its derivation from traditional styles. Worst of all, it lacked feeling. It was a synthesis in which both elements were the losers. It was not a 'modern' response but an atavistic one, a revival as reactionary in its way as that of the Hindu nationalists.

Through travel abroad, however, Indians were beginning to acquire a new awareness of world art, and at a time when the art movements of Europe were at their most dynamic. Between 1923 and 1928, Abanindranath's brother, Gogonendranath, experimented with cubism and produced paintings which might have come from anywhere, as they contained nothing characteristically Indian.

The problem which faced Indian artists in the first thirty years of the twentieth century was not so much the form of synthesis as the point of departure. Were Western art forms to be given an Indian nationality, or were Indian forms to take on a modern expression? Between about 1900 and 1920, the art of the Jains was rediscovered, as were other Indian styles which had survived in such parts of India as Rajasthan. These styles were not naturalistic. Flat planes were mainly used, and hot colours. There were frequent distortions. Indeed, they had a remarkably 'modern' look. Here, it seemed, was a technique (and an Indian technique, at that) which might be used to create an art which was modern and yet related to the Indian tradition. It was later to influence the Bengali painter, Jamini Roy.

Rabindranath Tagore, that entrepreneur of India's culture, turned in his sixties to the unconscious as a source for his paintings. His work has much in common with that of Paul Klee, though without the humour, and also contains reflections of other Europeans. Some Western critics – and in particular W. G. Archer – have been enthusiastic about Rabindranath's drawings and paintings and have seen in them both a genuinely modern and undoubtedly Indian content. There is no doubt that, in the arid desert that was modern Indian art in his time, Tagore's work stands out as vital.

Among Indian painters who sought not to explore their unconscious but to bring together a modern idiom and Indian reality are Jamini Roy and Amrita Sher-Gil. The intellectual climate in which twentieth-century Indian artists found themselves was dominated by ideas of nationalism and the struggle for freedom from the British. Just as, in the early part of the nineteenth century, the desire of British customers for picture postcards had sent Indian artists to subjects unknown to their predecessors, so, in the first half of the twentieth century, painters turned for their subjects to the Indian village in pursuit of that identity with the masses which they felt the need of as much as any politician. Amrita Sher-Gil (1913–41) was the daughter of a Sikh father and Hungarian mother. She studied in Paris for five years and adopted the un-Indian technique of painting in oils. Perhaps the most important European influence in her case was Paul Gauguin, though until about 1933 she was also profoundly influenced by the work of Cezanne. Back in India, Amrita Sher-Gil turned to the village for her subjects. But though she was drawn there by the peculiar situation of the last years of British India, the political and intellectual circumstances of the time had no real place for artists. An artist who portrays social conditions cannot do so in a vacuum; the realism lies not in the portrayal but in the hope of response. There was none for Amrita Sher-Gil – nationalism had no need for painters, and India's art-lovers were indifferent to social realism.

The use of water-colours in the early nineteenth century had inspired a type of bazaar painting at Kalighat, Calcutta. Its subjects were gods and goddesses. Its style was extremely free, shading was used to express volume, and the backgrounds were usually left blank. Kalighat paintings influenced the Bengali painter, Jamini Roy (b. 1887) who had begun as an academic artist in Western style. After 1932, however, Jamini Roy rejected his Kalighat sources and turned more to medieval miniature paintings and Bengali village art.

Though the British themselves played no seminal role in the beginnings of modern Indian art, the search for new idioms was an intellectual response to the impact of British rule. In the first half of the twentieth century, British art had very little to offer compared with the school of Paris, and in any case modern art was international in spirit. But the search for new forms of expression – from that of Abanindranath Tagore to that of Amrita Sher-Gil – was a product of the oppressive emotional climate of the final years of British rule.

*

The isolation of the British after the Mutiny was reflected in their architecture. Every building they erected in the debased and imitative Victorian style – town halls resembling Renaissance *palazzi* and railway stations disguised as Gothic cathedrals – was a gesture of contempt for indigenous architectural traditions. Some concessions were made to India by adding Mughal motifs and domes to neo-Gothic buildings, but the government, the principal builder, was not interested in living Indian architecture. In the large cities, what little private building there was, copied the style of public buildings.

Throughout the nineteenth century, however, there were still Indian architects and builders producing religious and private architecture of considerable vitality. Most of it was in the princely states or commissioned by princely rulers – a palace in the city of Benares, or a temple at one of the holy places of Hinduism.

The last twenty years of British rule saw a considerable amount of mainly commercial building in the major cities. Most of it was designed by foreign architects and followed the general pattern of contemporary European and American architecture, though it was occasionally embellished with Indian motifs. There was no synthesis because there was no inspiration. The growth of a modern Indian architecture using international idioms in a distinctively Indian manner had to wait until independence.

*Literature*

The founding of universities during the Mutiny began a wide diffusion of the works of English and European writers amongst educated Indians. When an entirely English-based education was opened to a large number of Indians with widely differing mother tongues, the chances of cross-fertilization became very much higher. In the absence of any other all-India language, English became even more important to intellectuals because it was the *only* means of communication between them. The number of English-language periodicals expanded considerably in the last years of the nineteenth century. Under the pressures of a growing and articulate nationalism, new Indian-owned daily newspapers in English came into existence. The language, as well as the idea, of nationalism was English, and many Indians came to use it with great fluency and ease.

In Indo-English poetry, two Bengali women – Aru Dutt, who died in 1874 aged twenty, and her sister Toru, who died in 1877 aged twenty-one – wrote poems which were very English in form though characteristically Indian in subject. Romesh Chandra Dutt, who was responsible for a number of historical works, published translations of the *Ramayana* and the *Mahabharata* which some Indian critics still believe to be good. They are, however, even making allowance for massive condensation, unfaithful to the originals, and are rendered in a facile Tennysonian metre which bears no relation to that of the Sanskrit.

Rabindranath Tagore, whose real place is in Bengali literature, produced English versions of some of his poems and wrote a number of prose works in English. The Hindu extremist – and, later, mystic – Aurobindo Ghose, was influenced by English literary styles and wrote with considerable facility a great many poems and critical works. These included a vast blank verse epic, *Savitri*, which took over fifty years to write and was published after his death. The poetess, Sarojini Naidu, who published her first collection of poems (*The Golden Threshold*) in 1905, has been compared with Elizabeth Barrett Browning, and there are certainly some affinities in their works. During the last years of British rule, there were numerous Indian poets writing in English but they did little more, in most cases, than reflect the latest European vogues with some fidelity.

The novel in English began to come into prominence after 1920, though there had been a number of rather mediocre examples before that date. Among the works worth remembering are K. S. Venkataramani's *Kandan the Patriot* (1932), Mulk Raj Anand's *The Village* (1939), and the works of

R. K. Narayan, including *The Dark Room* (1938) and *The English Teacher* (1945).

Indian writers in English (including politicians) hoped to reach a much wider English-speaking audience than that composed of English-educated Indians. Some of them achieved it, but the majority did not. It was only to be expected that, as English had opened the door to a wider world, Indians themselves would hope to influence that world. Politicians like Jawaharlal Nehru and Mahatma Gandhi succeeded in doing so, but it was mainly what they had to say that gave them an audience, not how they said it. It is a fair criticism of Indian creative writing in the English language to say that it was exoticism of subject combined with some facility of expression – rather than any genius – which led to publication in the West.

In the vernaculars, Bengali continued to lead the way. The English novel form was used by Bankim Chandra Chatterjee, whose models were Scott and Bulwer Lytton. Bankim Chandra wrote his first novel (*Raj Mohun's Life*) in English, but all his others were written in Bengali. They are emotion-charged historical works, highly rhetorical in tone. Bankim Chandra had quite a number of imitators.

Rabindranath Tagore, who was awarded a Nobel Prize for literature in 1913 was profoundly influenced by European poets. Unfortunately, he was also impressed by the windy mysticism of the Celtic twilight and the works of the Belgian dramatist, Maurice Maeterlinck.

From the 1880s onwards, a reaction against total acceptance of Western values – which was also expressed in religious revivalism and religious nationalism – had its effect in vernacular literature. In spirit, the reaction owed much to Western scholarship, which had discovered India's past. But the literature it produced was, with some exceptions, sentimental and weak.

In the last twenty years of British rule, large numbers of pseudo-psychological stories were written and published. Other writers based their works on such important English authors as Ethel M. Dell. Indeed, except for one or two outstanding figures, the state of literature in Indian languages at the end of British rule was low. The works of Bengali novelists and poets had been translated into other Indian languages, and pseudo-Tagores and Bankim Chandras emerged in most of them. Plots were lifted from such English writers as Mrs Henry Wood, author of the melodrama *East Lynne,* from Conan Doyle, and from many others less respectable.

The movement to synthesize Western style and Eastern subject continued. It produced such unlikely results as the Johnsonian essay in Marathi (V. S. Chiplunkar's *Nibandh Mala,* 1875). A number of translations of European works into the major Indian languages was one of the outstanding features of twentieth-century literature. The authors ranged from the most worthless of romance writers to Shakespeare, Ibsen, Tolstoy, Victor Hugo and George Bernard Shaw. In all the Indian languages, it is possible to find poems and stories, essays and novels imitating the styles of a wide variety of European writers. T. S. Eliot's *The Waste Land* is echoed in Kannada, in Adiga's *Gondalapura* (1943). Oliver Goldsmith's *Vicar of Wakefield* has its Telugu counterpart in Virasalingam's *Rajasekhera Chavitram* (*c.*1881). The Indian theatre, too, had its versions of European playwrights.

One of the most interesting features of the impact of the West was the way in which Indian languages were penetrated by English words and idioms. It was commonplace for ordinary speech to be peppered with fragments of English. Many writers used them in Indian-language works after making the necessary phonetic changes. Before the end of British rule, however, nationalist sentiment was turning against the 'defilement' of Indian languages by English – an attitude which has intensified since independence.

Whatever criticisms may be made (and they are many) of the effects of English ideas and models upon Indian literatures, they did bring a new vitality and a desire for change. On the whole, the results before the end of British rule were not encouraging, but a foundation had been laid for later experiments which have resulted in considerable progress being made since independence.

## NATIONALISM

The Mutiny made a profound and lasting impression on both British and Indians. The British reaction in India – despite the cooling words of Queen Victoria's proclamation of 1858, which had promised that there would be no discrimination against Indians in the public service – was to ensure such discrimination in practice, on what were purely racial grounds. The depth of British fears aroused by the Mutiny has been dealt with elsewhere (see page 194). The British in India did not dissimulate and their attitude appeared as what it was, a complete denial of the frequently stated hope of British liberals that cooperation with Indians would be the first step towards actual self-government. The Indians who were first nominated to the new councils represented the old governing classes. They were not the men whom Macaulay foresaw as 'Indian in colour and blood, but English in taste, in opinions, in morals and in intellect', who were to be the acknowledged legatees of British rule. On the contrary, such men as these were denied higher posts in the civil service. Racial discrimination was reinforced by economic discrimination. Most educated Indians had looked to government employment as the reward for their anglicization. Now, cut off from their background by education, they found themselves unacceptable elsewhere, and the rejection in financial terms was the most expressive of all. Economic discrimination was to be responsible for various nationalist reactions.

Racial – and therefore cultural – discrimination inevitably led to religious revivalism. Economic and political discrimination led both to moderation and extremism, to imitative ideologies and to Hindu nationalism. During most of the latter part of the nineteenth century, these two aspects of Indian reaction remained separate, but by the beginning of the twentieth century they had come together. In various guises, they have remained so ever since.

A third attitude – the desire to create some form of synthesis between Eastern and Western ethical values, first propounded by Ram Mohun Roy – influenced both sides. Ram Mohun founded the Brahmo Samaj ('Society of the Worshippers of God') and its work was continued after his death by, first, Debendranath Tagore (1817–1905), and then Keshub Chunder Sen – whose name is sometimes spelt as Keshab Chandra Sen – (1839–84). Debendranath sought to continue the purification of Hinduism which had been begun by Ram Mohun, while Keshub tried to create a genuine synthesis between Hinduism and Christianity (see page 296 ff.). The Brahmo Samaj influenced only a very small minority of Indians, but its role under both Debendranath and Keshub was seminal, for it helped to fashion the religious understanding of such men as Rabindranath Tagore and Mahatma Gandhi.

The activities of Debendranath and Keshub were primarily defensive. Those of Dayananda Saraswati (1824–83), however, were aggressive and full of Hindu self-confidence. Dayananda rejected Western ideas and proposed, instead of a synthesis, the revival of the old religion of the Aryans who had invaded India around 1500 BC and whose sacred books, the *Vedas,* were the foundation of Hinduism. Dayananda's teaching was revolutionary, for it claimed that there was no Vedic authority for most of the customs of Hindu society – rigidity of caste, untouchability, or child marriage. In 1875, he founded in Bombay the Arya Samaj ('Society of Noble Men').

To many orthodox Hindus, members of the Brahmo Samaj – the 'Brahmos', as they were called – seemed distinctly irreligious. Their attacks on Hinduism as a religion in need of reform seemed to be a capitulation to Western critics. Many Brahmos did, indeed, express contempt for several aspects of Indian life. They were themselves fully Westernized in their general behaviour. If they had chosen to become Christians (although very few educated Indians were, in fact, converted) orthodox Hindus could have ignored them. But they did not, and their desire to reform Hinduism by assimilating Western ideas appeared to be designed to subvert the very foundations of Hindu society.

In the eyes of most Hindus, the government of India *could not be* a secular government. In Hinduism, there is no divorce between religion and society. According to this reasoning, the British government of India was a Christian government. Whatever its disclaimers, its aim was assumed to be total conversion of Indians to Western ideas, both social and religious. Orthodox Hindus saw the Brahmos as secret agents, preparing the ground by undermining Hinduism in order to make way for Christian missionaries. So, too, the moderates' demand for political reform was viewed as an attempt to entrench in the system those who most approved of that system. If Westernized Indians became involved in the process of government, they would have a hand in further reforming legislation. There seemed, in this, to be an overt threat to orthodox Hinduism.

It was implicit in Dayananda's desire to cleanse Hinduism that it should be revitalized and so become a force which might resist Westernizing tendencies. But there was more to the aims of the Arya Samaj than that. The British had imposed on traditional Indian society a vast superstructure of Western law, economic organization and administration. Whatever orthodox religious leaders believed, the government after the Mutiny had no intention of taking aggressive action, overt or clandestine, against the traditional social order. But Western systems, in themselves, were continuously assaulting long-held customs and attitudes to life. For orthodox Hindus, there was no possibility of reconciliation. Cultural and religious freedom, they believed, could only be achieved through political freedom. As a contemporary Englishman put it, the logic of Dayananda's view was that 'the religion of India as well as the sovereignty of India ought to belong to the Indian people; in other words, Indian religion for the Indians, Indian sovereignty for the Indians'.

Another stage in what might be called the rehabilitation of Hinduism was represented by Ramakrishna Paramahamsa (1836–86) and by his disciple and propagandist, Vivekananda (1862–1902). To traditional Hinduism they added the ideas of social service and of self-reliance. Vivekananda's appeals on behalf of the downtrodden masses gave nationalist leaders an opportunity to express, in political terms, not just the demands of a minority but of the majority of India's people. In his response to these appeals, Gandhi, in the twentieth century, helped to give the nationalist movement an apparently broad base of resistance to British rule. Vivekananda's rousing speeches to the young men of India, urging them to dedicate themselves to changing the lives of millions of their poor and starving fellow-countrymen, were to give nationalist sentiment not only a sense of reality but of purpose – and of a purpose entirely Indian in character.

Hindu self-confidence was further bolstered by the work of the Theosophical Society founded in New York in 1875 by the Russian spiritualist, Madame Blavatsky. The society's wholehearted acceptance of Hinduism was expressed in a pseudo-intellectual manner which had considerable appeal for Indians who had been repelled by the emotionalism of Ramakrishna and Vivekananda. The society disseminated a wide – if mainly uncomprehending – knowledge of Hindu ideas to a large number of people in the West. The second president of the society was to be Mrs Annie Besant, who chose to be active in Indian politics and was even elected president of the Indian National Congress in 1917.

In the nineteenth century, none of these movements specified, or even advocated, political action. What they did was supply a series of ideas and emotions which had to wait for a political vocabulary in which they might be expressed, as well as for leaders capable of using that vocabulary. Meanwhile, the moderate elements – the liberals, the gradualists, the hopeful cooperators with the British – continued to found quasi-political movements designed to persuade the British to grant liberal institutions to India, institutions through which these moderates could play a part in the government of their country. Whatever their political platforms, such movements still tended to represent the limited interests of the educated classes. The moderate leaders were, generally speaking, men with a secular outlook who believed that religion could be separated from politics. And, despite everything, they continued to believe in the fundamental good faith of British intentions. Every time the British denied them the right to appointments at the higher levels of the civil service, they hid their embarrassment and, in their weakness, removed themselves even further from contact with the Indian masses.

Nevertheless, the moderates played an extremely important role in developing the Westernizing strand in the complex of Indian nationalism. In their attempt to find in Western society a spur for Indian action, they looked to a wider field than English liberalism. They saw, in mid-nineteenth-century Europe, examples of men who challenged the old order of things. Garibaldi, Mazzini, and the others who formed the Young Italy movement inspired some of them with great hopes. They pointed to patriotism and to nationalism in its European sense as great and vital forces.

Again, the initiative came from Bengal. The British Indian Association was so obviously a class-orientated association that the middle classes felt it unsuitable for the expression of their interests. A number of Bengalis suggested that a strictly Bengali organization should be formed, but this was thought to be too parochial. An attempt was made to force the British Indian Association to open itself to a wider membership by reducing its subscription, but this was not successful. In 1875, a new organization, the India League, was formed in Calcutta to coordinate the activities of a number of district associations. Its aims were 'to ascertain and propagate the views of the people as to how Indians could progress in the political and other fields; to discuss and adopt the means which we should consider proper for the good of our countrymen and for the diffusion of political education amongst them; to devise and adopt legitimate means for safeguarding the interests of different classes; to stimulate the spirit of nationalism among the people; to adopt means for the development of economic resources of the country.' The subscription (five rupees) was a tenth of what the British Indian Association asked, and artisans, cultivators and village headmen could join for a special subscription of one rupee – which was still quite a large sum.

A year after the India League was formed, another organization, the Indian Association, was also founded in

Calcutta. Among those present was Surendranath Banerjea (1848–1926), who had been one of the first Indians admitted to the Indian Civil Service but who had been dismissed in 1874 for what the secretary of state for India described as 'a palpable misuse of his judicial powers' and for being 'guilty of falsehood'. In fact, he had failed to correct a false report by a subordinate – a crime for which his English colleagues would have received no more than a departmental reprimand. Surendranath's appeal, when he presented himself in London, was dismissed, and he returned to India convinced that 'the personal wrong to me was an illustration of the impotency of our people'. He determined to dedicate the rest of his life to 'redressing our wrongs and protecting our rights, personal and collective'.

The idea of a truly all-India organization was very much in the minds of the men present at the founding of the Indian Association in 1876, 'for even then', wrote Banerjea, 'the conception of a united India, derived from the inspiration of Mazzini, or, at any rate, of bringing all India upon the same common political platform, had taken firm possession of the minds of the Indian leaders in Bengal'. An immediate attempt was made to identify the Indian Association with popular causes. The first crusade took up the complaint of third-class railway passangers at not having lavatories in the coaches. The association's agitation was successful.

The association held its first public meeting in March 1877 to protest at discrimination against Indian candidates for the Indian Civil Service. The age limit had been lowered from twenty-one to nineteen, and it was suggested at the meeting that examinations for the service should be held simultaneously in Britain and India, and not – as was the practice – in Britain alone. At the same meeting, Surendranath Banerjea was appointed a special delegate whose duty was to visit other parts of India. He left Calcutta in May 1877 for an extended tour, during which he spoke at many public meetings. Surendranath made considerable impact on his audiences. It was necessary, he said at a meeting in 1878, to preach 'the great doctrine of peace and good will between Hindus and Musulmans, Christians and Parsees, aye between all sections of the great Indian community. Let us raise aloft the banner of our country's progress. Let the word "Unity" be inscribed there in characters of glittering gold. ... There may be religious differences between us. There may be social differences between us. But there is a common platform where we may all meet, the platform of our country's welfare.' Under Surendranath's influence, a number of organizations were established in different parts of India, designed to act in concert with the Indian Association.

The association continued to agitate against discriminatory action by the government – against the Vernacular Press Act of 1878, against the removal of import duties on Lancashire cotton, and against continued discrimination in the public services. In 1880, it even sent a representative to Britain to help appeal to the electorate on behalf of the Liberal Party, in which many Indians had placed their hopes of a new deal.

In 1883, the Indian Association took advantage of an industrial exhibition in Calcutta to arrange a national conference, hoping to attract some of the many leading Indians who were expected in the city for the occasion. Early in the same year, Surendranath Banerjea had been imprisoned for two months on a charge of contempt of court, and this had brought his name to the attention of a wider public. But when the 'national' conference took place, it was still very much a local affair, three-quarters of the delegates coming from Bengal. Much emphasis was placed on the desirability of parliamentary government for India, and one speaker – the English writer, Wilfred Scawen Blunt – noted at the end of the conference: 'So ended the first session of the Indian Parliament. May it be memorable in history.'

The Indian Association held its second meeting in Calcutta in 1885. At the same time, another body was holding its first meeting, in Bombay. This was the Indian National Congress, which was to lead the country to independence.

Congress had its origin not so much in the spontaneous desires of Indians as in the considered policy of the government.

After the disturbing events of Lord Ripon's administration – particularly the British community's success in resisting legislation to permit Europeans to be tried by Indian judges – there were signs of considerable unease amongst educated Indians. The Indian Association had protested vigorously against the government's capitulation in face of civil service and British community disapproval. To educated Indians, it seemed as if even a Liberal viceroy was helpless against the conservatism of the British in India. The proposed Bill, known as the Ilbert Bill (after the Law Member, Sir Courtenay Ilbert), aroused both sides to such an extent that the British-owned Calcutta newspaper, *The Englishman*, declared: 'We are on the eve of a crisis which will try the power of the British government in a way in which it has not been tried since the Mutiny of 1857.'

When Lord Dufferin arrived as viceroy in 1884, his first task was to try and quieten the unrest caused by Ripon's well-intentioned but basically weak administration. Dufferin soon developed a dislike for educated Indians. 'I have already discovered', he wrote to the secretary of state in February 1885, 'that the Bengalee Baboo is a most irritating and troublesome gentleman, and I entirely agree with you in thinking that we must not show ourselves at all afraid of him. He has a great deal of Celtic perverseness, vivacity and cunning, and seems to be now employed in setting up the machinery for a repeal agitation, something on the lines of O'Connell's Patriotic Associations.' Dufferin preferred to try and win the cooperation of the landed and other conservative elements.

Something, however, had to be done in another direction. The tendency towards political association among the predominantly Hindu middle classes demanded some form of neutralizing encouragement. The actual degree of government involvement in the birth of the Indian National Congress is, however, the subject of considerable controversy. The moving spirit was a former civil servant, Allan Octavian Hume, and it has been suggested that he and Lord Dufferin were entirely responsible. But there is no satisfactory evidence for this. There seems little doubt, however, that Dufferin welcomed Hume's idea of 'a safety valve for the escape of great and growing forces, generated by our own actions', and gave the proposal his support.

Hume himself, it is claimed, was motivated by having seen in the government's Intelligence archives seven large volumes containing reports from all over India relating to the state of unrest. According to a memorandum allegedly preserved in Hume's papers: 'Innumerable entries referred to the secretion of old swords, spears and matchlocks, which would be ready when required. It was not supposed that the immediate result in its initial stages would be a revolt against our Government, or a revolt at all in the proper sense of the word. What was predicted was a sudden, violent outbreak of sporadic crimes, murders of obnoxious persons, robbery of bankers, looting of bazaars. In the existing state of the lowest half-starving classes, it was considered that the first few crimes would be the signal for hundreds of similar ones, and for a general development of lawlessness, paralysing the authorities and the respectable classes. It was considered certain also, that everywhere the small bands would begin to coalesce into large ones, like drops of water on a leaf; that all the bad characters in the country would join, and that very soon after the bands obtained formidable proportions, a certain small number of the educated classes, at the time desperately, perhaps unreasonably, bitter against the Government, would join the movement, assume here and there the lead, give the outbreak cohesion and direct it as a national revolt.'

If such evidence actually did exist – and no one else ever admitted to having seen it – Hume's desire to divert the educated classes towards a gradualist attitude could have been motivated by purely liberal and humanitarian feelings. The memory of the Mutiny was still strong in India, and no right-thinking person wanted a repetition of it. But, as such a view coincided with British self-interest, a Machiavellian interpretation has been put upon it.

Any organization which polarized moderate and basically 'loyal' opinion was desirable from the government's point of view. Dufferin and many others were fully aware that, in a fundamentally divided society, there was really no need for the British to initiate division. All classes of Indians – and the middle classes were no exception – would do it for them. Inter-communal and inter-class antagonisms were self-perpetuating. The government's real concern was to minimize violence and it seems very unlikely that, in 1885, it really considered it possible for the educated classes (already thoroughly alienated from the masses) actually to take control of a basically agrarian rebellion, as Hume suggested. However, in the face of growing revivalist tendencies amongst Hindus, it was obviously sensible to encourage organizations of moderates. The government's policy was to maintain, and if possible extend, the division between moderates and extremists, and so it remained until the defeat of the moderates in 1918.

The first meeting of the Indian National Congress took place in Bombay in December 1885. The names of seventy-two delegates were recorded, though more were probably present, including some Muslims. When the session of 1886 came, however, the secretaries of two Muslim bodies – the Mohammedan Association, founded in Calcutta in 1856, and the Central Mohammedan Association, founded in 1877 – refused to attend. Basically, the Muslims were not antagonistic to Congress, merely indifferent to it. This attitude, however, did not last long.

In 1888, Hume, fully aware that Congress was national only in the sense that its members came from different parts of India, decided to engage in aggressive propaganda designed to rouse some political awareness in the masses. His propaganda included the preparation of what was called the *Tamil Catechism* – of which some thirty thousand copies were distributed in Madras – and other versions in Urdu and English. The catechism included an attack upon the civil service and, though the strictures were extremely mild, the government chose to believe that they were inciting hatred against it. Hume was officially informed of the government's displeasure. The propaganda was not particularly effective among Hindus, but it antagonized certain elements of Muslim opinion.

Syed Ahmed Khan, leader of the educated Muslims, founded in 1888 the United Indian Patriotic Association, whose primary aim was to combat the influence of Congress. One of its objects was 'to strengthen the British Rule, and to remove those bad feelings from the hearts of the Indian people which the supporters of Congress are stirring up throughout the country, and by which great dissatisfaction is being raised among the people against the British Government'. The majority of its members were Muslims and it expressed its anti-Congress feelings with a distinctly anti-Hindu bias – though this was justified by members on the grounds that Congress was directed by Bengalis, who were antagonistic to Muslims. Syed Ahmed's principal fear was that the pressure for democratic institutions would lead to the Muslim minority being dominated by the Hindu majority. 'If at any future time', he wrote in 1886, 'there should be a Parliament with Hindus and Mohammedans sitting on the two sides of the house, it is probable that the animosity which would ensue would far exceed anything that can be witnessed in England. For the safeguard of the English system is – that the party in power is always in dread of being left in a minority by the defection of some of its adherents, but this safeguard would not exist in India because a Hindu would not turn Mohammedan and *vice versa.* Moreover the Mohammedans would be in a permanent minority and their case would resemble that of the unfortunate Irish members in the English Parliament, who have always been outvoted by the Englishmen. The majority in Parliament has absolute control and a study of the habit of assemblies points to the conclusion that bodies of men are less generous in regarding opponents than individual rulers are. If this were so, and one side were perpetually outvoted, there is only too much fear that the minority would ultimately take the matter into their own hands and see if they could gain by force what they were unable to obtain by constitutional means.'

The attempts made to persuade Muslims not to support Congress were, however, none too successful. At the Congress session of 1888, there were 222 Muslims out of a total of 1,248 delegates. Congress Muslims, too, were strongly antagonistic to Syed Ahmed, whose main purpose was to keep Muslims *out* of politics and to withhold their support from the democratic, liberal and fundamentally secular aims voiced by Congress. Syed Ahmed did not really fear the organized middle classes – only that they might be successful in persuading the government to grant democratic institutions, which would then, he thought, be used by extremist Hindus to discriminate against Muslims.

Unfortunately, there was enough evidence of Hindu revivalism to confirm his worst fears. The activities of Swami Dayananda and others had distinctly anti-Muslim overtones, especially after the Cow Protection Society was established in 1882. This was directed against Muslims, who ate beef, as well as against Christians and the government which permitted the slaughter of cows. But Dayananda did not openly take religion into politics. That was left to others.

As in the case of most aspects of political action in India, the seeds of Hindu nationalism were first sown in Bengal. The works of Bankim Chandra Chatterjee – who had been one of the two students to graduate from the new Calcutta university in 1858 – supplied some of the inspiration. Bankim Chandra was a member of the civil service until 1891. It is a comment on the limitation placed on Indians in government service that he was appointed only as deputy magistrate and that he never advanced in rank.

Bankim Chandra wrote in Bengali, using English literary forms. In his work, he praised Hindu religious sentiments and glorified the Hindu past. His poem, *Bande Materam* ('Hail to the Mother'), became the anthem – the *Marseillaise*, even – of Hindu nationalism, identifying love of the mother country with love of god. Though for Bankim Chandra, the motherland was Bengal, it soon came to mean India and, specifically, Hindu India. In his novel, *Amandamath* ('Abbey of Bliss'), he claimed that British rule was the essential prelude to a revival of Hinduism. Bankim Chandra Chatterjee was the prophet – and, in a sense, the ideologue – of cultural and religious nationalism, and his work profoundly influenced the young Bengalis who were to turn to terrorism as their form of nationalist expression.

This looking backwards to see a reflection of the future was at the base of the ideas of the man who was to unite religious sentiment with positive political action. He was not a Bengali, but a Maratha, a member of the race which had resisted British expansion at the beginning of the nineteenth century as it had resisted the Mughals in the seventeenth. Bal Gangadhar Tilak (1856–1920) had received a Western-style education at the Deccan College in Poona. His reading was wide, taking in most of the Hindu classics as well as the works of Hegel, Kant, Mill, Bentham, Voltaire and Rousseau. He was early determined to take up a political career and believed that the way to acquire most influence was to establish schools where patriotism and sacrifice could be taught. He had no objection to Western science, but believed that it should be absorbed and restated in Hindu terms.

For a time, Tilak co-operated with moderate elements in Bombay but, realizing that they had no mass support, he soon turned his attention to creating it for himself. He acquired a newspaper, the *Kesari* (the 'Lion'), and through it began to promote two new annual festivals, one dedicated to the Hindu god, Ganesha – known in western India, where he was held in particular esteem, as Ganapati – and the other honouring the Maratha hero, Sivaji, who had been the most consistent opponent of the Mughal empire. Both festivals were obviously anti-Muslim. The Sivaji festival was given even more point by the fact that it was held at the same time as the Muslim religious festival of Muhurram.

Tilak's propaganda activities and the spread of cow protection societies helped to cause considerable unease. In the North-West Provinces in 1893, there was Hindu rioting in certain districts and British troops had to be called out to restore order. Soon, there were similar riots in Bombay. The government seemed to think that Congress was behind the troubles. It was reported that trials had been held in imitation of normal courts of law, and that *chapatis* were being passed (the cakes of Indian bread which had been circulated just before the outbreak of the Mutiny). There was a great deal of violent writing in vernacular newspapers. In 1897, Tilak used the insensitive actions of plague officers to arouse Hindu feelings.

Bubonic plague had swept Bombay, killing some twenty thousand people, and in the spring of 1897 the scourge spread through the countryside until it reached Poona. There the Plague Commissioners adopted determined and brutal measures – exactly what the situation required. Unfortunately, they carried them out without giving any explanation or attempting to involve the people themselves in implementing them. The chief plague officer – one Mr Rand, who was the assistant Collector of Poona – used British troops to destroy property which was believed to be contaminated. It was arranged that men, women and children from infected areas should be segregated into special camps. While searching houses for people infected with the disease, the soldiers damaged shrines, sometimes looted property, frequently sent off to camps people who were in fact free from the plague. To the people of Poona, already unnerved by the hideous epidemic, Rand and his men seemed to be engaged on a senseless reign of terror. Plague Commissioners came to be dreaded more than the plague itself. The rich fled the city, and panic and alarm roamed the streets.

Tilak protested against what Rand and his men – this 'vast engine of oppression,' as he called them – were doing. He warned the authorities that popular resentment was running high. 'What people on earth, however docile,' he thundered in the *Kesari*, 'will continue to submit to this sort of mad terror?' In June 1897, Rand and his assistant were shot dead. A few weeks later, Tilak was arrested on a charge of sedition and, after a travesty of a trial, sentenced to eighteen months' imprisonment.

The news of Tilak's 'martyrdom' spread throughout India, and his ideas became known to a large number of that new class of young, partly Western-educated Indians who were suffering acutely from economic and social frustration. Religious nationalism had a very wide appeal. It gave to the

Brahmins – the highest caste and, consequently, the natural leaders of the Hindu community – a vocabulary with which to resist the challenge to their traditional social and political influence which was implicit in British rule. It offered the unemployed middle classes an outlet for their economic despair as well as a firm anchor within the traditional order from which their education had seemed to cut them loose. In the case of the peasants, the new nationalism mobilized the very gods of the Hindu pantheon in their defence and encouraged them to participate in a kind of religious crusade. And to young hot-heads it offered the excitement of violence, of action rather than words.

Nevertheless, religious nationalism had little appeal for those members of the middle classes – the doctors, the lawyers, the schoolmasters and businessmen – who were members of Congress and, after the Councils Act of 1892, of the legislative councils. Generally speaking, these men had little sympathy for the peasant and his troubles. It is an interesting fact that, throughout the whole period of the struggle for freedom, a large proportion of moderate nationalists came from the legal profession; their respect for the law reinforced other pressures in favour of legitimate means of agitation. By 1899, according to a confidential government report, almost 40 per cent (5,442) of the 13,839 delegates to the Indian National Congress were from the legal profession. The other large groups consisted of 2,629 representing landed interests, and 2,091 from the commercial classes. The remainder was made up almost entirely of journalists, doctors and teachers.

Congress, like the British Indian Association, was opposed to any reform of tenants' rights, for although the legal profession might be indifferent to landlord and peasant alike, much of Congress's financial support came from large landed proprietors. The commercial classes formed another interested party. They felt themselves oppressed, and believed that British rule did not favour indigenous capitalists. They were only partly right because, though British rule undoubtedly favoured British business undertakings and did not actively encourage the growth of indigenous industry, development had been restricted primarily by lack of Indian capital and enterprise. Furthermore, the Congress attitude to industrial reform, for example, showed that its members were no friends of the workers.

The coming together of the educated classes, deprived of higher posts in the civil service, and of the businessmen who regarded themselves as discriminated against economically, was of profound importance in the struggle for freedom. It brought much-needed funds, as well as adding a further pressure in favour of non-violent reforms rather than bloody revolution, for Indian businessmen also brought the innate conservatism characteristic of capitalists of all races.

This upper middle-class minority – which, in the early days of the freedom movement (1886) numbered about 300,000 in a population of 180,000,000 – saw representative institutions as the only possible system which might satisfy its demands. It was not concerned with whether the British government was morally good or bad, but only with the fact that it was there – depriving educated Indians of their rightful jobs and profits.

Congress continued to represent this section of Indian society. Religious nationalism, on the other hand, was to have its appeal to the growing, partly-Westernized, lower middle class. It was on these people that Westernization had a destructive effect. Being inadequately educated in an alien cultural tradition, they found themselves uneasy in their own. They became afraid of Western-style changes and saw no advantage for themselves in representative government, which they anticipated would favour the fully-Westernized upper middle classes rather than themselves.

The period up to 1905 was essentially one of frustration. Congress appeared to be getting nowhere with its gradualist demands. Religious nationalism was spreading its influence but was hardly in a position to challenge the government by force. Muslims, who had been advised by Syed Ahmed to keep out of politics, did not seem to be gaining anything by their loyalty to the British. The situation was ripe for the acceptance of another European institution – the secret society. The major influences were the Carbonari of Italy and the Irish Sinn Fein. The appeal of such societies was mainly romantic, for even such revivalist leaders as Tilak did not approve of terrorism or accept that it could lead to Indian freedom. Tilak believed in mass agitation, not in the isolated murder of British officials. Terrorism, indeed, was to remain only a tributary stream in the current of Indian nationalism. But the deeds of terrorists were followed avidly by young and old, and the idea of liberating India by force remained the hope of some nationalists right to the end of British rule.

Under the pressures of extremism, the fortunes of the moderate leaders of Congress suffered continuous decline. Their loyal and peaceful agitation was regularly rebuffed by the British. The moderate leaders, however, were men of very real quality. Their tragedies were the depth of their Westernization and their trust in British good faith. (Not that this prevented them from criticizing British rule in India.) Dadabhai Naoroji (1825–1917), for example – a Parsee who was president of Congress in 1886, 1893 and 1906 – lived for some time in England and had the distinction of being elected to the House of Commons in 1892 on a Liberal ticket. His aim was to convince the British, and particularly the legislators in Britain itself, that they should grant liberal institutions in India. Mahadev Govind Ranade (1842–1901), who was a judge for thirty years and barred by his position from political activity, concentrated on social and economic reform, and his activities persuaded others who were politically active that such reforms could not be divorced from political action. Gopal Krishna Gokhale (1866–1915) believed implicitly in gradualist reform and in co-operation rather than revolution. In 1905, Gokhale founded the Servants of India Society. 'Its members,' he said, 'frankly accept the British connection, as ordained, in the inscrutable dispensation of Providence, for India's good. Self-government on the lines of English colonies is their goal. This goal, they recognize, cannot be attained without years of earnest and patient work and sacrifices worthy of the cause.' These men all believed in service and in the working out of the pattern of British rule –

through education and the assimilation of ideas, to self-government.

They were, however, engulfed by frustration, a reaction to their fundamental ineffectiveness. The British might have responded to them – and if they had, the history of India in the twentieth century would have been different. But they did not. The concessions asked for quietly and temperately by the moderates were given to others, and under duress. Some historians have seen, in the democratic framework of independent India, the triumph of the Liberals, but this may not be the verdict of the future. Their ideas certainly had some influence on the man who laid the foundations of independent India, Jawaharlal Nehru, but whether these foundations are permanent remains to be seen.

In 1905, the divorce of the moderate leaders from the trend of the times had become almost absolute. Their reasonable demands impressed neither the government nor other nationalist bodies. In the emotional excitement of Hindu revivalism, secret societies, and growing economic frustration, their ideas appeared spiritless and futile.

For the very best of administrative reasons, the British decided to divide the vast province of Bengal in 1905. This move appealed to the government on other grounds than purely administrative ones. Lord Curzon – who viewed the matter purely in terms of efficiency – did not consider Indian responses important, primarily because he did not believe that Indian nationalism posed any real danger to the British. Others, less Olympian, thought otherwise. The lieutenant-governor of Bengal thought partition would be a blow to Bengali nationalists. He was right, and when partition was announced extremist agitators recognized that here was a situation which could be emotionally exploited. Extremists began agitation, and the moderates, fearful of being left behind, joined in. Here at least was a great and specific issue which could give unity of purpose to all sections of the nationalist movement.

Two weapons were to be used in the campaign, terrorism and the economic boycott. The boycott began in August

1904. It was widely supported, especially by Indian mill-owners, and the wearing of homespun cloth became one of the manifestations of the struggle for freedom. Secret societies were formed among students; bomb-throwers and political assassins became popular heroes and their funerals scenes of hysterical emotion. A number of murders occurred, the first in Muzaffapur in 1908. For his comments in the *Kesari*, Tilak – who had been active again after his release from jail – was sentenced to six years' imprisonment on a charge of incitement to murder.

Terrorist activity was not confined to India. In 1909, Sir Curzon Wyllie was murdered by a Punjabi at the Imperial Institute in London. This at least brought home to the British public the existence of a nationalist movement in India.

Extremist ideas had, in fact, captured Congress. At the meeting at Benares in 1905, Tilak, Lala Lajpat Rai (1865–1928), who led the Punjab delegation, and Bipin Chandra Pal (1858–1932), who headed the delegation from Bengal, jointly expressed the mood of the impatient. Tilak's slogan, openly opposed to the moderates and their appeals for concessions, was 'militancy – not mendicancy'. But the extremists were unable to take over actual control of Congress, partly because of Dadabhai Naoroji, who was brought in for the 1906 meeting to effect a compromise. Congress's moderate leaders officially accepted most of the extremists' ideas but expressed them in rather gentler terms.

The almost entirely Hindu agitation against the partition of Bengal was bitterly resented by certain Muslims. The partition had at least given the predominantly Muslim population of East Bengal a new sense of freedom. Conservative Muslims decided that they needed some kind of political organization to counteract the effects of Congress, and in 1906 the Muslim League was formed. In the same year, a Muslim delegation appealed to the viceroy for a guarantee of a separate electorate for Muslims in the coming reforms.

The outbreak of the first world war gave nationalists a new sense of direction. The moderates in Congress hoped that new reforms would be granted. There was even an alliance in 1916 between Congress and the Muslim League. But the slowness with which the British government moved towards reform discredited the old moderate leadership – although it did not in fact destroy moderation.

In 1920, after the death of Tilak, control of Congress was taken over by Mahatma Gandhi, who drew for his philosophy of action on the most diverse of sources. The freedom movement now concentrated on the single task of putting an end to British rule. Nationalist activity, however, continued to take the forms of the past. Gandhi, for all that has been read into his life, was essentially a Hindu reformer who believed that no lasting reform was possible while an alien government ruled India. He was a Hindu nationalist who differed from the extremists in his firm belief that loving blackmail was better than murder, that the British could be shamed into leaving India. Gandhi had received a Western education and had studied law in England. He was profoundly influenced by the pacifist anarchism of the Russian, Kropotkin. Tolstoy suggested to him the idea of passive resistance, though it was already present in the Hindu tradition. He firmly believed that large-scale violent action would only provoke large-scale oppression. By willingly submitting to suffering – to police violence and to imprisonment – he believed that Indians would make the British feel embarrassed and begin to question the rightness of their actions. No more improbable political philosophy has ever been accepted as the ideology of rebellion.

Gandhi expressed his approach as 'non-violent non-cooperation'. Though his idea was to encourage as many people as possible to break those laws which he believed were against the interests of the masses, and to do so peacefully, such action as did take place frequently led to violence. As far as 'non-cooperation' was concerned, Gandhi was actually cooperating with the British in maintaining civil peace by keeping Congress to what was, generally speaking, a non-violent policy. His philosophy was not accepted by everyone, but because of his saintliness, his overwhelming honesty, and his personal identification with the masses, he overpowered men who thought in violent terms.

Gandhi was a remarkably good judge of character, and he was able to see in Jawaharlal Nehru (1889–1964) the liberal moderate hidden behind socialism and Marxist jargon. Gandhi himself, though he made many qualifications, rejected Western ideas and values. He was opposed to Western science and economics, and not particularly interested in political institutions. He accepted that democracy meant 'the awakening of the poorest of the poor,' but, believing in the moral content of the democratic system, left it to others to consider the problems of establishing it. By giving his personal support to Nehru, Gandhi ensured that, at the moment of independence, the hopes of the Indian moderates – who had themselves played no real part in the freedom movement after 1918 – were in fact fulfilled. At independence, India took democracy as it took everything else the British had to leave. Not, indeed, that there was any real alternative. The institutions of parliamentary democracy existed, and were functioning. As Congress had demanded them, it was hardly likely that it would reject them.

Gandhi, with his primary interest centred on radical religious and social reform, continued the tradition of such revivalists as Swami Dayananda. He looked to the Indian and, specifically, Hindu tradition for the instruments of reform. Essentially, he looked backwards to mythical eras of innocence and universal good. In the disintegration of Hindu life, he observed the evil effects of Western secular ideas. But he was shrewd enough to see that only by appealing to the justice implicit in such ideas could the British be made to give up India.

Gandhi's views appear – and, indeed, were – contradictory. The saint and the politician are an uneasy mixture. Nevertheless, he gave to Congress the appearance of a mass identity. Congress, by being non-ideological in the political sense, could contain all ideologies and allow no preponderance to any. Nehru, in spite of his impatience and revolutionary tongue, never broke away from Gandhi or from Congress, because he knew that the alternative was genuine revolution and this was repugnant to him. Others, revolted by Gandhi's medievalism and his indifference to the modern world, moved away into more positive action.

The most important of such men was Subhas Chandra Bose (1897–1945). After being president of Congress in 1938, he ran for a second term against the wishes of Mahatma Gandhi and was forced to resign. Many Congressmen, including Nehru, were soon condemning Bose as a fascist. Indeed, he had for some time been propounding a synthesis between fascism and communism. 'In spite of the antithesis between Communism and Fascism', he wrote in 1934, 'there are certain traits common to both. Both Communism and Fascism believe in the supremacy of the State over the individual. Both denounce parliamentarian democracy. Both believe in party rule. Both believe in the dictatorship of the party and in the ruthless suppression of all dissenting minorities. Both believe in a planned industrial reorganization of the country. These common traits will form the basis of the new synthesis. That synthesis is called by the writer "Samyavada" – an Indian word, which means literally "the doctrine of synthesis or equality". It will be India's task to work out this synthesis.'

In 1941, after a dramatic escape from house arrest, Bose reached Germany and there formed the nucleus of an Indian national army. In 1943, he went to Tokyo and took over an organization known as the India Independence League, which had been founded in Japan as far back as 1916. Bose organized an Indian National Army from among prisoners of war, and hoped to arrive in India with the vanguard of the Japanese armies. This, however, was not to be, and in 1945 he died on Formosa from injuries received in an air crash. Bose was perhaps the only genuinely revolutionary Indian nationalist leader, and took a genuinely revolutionary road. He had no faith in gradualism or in parliamentary democracy as a system suited to economically and socially backward countries. He was deeply influenced by the romantic fascism of Nazi Germany, yet he represented the continuing achievement of religious and cultural nationalism. Though many of his political ideas came from Germany, Italy and the Soviet Union, his model for an independent India was based on the Turkey of Kemal Ataturk. When a strong central authority had solved the problems of social change, then, perhaps, the masses would be ready for democracy.

Bose's view that democratic institutions were irrelevant to Indian conditions was shared by men who wanted to overthrow the British by violence inside India. The terrorist tradition continued to have its appeal. In the early years of the twentieth century, centres had been established abroad – in London, Paris and New York – where revolutionary literature could be prepared. Inside India, Vinayak Damodar Savarkar (1883–1965) had founded the Hindu Mahasabha in 1919. Savarkar had a terrorist past and he was strongly critical of Gandhi and of Congress.

In the 1920s, the Mahasabha was openly anti-Muslim, and part of its public platform was that Indian Muslims must be reconverted to Hinduism. In 1925, its programme was described by Lala Lajpat Rai, who was then its president. '1. To organize Hindu Sabhas throughout . . . the country. 2. To provide relief to such Hindus . . . who need help on account of communal riots . . . 3. Reconversion of Hindus who have been forcibly converted to Islam. 4. To organize gymnasiums for the use of Hindu young men and women. 5. To organize Sevasamitis (social service units). 6. To popularise Hindi. . . . 7. To request the Trustees and Keepers of . . . . Hindu temples to allow halls attached to the temples where people may gather to discuss matters of social and religious interest. 8. To celebrate Hindu festivals in a manner which may conduce to the promotion of brotherly feelings amongst the different sections of the Hindus. 9. To promote good feelings with Mohammedans and Christians. 10. To represent communal interests of the Hindus in all political controversies. 11. To encourage Hindu boys to take to industrial pursuits. 12. To promote better feelings between Hindu agriculturists and non-agriculturists. 13. To better the condition of Hindu women . . .'. Until the late 1930s, many members of the Mahasabha were also members of Congress. Two of the early Mahasabha leaders even became presidents of Congress. After 1939, however, the Mahasabha reflected Savarkar's hatred of Congress and engaged in public attacks on Congress leaders.

In the second world war, Savarkar, then president of the Mahasabha, coined the slogan 'Hinduise all politics and militarise Hindudom'. His strongly anti-Muslim attitude infected most members of the Mahasabha, and one of his close associates, N. V. Godse, assassinated Mahatma Gandhi in 1948 in revenge for what he felt was Gandhi's betrayal of Hinduism by accepting partition. Savarkar's ideas – Hindu nationalism, aggressive and authoritarian – helped to create Hindu political organizations in independent India whose appeal to patriotic and religious sentiment gave them a potentially powerful position in Indian politics.

Under British rule, communism had very little influence in India though it greatly appealed to some Indian intellectuals. Marxism, that most secular of modern ideologies, found the groundwork for some of its activities already done by the politico-religious secret societies of Bengal. A number of Marxist parties, both communist and non-communist, were established. Some of these existed actually inside Congress. When Subhas Bose left Congress, he attempted to organize a Forward Bloc to unite all the leftist groups. The bloc was banned in 1942, by which time Bose was in Germany. Communist parties, though some of their leaders attempted to form peasant organizations, played very little part in political activities in the last years of British rule.

The fact that Congress was dominated by Gandhi, however eccentric his Hinduism may actually have been, convinced the majority of Muslims that Congress was a Hindu organization. The secularists within Congress increased Muslim fears by their open detestation of the communalist nature of Muslim political ideas. Ironically and tragically, the refusal of such men as Jawaharlal Nehru to accept the validity of Muslim fears only intensified them. Gandhi's declaration of belief in Hindu-Muslim unity was thought to be merely a ruse, and the statements made by Hindu nationalists were taken to represent the general view of Congress, regardless of what its leaders might claim. Furthermore, Congress's continued support for parliamentary democracy emphasized the early fears of such Muslims as Syed Ahmed Khan that majority rule would mean Hindu rule. In the Indian situation, religion and politics could never be divorced.

As the possibility of majority rule in a self-governing India was reinforced by democratic concessions, Muslims looked for some kind of protection. While the British remained, the Muslims believed that the central government would not discriminate; it was still an authoritarian government and not under the influence of the Hindu majority. But remove the British, and Muslims feared that they would occupy a permanently minority position. The idea of a separate Muslim state had existed in the nineteenth century. In the twentieth, it appeared to be a necessity. Nevertheless, an outright political commitment to the creation of a separate state was slow in growing, partly because Muslim leaders were reluctant to accept that the British, who had favoured minorities in the 1909, 1919 and 1935 reforms, would really desert them. In 1933, Chaudhuri Rahmat Ali coined the name 'Pakistan' for the sovereign Muslim areas he suggested should be created inside India. The word – which also means 'land of the pure' – was made up from the initial letters of the Punjab, Afghania (Rahmat Ali's name for the North-West Frontier Province), Kashmir and Sind, with the suffix of -tan to represent Baluchistan. (When the word Pakistan is written in Urdu, there is no 'i' in it.)

Rahmat Ali's emotionally expressed ideas had no effect when they were first published, but when Muhammad Ali Jinnah (1876–1948) – a highly-Westernized Muslim lawyer who had left Congress partly because there were no personal opportunities in it for him, and partly because he recognized that Muslims needed a sense of political identity – gave new life to the Muslim League, it was almost inevitable that the Pakistan idea should be taken up.

The general trend of Muslim politicians after the abortive pact with Congress in 1916 had been to continue the demand for constitutional safeguards from the British. But the poet and philosopher, Muhammad Iqbal (1873–1938), gave to Muslim intellectuals a new and inspired view of Islam. By suggesting in 1930 that, if Islam was to be preserved, it was necessary to create Islamic political institutions operating in sovereign Muslim areas, he supplied the ideological framework for Pakistan.

A more active attempt to create a sense of Muslim identity had been made by the Khilafat movement, which gained momentum during the first world war in response to the defeat of Turkey. Muhammad Ali (1879–1930), one of the original members of the Muslim League, symbolized the feelings of Indian Muslims at the treatment of their co-religionists. He was jailed by the British during the war, and after the dismemberment of the Turkish empire by the Treaty of Sèvres, was able to arouse the Muslim community which, in its fear of militant Hinduism, had begun to look to the greatest Islamic community outside India. At first, the Khilafat movement had the support of Gandhi and Congress, and they cooperated in action against the government. There was, however, a militant section of the Khilafat movement which was not averse to public violence. It was this section whose propaganda persuaded a large number of Muslims to emigrate to Afghanistan; when they arrived, they found neither organization nor welcome, and many were forced to return to India. In August 1921, the Moplahs – a Muslim community in Malabar – started a holy war against Hindus and, by doing so, revived scarcely latent communal tensions.

When the caliphate in Turkey was abolished in 1924 by Kemal Ataturk, the Khilafat movement ceased to exist. Muhammad Ali himself became more and more convinced that Congress was dominated by Hindus. When, in 1930, Congress began its second civil disobedience campaign, he advised Muslims not to support it.

Muhammad Ali gave Muslims the taste of mass action, Iqbal supplied an ideology, Rahmat Ali the name of a country, and Jinnah the reality of independence. In 1940, under Jinnah's leadership, the Muslim League accepted the principle of a separate state for India's Muslims. 'Mussalmans,' he said, 'are a nation according to any definition of a nation, and they must have their homelands, their territory, and their state. We wish to live in peace and harmony with our neighbours as a free and independent people. We wish our people to develop to the fullest our spiritual, cultural, economic, social, and political life in a way that we think best and in consonance with our own ideals and according to the genius of our people. Honesty demands and the vital interests of millions of our people impose a sacred duty upon us to find an honourable and peaceful solution, which would be just and fair to all. But at the same time we cannot be moved or diverted from our purpose and objective by threats or intimidations. We must be prepared to face all difficulties and consequences, make all the sacrifices that may be required of us to achieve the goal we have set in front of us.'

Jinnah hoped to achieve a Muslim state by refusing to accept anything else. This left the creation of Pakistan to the British who, at the end, remained faithful to the principle of separate electorates – and partitioned India. It was a long shot on Jinnah's part, but it came off.

Other Muslims thought more in terms of positive action. One movement was known as the Khaksars, a para-military organization (founded in 1931) with social service leanings. Its founder, Mashriqi, is said to have been a brilliant scholar at Cambridge, and he propounded the thesis that Islam was the law of natural progress. 'Islam becomes,' he said, 'the most successful and universal principle of nation-building and all religious and moral injunctions become means serving that end. It becomes, so to speak, the infallible and divine sociology.' The Khaksar movement professed a sort of Muslim communism (the word 'khaksar' means 'humble'). Its symbol was the spade. It also believed in military training. The Khaksars were involved in civil disturbances in Lucknow in 1939, and in March 1940 attempted a *coup d'état* in Lahore (Punjab). Mashriqi, though he denied having had anything to do with the attempt, was arrested and the Khaksar movement was banned. Mashriqi tried to turn the movement back to social service, and in 1943 he was released from jail. By the end of British rule, the Khaksars had abandoned their militant views and become what was virtually a pressure group within the Muslim League.

All the political movements of British India – the moderates, the extremists, the Hindu revivalists and the Muslim nationalists – were dominated, in the main, by middle-class, Western-educated leaders. The variety of their responses to the impact of Western ideas ensured the widest variety of political expression. In the twentieth century, they realized that any goal of self-government could only be reached with the support of the masses. Unfortunately, there was no way of achieving such mass support for the alien concepts of Western liberalism without resort to religion, and this inevitably led to communal violence. The middle classes created India's political life. Through their actions, they won freedom. But they also created the division of India – and that is a tragedy which has still not worked itself out.

# PART THREE

# *India and the West*

# 1

# *Indian Influences on Western Life and Culture*

FROM the very earliest times, India has made its contribution to the texture of Western thought and living. Throughout the literatures of Europe, tales of Indian origin can be discovered. European mathematics – and, through them, the full range of European technical achievement – could hardly have existed without Indian numerals. But until the beginning of European colonization in Asia, India's contribution was usually filtered through other cultures.

Direct contact did not bring understanding; travellers' tales, rather, increased the sense of wonder. Even commerce helped to feed the imagination, for its trading cargoes – of bezoar stones, musk, silk and pearls – were luxuries, exotic and non-European. The 'gorgeous East' became an essential part of the Western view of India, influencing the ideas of merchants as well as of poets.

In the second part of the eighteenth century, works of travel, memoirs and histories increased enormously in number, and from them Europe began to assemble an image of India less concerned with physical wonders than with ideas. The philosophers, always on the lookout for some ideal civilization, first thought they had found it in China, then began to consider India a more likely place. By 1775, Voltaire was convinced that Western astronomy and astrology had come from somewhere along the River Ganges. The French astronomer, Bailey, who was guillotined during the French Revolution, maintained that the Brahmins of India had been tutors of the Greeks and, through them, of Europe. Towards the end of the eighteenth century, there was a general feeling amongst

European intellectuals that Indian civilization was of great antiquity – but it was only a feeling, for they did not have access to Indian literature. Very little was known about it, and no translations from Sanskrit, the literary language, had appeared.

The first adaptation of a Sanskrit work into a Western language had appeared as early as 1651; this was of a collection of lyrics by the poet Bhartrihari, who died *c.* AD 651. The adaptation was, in fact, a paraphrase in Dutch prose of a version in Portuguese. The existence of Sanskrit had been known for some time in the West, but as it was a sacred and liturgical language used only by the priestly caste for ritual observances, it was difficult to find a Brahmin willing to teach it to a European. Jesuit missionaries had acquired some knowledge of the language, and it was a work compiled by them – *L'Ezour Vedam*, a highly inaccurate version of the *yajur veda* – which was to influence Voltaire. In 1762, a young Frenchman, Anquetil Duperron – who had discovered a manuscript in a Paris shop and had gone out to India as a soldier in the service of the French East India Company in order to learn how to decipher it – returned to Paris with a number of manuscripts, one of which was a Persian version of sixty sections of the ancient Hindu work, the *Upanishads*. This he published in 1801–2 in a peculiar mixture of Persian, Latin and Greek. Duperron's work, known as the *Oupnekhat*, so affected the German philosopher, Schopenhauer, that he later claimed: 'It has been the solace of my life, it will be the solace of my death.'

The real revelation of Sanskrit literature, however, was to come as a byproduct of the establishment of direct British rule in Bengal. Warren Hastings encouraged the study of Sanskrit for a purely practical purpose – to ascertain the nature of Hindu law. A number of digests were first prepared, but these were found to be inadequate and it proved necessary to go to the original sources. Nevertheless, the first published translation from the Sanskrit was not of a law book, but of the great philosophical poem, the *Bhagavad Gita*. This appeared in 1785, and was the work of Charles Wilkins (1749–

1836). The *Bhagavad Gita*, is a series of dialogues between the god Krishna and the hero, Arjuna. They are fundamentally concerned with the moral problem of how men may govern their actions and are expressed in extremely esoteric terms. In his preface, Wilkins noted that the work was only imperfectly understood even by the most learned Brahmins of the time. It was even less likely to be understood by Europeans, and its publication had no immediate impact.

William Jones's translation of the play *Sakuntala,* by the dramatist Kalidasa (*c.* AD 400), was a very different matter. Jones, who had been appointed a judge at Calcutta in 1783, helped to found the Asiatic Society of Bengal in the following year. He first translated *Sakuntala* into Latin, maintaining that it was the only European language which had any resemblance to Sanskrit. He then translated the Latin version into English, and it was this, first published in 1789, which was later translated into other European languages. To his translation, Jones added no notes and only a very short preface, assuming perhaps that his English readers would already be sufficiently acquainted with Hindu mythology and Indian life through the publications of the Asiatic Society. Some of them undoubtedly were, and there are traces of Indian ideas in the works of Shelley and Wordsworth, among others. But the real effect of Jones's work and of other translations from Sanskrit was to appear in the poets and writers of early nineteenth-century Germany.

The passionate enthusiasm with which the German romantics were to grasp at India and Indian ideas owed a great deal to the pioneer work of Johann Gottfried Herder (1744–1803). He had early acquired from works of travel a reverence for India which was reinforced by the translations of Wilkins and Jones. In his preface to the second German edition of *Sakuntala* (first translated by Forster in 1791), Herder maintained that, on the Ganges, that river of paradise, the golden age actually did exist.

The discovery of Indian ideas came at a time of profound intellectual upheaval in Europe. The French Revolution and its aftermath shook even more than the social and political foundations of Europe. Writers and philosophers had become receptive to new modes of thought, and India seemed capable of satisfying them. Paris was then the centre of oriental studies, and one of the East India Company's servants, Alexander Hamilton, had been detained there by the outbreak of hostilities between Britain and France. Hamilton was something of a Sanskrit scholar, and came in contact with A. L. de Chézy, who had taught himself the language. From these two men, Friedrich Schlegel – who had journeyed to Paris in 1802 in quest of the new Indian vision of life and happiness – acquired a knowledge of Sanskrit. In 1803, he was able to claim that he had become such an expert copyist of Sanskrit characters that he could have earned his living as a scribe in India.

The reaction of German writers to India followed two distinct lines. Schlegel represented a longing for harmony between the arts and sciences, for that unity of philosophy, religion and art which had existed in the Middle Ages but which had been broken by the progress of Western civilization. Schlegel and those who thought like him believed that such a unity still existed in India, and that Hinduism represented a synthesis of personal, social and political life. They thought that the Hindu world offered a concrete ideal, a genuine example for a politically divided Europe. They were sure that, through a meeting of the cultures of East and West, the most profound revelation of the human spirit could be achieved. This vast structure of hopes was based upon the most meagre of foundations. In the mind of the romantics, legend had taken on the lineaments of reality.

They did, in fact, realize this at the time, and it was their desire to reinforce assumptions with fact – or, rather, with a wider range of data – which produced the second line of interest in Germany, that of comparative linguistics. Unwilling to receive Indian ideas only by way of translation, the romantics encouraged the scholarly study of Sanskrit. Ironically, this withered the ideal. Friedrich Schlegel, disillusioned, turned away from India. Others, such as the mythologist Friedrich Majer (1772–1818) and the philosopher Schelling (1775–1854), whose thought has a particularly Indian cast, kept the image alive. But even to them, it was no longer the image of a golden age.

India had considerable influence on German creative writers. Goethe, though not overwhelmed by India, received *Sakuntala* with enthusiasm. The prologue to *Faust* is modelled on that of Kalidasa's play. Goethe also utilized other Indian themes and, though he found the Hindu gods repulsive, he did not object to idealizing suttee in his play *Gott und die Bajadere* (*God and the Dancing-girl*). The poetess Karoline von Gunderode (1780–1806) converted suttee into an almost erotic rite of love, in which the lovers are united in the eternal embrace of nature. The dramatist Schiller (1759–1805) borrowed from Kalidasa's poem *Meghaduta* (*The Cloud-Messenger*). E. T. A. Hoffman (1776–1822) used India to supply the fantastic imagery of some of his stories; in *Der Goldene Topf*, Sanskrit becomes a magical language whose script resembles the forms of nature itself. By the time of Heinrich Heine (1799–1856), however, India's power over the German literary imagination had fallen into decline. The commonplaces of Sanskrit literature – the sacred river, the lotus blossom, the love of animals – became symbols, part of the poetic vocabulary and no more.

India had no great effect upon French writers beyond supplying an occasional exotic image, despite the fact that French oriental scholarship was of a particularly high order and there was constant intercourse between scholars and poets. This was mainly because the French intellectual climate was very different from that of Germany. French romanticism was not so much a quest for eternal truth as a search for new literary forms and language. Josèphe Méry, whose novels *Les Damnés de l'Inde* and *La Guerre du Nizam* went into many editions in the mid-nineteenth century, was described in his time as the most Hindu poet who ever existed. It is difficult, today, to see why.

It was the American poets of the transcendentalist school who were to be the real heirs of German romanticism and its enthusiasm for Indian ideas. This came about principally through Thomas Carlyle (1795–1881), the Scots historian and essayist, and his translations and criticism of some of the German poets. The American transcendentalists, of whom the most important was Ralph Waldo Emerson (1803–82), fundamentally represented a reaction against the puritan prejudices and the materialistic philistinism of the emergent American society. The sources of their ideas were an odd mixture of Plato and Swedenborg, German idealism, Carlyle, English poets such as Coleridge and Wordsworth, and translations of oriental literature. Emerson had some acquaintance with Sanskrit texts, and his view of the omnipresent deity and of the human personality as a passing phase of Universal Being is contained in what is almost a paraphrase of part of the *Bhagavad Gita*, his poem *Brahma*. Emerson's lines:

> If the red slayer thinks he slays
>   Or if the slain thinks he is slain
> They know not well the subtle ways
>   I keep, and pass, and turn again.

are very close to Krishna's words to Arjuna: 'He who deems This to be a slayer and he who thinks This to be slain, are alike without discernment; This slays not, neither is it slain.'

As the British became more sure of their position in India and developed a sense of mission, there grew up a contempt for Indian culture. This was partly due to cultural arrogance on the part of the British, who dismissed Indian literature as pagan rubbish and Indian science as primitive nonsense. Macaulay disposed of 'the whole native literature of India' as 'medical doctrines which would disgrace an English farrier – Astronomy, which would move laughter in girls at an English boarding school – History, abounding with kings thirty feet high, and reigns thirty thousand years long – and Geography, made up of seas of treacle and seas of butter.' Such an attitude tended to discredit Indian culture in the eyes of Victorian England, and to give eccentric and non-conformist overtones to any interest in it. There are very few references to India, let alone Indian influences, in English creative literature, although in the twentieth century a growing interest in Eastern philosophy – which had begun in the 1890s – influenced the work of such poets as W. B. Yeats and 'AE'. Towards the end of his life, the latter, in collaboration with an Indian, produced a version of the *Upanishads* (1937).

Fortunately, the attitude of Macaulay and others did not affect scholarly research which, since it satisfied the Victorian criterion of scientific curiosity, was not regarded as eccentric in its Indian manifestation. In 1870, there began in France the publication of the *Bibliothèque Orientale*. Four years later, in England, came the great series of *Sacred Books of the East*, under the editorship of Friedrich Max-Muller (1823–1900). Between them, these two series were to make the Hindu scriptures available for the first time to the general reader. In 1875, James Fergusson published his *History of Indian and Eastern Architecture*, the first important work on the subject. The new interest in Hindu literature and art had its parallel in the study of Pali literature and of the Buddhist scriptures written in that language.

The message of the Buddha was little known before the middle of the nineteenth century. Brian Hodgson, the British representative in Nepal, had indeed collected Buddhist manuscripts there in the early years of the century, and James Prinsep, another servant of the East India Company, had deciphered inscriptions of the Buddhist emperor, Asoka. But these were known only to a very small number of Europeans until Eugène Burnouf published his immensely influential *Introduction à Histoire de Bouddhism Indien* in 1844. R. Spence Hardy's *Manual of Buddhism* appeared in 1853, and five years later a popular life of the Buddha by Barthelemy Saint-Hilaire was published in France.

The discovery of the Buddhist scriptures went on, and their influence can be traced in the works of such disparate personalities as Richard Wagner and Tolstoy, as well as in the paintings of Odilon Redon (1840–1916) and others. Perhaps the most superb example of Buddhist influence can be found in the works of Herman Hesse, particularly his mystical novel *Siddartha* (1926). In the case of Wagner, both Buddhist and Hindu ideas had a tremendous appeal. His knowledge of

Buddhism was acquired almost entirely from Burnouf. Wagner absorbed Indian ideas and transformed them to suit his aesthetic purpose. They appear in the libretti of such operas as *Parsifal* (1882), in which he used an episode from the great epic of the *Ramayana* (*c.* 400 BC). In a sense, he succeeded in producing a synthesis of East and West, and from it derived the materials of a universal drama. In this, he was in a direct line from the early German romantics.

In the works of European philosophers, there is a continuing thread of ideas which are Indian in origin. Some of these ideas can be traced in the works of the racialist 'historians', beginning with Arthur de Gobineau (1816–82) and his *Essai sur l'Inégalité des Races Humaines* (1853–55), and developing through the theories of the violently pro-German Englishman, Houston Stewart Chamberlain (*Grundlagen des neunzehnten Jahrhunderts,* 1899) to those of Alfred Rosenberg, the 'philosopher' of Nazism, who invented an Indian proverb to the effect that 'right is what Aryan men consider to be right'.

Gobineau originally argued that the races of the world were unequal, that by mingling they changed character, and that the white races – the Aryans – were superior to all. Gobineau drew many of his ideas from his own interpretation of the history of the 'Indo-Aryans,' a tribe of light-skinned, blue-eyed nomads who invaded northern India about 1500 BC. The Indo-Aryans were extremely colour-conscious and passed laws to preserve themselves from the defiling blood of the dark-skinned peoples they had conquered. But the races mixed nevertheless. Gobineau pointed at the India of his own day to demonstrate what happened to a race which did not protect the purity of its blood. The Indo-Aryans had compromised with circumstance and intermarried, only in the course of time to be conquered by the more virile Aryans of the West. The 'Aryan family,' said Gobineau, was 'the most noble, the most intelligent, the most dynamic.' To Gobineau's support came the science of comparative linguistics, which discovered that a number of European languages had something in common with Sanskrit. This led to a suggestion that all the languages concerned had a common *Aryan* root. Gobineau believed that, of all the Aryans, the Germanic tribes were the purest. Chamberlain took this belief, added to it the discoveries of comparative linguistics, and declared that the German race consisted only of those who spoke the German language – a curious theory, whose logical extension would be that an English-speaking Bengali from Calcutta is English by race. From Chamberlain, the ominous ideas of blood and race were taken up by Hitler and Rosenberg, to end (it is to be hoped) in the crematoria of Dachau and Buchenwald.

Madame Blavatsky (1831–91) was another myth-maker whose work had considerable – though fortunately less perverse – influence on European thought in the late Victorian period. In 1880, in the company of an American, Colonel Olcott, with whom she had worked during a series of spiritualist seances she had given in the United States, Madame Blavatsky went to India. From there, she was able to reveal to those Westerners who had become disillusioned with orthodox religion and were on the lookout for some other means of satisfying their appetite for miracles, that the world was under the guidance of a number of *mahatmas* residing at some imprecise location in Tibet. The Theosophical Society which she had founded in New York in 1875 propagated an elaborate and rather insecurely-based philosophy owing much to Hinduism, though it was largely dressed up in Christian terms. The society had a considerable vogue under its second president, Mrs Annie Besant (1847–1933), who was, in fact, to play a helpful role in the cause of Indian nationalism. Though the society's view of Hinduism was unscholarly and uncritical, it did persuade a large number of people in the West to read some of the Hindu classics.

It was, however, left to Swami Vivekananda (1862–1902) to create the popular image of India and to supply the vocabulary with which Indian ideas have been expressed in the West. Vivekananda, a disciple of the Bengali ascetic and visionary, Ramakrishna Paramahamsa, wrote in English. He produced an idealized vision of India – spiritual, non-violent, the repository of life's secrets – which has had a persistently misleading effect. Another man who was to contribute to Western misunderstanding of Hindu ideas was the Hindu reformer and nationalist leader, Mohandas Karamchand Gandhi (1869–1948), though he did so less by intent than by the uncritical assessment of those who believed (and still believe) that his 'philosophy of non-violence' was the instrument of Indian independence.

*

The influence of Indian art and architecture in the West has been slight. The true appreciation of Hindu sculpture and Mughal miniatures, for example, had to wait until the twentieth century, and it remains to this day primarily a connoisseur's interest.

The expansion of British dominion attracted a number of British artists to the Company's territories in India. Their drawings of scenery and buildings were published in Britain. Between them, artists and engravers produced an idealized view of Indian architecture and topography.

Thomas and William Daniell – whose collection of coloured aquatints, *Oriental Scenery*, was published between 1795 and 1808 – illustrated many Indian buildings, and Thomas Daniell collaborated in designing an Indian villa at Sezincote in Gloucestershire (1806). Daniell was responsible for a temple, a bridge and a fountain, while Samuel Pepys Cockerill – surveyor to the East India Company – produced the plans for the house, which was based on the tomb of Haidar Ali Khan in Hyderabad.

In 1807, George, Prince of Wales, visited Sezincote and later commissioned the landscape gardener, Humphry Repton (who had laid out the gardens at Sezincote), to advise on reconstructing the prince's pavilion at Brighton in the Indian style. The prince had already employed William Porden, one of Cockerill's pupils, to design stables at the pavilion, and these bore a distinct resemblance to Sezincote. Repton's designs, which also owed much to Sezincote, were not carried out because the prince was short of money, but in 1815 John Nash, the prince's personal architect (who had once been in partnership with Repton), was commissioned to re-design the pavilion. The result, which still stands today, was an exotic tribute to the romantic image of India.

The pavilion at Brighton influenced two other buildings. The American circus proprietor and impresario of the bizarre, P. T. Barnum, had the design adapted (extremely loosely) for his home, 'Iranistan,' at Bridgport in Connecticut, which was completed in 1848 but has since been destroyed. An even more curious adaptation had been constructed a few years earlier (between 1837 and 1840) at Alupka in the Crimea. This building was commissioned by Count Woronzow-Daskow to designs by the English architect, Edward Blore, and is a mixture of the Oriental and the Gothic. The building still survives; indeed, it was used by the late Winston Churchill during the Yalta conference of 1945. But apart from some early buildings with Indian-influenced detail and a mid-nineteenth-century castle in Portugal, Indian architecture had little other influence upon that of the West.

*

During the early period of European trade with India, the principal items imported from that country were textiles such as the extremely fine muslins from Dacca in Bengal. Their appeal lay in their texture, and though there was a well-known range of 'Indian' designs these turned out to have been supplied from Europe in the first place. Later, European factories even came to reproduce them. Part of the reason for the lack of interest in Indian wares was that *chinoiserie* and classical designs were predominant in the eighteenth century. But it also had a good deal to do with the temperament of the returning English merchant who, having made his fortune in India, came home to spend it. The 'nabobs', as they were called, were anxious to be absorbed into English society. There, merchants were viewed with some distaste, as were eccentricities – in oriental or any other shape. There was little point, or advantage, in displaying such eccentricities, either in business or in art. The nabobs aped current fashions among the British nobility and chose a Palladian mansion rather than an Indian villa. If they brought back with them some Eastern wares, these were usually Chinese.

Such Indian influences as did appear were mainly in the field of pattern. The characteristic Kashmir design of the teardrop was to live on in the so-called 'Paisley pattern'. Kashmir shawls had been imported into Europe at a very early stage and soon inspired imitations. The first were produced at Norwich in 1784, though the products were not actually shawls but embroidered neckcloths intended for export to the new United States of America. Other imitations were produced in Edinburgh and, about 1808, in Paisley, near Glasgow. At the beginning, attempts were made to bring the Kashmiri shawl-goat – which produced extremely soft wool – to Britain, but the experiment was not successful. In France, the Empress Josephine possessed between three and four hundred Kashmir shawls, and the demand among fashionable ladies increased to such an extent that French manufacturers began to make imitations. By the middle of the nineteenth century, trade in Kashmir was dominated by French merchants and Kashmiri weavers were producing their patterns from designs originally born in France. France itself was producing shawls with designs supposedly imitating genuine Kashmir, and these in turn were copied by weavers in Paisley – the final product being a particularly fine example of cultural synthesis!

The Great Exhibition of the Works of Industry of all Nations which was held in London in 1851 inspired considerable interest in the 'industrial arts'. A number of Indian wares displayed in the Crystal Palace attracted a great deal of attention, and Indian designs began to appear on brassware, textiles, and in jewellery. But the influence was not creative, and most of the products merely added a touch of the exotic to the bric-a-brac of the average middle-class Victorian home.

*

The returning nabobs and their successors in the civil and military services of India brought back with them a liking for certain Indian dishes, and introduced them into the repertoire of British cooking. By as early as 1773, curry had become a speciality of at least one London coffee house – though even curry owed something to the West, for one of its principal ingredients, chilli (or red pepper), had first been introduced into India by the Portuguese. Mulligatawnay soup – the name is a corruption of *milagu-tannir*, the Tamil for 'pepper water' – has had a long life in Britain, though not perhaps as wide a diffusion as curry, which with the advent of commercial curry powder, has become a convenient way of disguising left-over cold meats. With polo, introduced into England in 1870, and the pyjama (from the Hindu *pae-jama*, 'leg-clothing'), the influence of things Indian on European, and in particular, British life seems very small for so long a connexion. Cultural penetration is often subtly expressed and underground in its effect, but the 'revelation' of India which took place over the years of British rule added up to little more than an imperfect acquaintance with a few examples of Hindu literature, yogic exercises, and the exotic belief that somewhere in the labyrinth of Hindu metaphysics lay some marvellous panacea for the ills of the Western world.

The reasons are not hard to find, but one of the factors which contributed was that the men and women who 'interpreted' India to the West were almost all Europeans. Very few Indians tried to explain Indian ideas, and it must be admitted that, when they did, they brought little enlightenment.

On the whole, except in the case of a few scholars and writers, the public's view of India remained fairly constant throughout the nineteenth century and until the end of British rule. It was a land of vast extremes of poverty and riches, of rajas, jewels, dancing girls – and Mahatma Gandhi. Fundamentally, it is a view that has changed very little, even since independence.

## 2

# *An Example of Cultural Penetration: Indian Words in English*

As the British established their connexion with India they were, not unnaturally, forced to acquire at least some casual knowledge of the languages used by the people with whom they first traded and then came to rule. The British are said to be bad linguists. Though there is little justification for such a *canard* – unless 'bad' is taken to mean 'lazy' – it is nevertheless true to say that very few merchants or administrators in the first half-century learned to speak a local language with any degree of fluency. There were exceptions, of course. Warren Hastings, for example, composed rather bad verses in Persian. But in general the Company's servants relied upon interpreters in their commercial and social relations with Indians.

They did, of course, learn the meaning of a large number of words – commercial, judicial and revenue terms – and mixed them with their normal speech. The Company's records are full of sentences peppered with Indian words in a wide variety of transliterations. Edmund Burke was driven to complain in the House of Commons that this hybrid language was probably 'of necessary use in the executive department of the Company's affairs; but it is not necessary to Parliament. A language so foreign from all the ideas and habits of the far greater part of the members of the House, has a tendency to disgust them with all sorts of inquiry concerning this subject. They are fatigued into such a despair of ever obtaining a competent knowledge of the transactions in India, that they are easily persuaded to remand them . . . to obscurity.' Nevertheless, many of these words made their way into the English language, and not only into the language of poets but into the common speech of everyday life.

The first words to be absorbed into the English language were mainly the names of things, like calico – after the port of Calicut, from which much of India's cotton cloth was exported to Europe in the seventeenth century – and cummerbund, a waist-sash. Although there were many more (the *Oxford English Dictionary* lists over three hundred words which entered the language from India in the seventeenth century), most have disappeared from normal speech. Such words as mogul, bungalow, pundit, shampoo, and cot have, however, become completely naturalized.

The eighteenth century saw a distinct increase in the number of words relating to political and military affairs – a situation brought about by the changing nature of the role played by the British in India during the collapse of the Mughal power. Of the words which have survived into modern speech, perhaps the most historically pertinent is loot (from the Hindu *lut*, plunder). Another word which indicated the widening of European horizons was 'jungle'. Veranda, bangle and buggy were also imported during the eighteenth century, as was chee-chee – a disparaging term applied to half-castes. The honour of first using it in literature apparently belongs to the journalist Hicky. It appeared in his *Bengal Gazette* in March 1781:

> Pretty little Looking-Glasses,
> Good and cheap for Chee-chee Misses.

Not surprisingly, the nineteenth century brought a large number of Indian words into the English language, particularly words which reflected the growing interest in Indian philosophy and literature. In ordinary English speech, however, such words as thug – which originally meant a particular class of professional robber and murderer, the extent of whose operations was only discovered by the British in the first decades of the nineteenth century – had already taken on the colloquial meaning of 'ruffian' or 'cut-throat' as early as 1839. The use of the word 'damn' in the expression 'don't care (or give) a damn' seems to have originated in the word *dan*, a copper coin of very small value.

The first world war added new words, and new meanings for old ones. This is particularly apparent in army slang. One new word was 'blighty', used to mean 'home' (i.e. Britain) by troops serving abroad. Others were 'cushy' – meaning easy, or comfortable – and 'char', referring to tea. The war gave wider currency to a number of words, including buckshee, puggled (from the Hindu *pagal*, mad or crazy), and wallah.

Although the second world war brought very few new words, it did distribute them widely among the large numbers of British and American troops who passed through India or were stationed there. Among today's survivals are 'phut' ('it went phut', meaning it stopped working or collapsed) which came from the Hindi *phatna*, to burst, and 'dekko' ('let's have a dekko') from the Hindi *dekho*, the imperative of the verb *dekhna*, to look.

*

The use in literature of words of Indian origin preceded actual contact with India and Indian life. Most of these words – even the word 'India' itself – came via Greek, Latin or French, and were mainly confined to the names of things, such as pepper, beryl and camphor. The works of English travellers, which began to appear in the seventeenth century, supplied not only colourful and exotic backgrounds and tales, but also some of the language needed to reinforce the exoticism. Strange-sounding place names obviously attracted the poet, John Milton:

> Of Cambalu, seat of Cathaian Can,
> And Samarkand by Oxus, Temir's throne,
> To Paquin of Sinaean kings, and thence,
> To Agra and Lahor of Great Mogul.
>
> *Paradise Lost*, xi, 388

The eighteenth century, with its growing awareness of

India and the consequences of establishing British rule in Bengal, brought a number of words into the vocabulary of English men of letters. Some were used precisely, and for a precise purpose, as when Edmund Burke used them in his speeches to the House of Commons; though he complained about them at the same time, he could not avoid using them. Perhaps the most popular Indian word in eighteenth-century literature was 'nabob' (from *nawab*, a Muslim prince), which was applied to returning servants of the East India Company as a term of abuse. Even such words as 'nabobess' and 'nabobry' were invented. Laurence Sterne produced a feminine version of Brahmin ('Bramine') which he applied to Eliza Draper, the wife of a Company servant. Robert Burns seems to have made the first literary use of the word 'toddy' – a mixture of whisky or some other spirit with sugar and hot water – corrupted from the Hindi *tari*, the fermented sap of the palm tree

The lads an' lasses, blythely bent,  
To mind baith soul an' body,  
Sit round the table, well content,  
An' steer about the toddy.

*Holy Fair* (1785)

The nineteenth century produced a special category of English literature which is best described as 'Anglo-Indian' and has been discussed elsewhere (see pages 56 ff. and 200 ff.). Naturally, writers of this school, who include Edwin Arnold and Rudyard Kipling, utilized a large number of Indian words in their works. Others, such as Jane Austen, Shelley, Carlyle, Dickens and Robert Louis Stevenson, occasionally used Indian words. Sir Walter Scott went further and wrote a novel about India, *The Surgeon's Daughter*, which displays an accurate knowledge of the meaning of Indian words, acquired apparently from a neighbour, Colonel Ferguson of Huntly Burn. Scott describes him in the novel – under the name of Colonel Mackerris – as 'one of the best fellows who ever trod a Highland moor or dived into an Indian jungle'.

Among other writers, Southey (*The Curse of Kehama*),

Byron (*The Giaour*), and Thackeray used Indian words, Southey in particular without much appreciation of their real meaning. Thackeray, however, was born in India and had a wide vocabulary of Indian words although he left the country when he was still a child. He often bent such words in order to make them and the characters who used them objects of fun – as when he used the word 'catamaran' (raft) to describe Mrs Mackenzie in *The Newcomes*- 'an infernal tartar and catamaran'. In the same novel, mulligatawnay became a place name. Elsewhere, Thackeray gave characters such names as Mr Chutney (*Vanity Fair*), General Sir Rice Curry, KCB (*A Shabby Genteel Story*), and Colonel Goldmore (*Barry Lyndon*) from the gold *mohur*, an Indian coin.

The present century has produced, in some areas, a greater understanding of India but very little desire to use Indian words for fun. E. M. Forster's *A Passage to India* uses very few Indian words, probably because of the author's inability – in spite of the uncritical praise lavished upon the work – to understand either India itself or the world of the British in India. Edward Thompson's unjustly neglected novels, *An Indian Day, Night Falls on Siva's Hill* and *A Farewell to India,* reflect a changing and essentially political vocabulary in which *swaraj* (freedom) and swarajists, *swadeshi* (home-produced) and other such words represent the new world of Indian nationalism.

Among other writers, the words used are mainly taken from Indian metaphysics. They appear in such poems as T. S. Eliot's *The Waste Land,* in the philosophical works of Aldous Huxley, and in the literature produced by the popularizers of yogic exercises. Indian words which still retain their virility in common speech are used without conscious knowledge of their origin. These are examples of genuine cultural penetration. They represent one of the very few permanent legacies of the British connexion with India.

# *Epilogue*

IT should be clear from the preceding pages that the impact of British rule upon the complex societies of India was essentially disruptive. The processes of government, of law, of economic theories and practice, all tended to distort – and in some cases to break – the traditional web of human relationships. But there was nothing total about the impact. Hindu and Muslim society was not destroyed. The processes of change begun under British rule are still going on, though with much greater vigour because of the rapid increase of modernization after independence. Vast social changes are implicit in the modernizing process itself – as the British discovered from the Mutiny of 1857 and the rise of nationalist movements.

The impact of Western ideas, which the British funnelled into Indian society, was to produce two basic reactions – atavism and acceptance – and the struggle between them still continues in present-day India. The cow protection agitation of 1966 was similar in purpose to that of 1882. It would, however, be foolish to suggest that the circumstances are the same. They are not, and not only because there is no longer an alien government ruling India. In the 1880s, there could well have been a turning back to the old forms of Indian government, to reaction rather than modernism. Today, however, there can be no reversion, even though the modernizing process could be modified. The real purpose behind religious revivalism today remains what it was in the past, a desire to change the basis of political life.

It was in politics that the British impact on India had its most profound effect. Indeed, in other areas, in for example the arts and learning (other than scientific), the British contributed very little to India. They inspired either imitation or revivalism – neither of which has been particularly creative. They did give to a small, anglicized class attitudes to life unrelated to their milieu and to which there has been considerable reaction since independence. But it was that class, created and sustained by the British, which reflected the positive effects of British rule. It was the middle classes who took to modern entrepreneurial techniques. It was they who demanded English education and, later, Western-style liberal reforms. They appeared, in the end, to triumph when India chose parliamentary democracy at the time of independence. It is because of the intense political activity of the last thirty years of British rule – and of political activity expressed in the vocabulary of Western liberalism – that, despite the tensions of independence, the representative principle appears to be firmly established in the minds of millions of Indians.

Implicit in the tenets of liberal democracy is the rule of law. Inefficient courts and the inappropriateness of their procedure often led, and still lead, to travesties of justice, but the basic principle that law controls the limits of government is entrenched in India.

It may seem very little after 175 years of direct British rule to have left behind only a system of government and of law, neither of which – according to some critics – works very well. But they were not abstract systems. They were supported by an administrative framework which survived the transfer of power. Unlike the other European imperial powers in their Asian possessions, the British deliberately constructed the scaffolding of a modern state in which Indians themselves played an indispensable functional role. When the small British element was withdrawn in 1947 the scaffolding did not collapse, even under the pressures of partition.

The period that has elapsed since independence is not long enough to suggest any firm conclusions about the effect of the British impact on India. There have been great superficial changes in India since independence. Modern industry, for example, has been greatly expanded. Cities look different – more modern and more progressive. Yet the countryside and the life of the peasant seem very little different from what they were in 1947. In this sector, the changes have been more subtle, less obvious to the eye. In India today, there is, however, a sometimes elusive sense of continuity, as if modern India began not in 1947 but some time during the British connexion. It is here, indeed, that the legacies of British rule take on meaning. In spite of all the criticisms of India today, it represents a basically stable political system, in direct contrast with the situation in other former colonial possessions.

# *A Selection of Books for Further Reading*


## THE BRITISH IN INDIA

BEARCE, G. D. *British Attitudes towards India* 1784–1858. London 1961

BROWN, H. *The Sahibs*. London 1948

BUCKLAND, C. T. *Sketches of Social Life in India*. London 1884

CAMERON, R. *Shadows from India*. London 1958. [Architecture]

CHATTERJEE, A. C. *British Contributions to Indian Studies*. London 1943

CUMMING, SIR J. (ed.) *Revealing India's Past*. London 1939

OGDEN, E. A. *A Sketch of Anglo-Indian Literature*. London 1908

SINGH, BHOPAL *A Survey of Anglo-Indian Literature*. London 1934

SPEAR, T. G. P. *The Nabobs*. Oxford 1963

## GOVERNMENT

ASPINALL, A. *Cornwallis in Bengal*. Manchester 1931

BEAGLEHOLE, T. H. *Thomas Munro and the Development of Administrative Policy in Madras 1792–1818*. Cambridge 1966

BENNETT, G. *The Concept of Empire from Burke to Attlee, 1774–1947*. London 1953

CHESNEY, SIR G. T. *Indian Polity: A View of the System of Administration in India*. London 1868

CURTIS, L. *Dyarchy*. London 1920

DHARKAR, C. D. (ed.) *Lord Macaulay's Legislative Minutes*. London 1946

EMBREE, A. *Charles Grant and British Rule in India*. London 1962

FURBER, H. *John Company at Work*. Cambridge 1948

GOPAL, S. *The Permanent Settlement in Bengal and its Results*. London 1949

GWYER, M., and APPADORAI, A. *Speeches and Documents on the Indian Constitution 1921–1947*. London 1957

ILBERT, SIR C. *The Government of India*. Oxford 1922

METCALF, T. E. *The Aftermath of Revolt: India 1857–1870*. Princeton 1964

MISRA, B. B. *The Central Administration of the East India Company 1773–1834*. Manchester 1959

MONKTON-JONES, M. E. *Warren Hastings in Bengal*. Oxford 1918

MOORE, R. J. *Liberalism and Indian Politics 1872–1922*. London 1966

MOORE, R. J. *Sir Charles Wood's Indian Policy 1853–1866*. Manchester 1966

STOKES, E. *The Utilitarians and India*. Oxford 1959

STOKES, E. *The Political Ideas of English Imperialism*. Oxford 1960

## LAW

ABDUR RAHIM *The Principles of Muhammedan Jurisprudence*. London 1911

BADEN POWELL, B. H. *Land Systems of British India*. London 1892

GUPTE, S. V. *Hindu Law in British India*. Calcutta 1947

MAYNE, J. D. *A Treatise on Hindu Law and Usage*. London 1914

RANKIN, SIR G. *Background to Indian Law*. Cambridge 1946

STOKES, SIR W. *The Anglo-Indian Codes*. Oxford 1887

## ECONOMIC LIFE

ANSTEY, V. *The Economic Development of India*. London 1949

BUCHANAN, D. H. *Development of Capitalist Enterprise in India*. New York 1934

DUTT, R. C. *The Economic History of India in the Victorian Age*. London 1906 and later editions

GADGIL, D. R. *The Industrial Evolution of India in Recent Times*. Bombay 1942

HOWARD, A. and G. L. C. *Development of Indian Agriculture*. London 1929

KNOWLES, L. C. A. *Economic Development of the British Overseas Empire*. London 1924

PILLAI, P. P. *Economic Conditions in India*. London 1925

SARKAR, J. *Economics of British India*. Calcutta 1917

STRICKLAND, C. F. *An Introduction to Co-operation in India*. London 1938

TRIPATHI, A. *Trade and Finance in the Bengal Presidency 1793–1833*. Bombay 1956

## SOCIAL POLICY

BALLHATCHET, K. A. *Social Policy and Social Change in Western India*. Oxford 1959

CRAWFORD, D. G. *A History of the Indian Medical Service 1600–1913*. London 1914

DATTA, K. K. *Survey of India's Social Life and Economic Conditions in the 18th Century*. Calcutta 1961

GEDGE, E. C., and CHOKSI, M. *Women in Modern India*. Bombay 1929

INGHAM, K. *Reformers in India*. London 1956

KAPADIA, K. M. *Marriage and Family in India*. Bombay 1958

PATON, W. *Social Ideas in India*. London 1919

## EDUCATION

HOWELL, A. *Education in India prior to 1854*. Calcutta 1872

MAYHEW, A. *The Education of India*. London 1926

TREVELYAN, C. E. *On the Education of the People of India*. London 1838

## CULTURAL AND RELIGIOUS LIFE

ARCHER, M., and W. G. *Indian Painting for the British 1770–1880*. London 1955

ARCHER, W. G. *India and Modern Art*. London 1959

BARNS, M. *The Indian Press*. London 1940

CHAND, TARA *The Influence of Indian Islam on Indian Culture*. Ahmedabad 1936

DUTT, R. C. *The Literature of Bengal*. Calcutta 1895

FARQUHAR, J. N. *Modern Religious Movements in India*. New York 1919

KHANDALAVALA, K. *Indian Sculpture and Painting*. Calcutta 1939

LATIF, SAYID ABDUL *The Influence of English Literature on Urdu Literature*. Calcutta 1924

MAJOOMDAR, P. C. *The Life and Teachings of Keshub Chunder Sen*. Calcutta 1887

RADHAKRISHNAN, S. *Eastern Religions and Western Thought.* London 1940

SADIQ, MUHAMMAD *A History of Urdu Literature.* London 1964

SEN, P. K. *Biography of a New Faith.* Calcutta 1950. [Brahmo Samaj]

SMITH, W. C. *Modern Islam in India.* London 1948

YUSUF ALI *A Cultural History of India.* Bombay 1940

## NATIONALISM

ALBIRUNI, A. H. *Makers of Pakistan and Modern Muslim India.* Lahore 1950

ANDREWS, C. F., and MUKERJI, G. *The Rise and Growth of Congress in India.* London 1938

AZIZ, K. K. *Britain and Muslim India.* London 1963

BOSE, S. C. *The Indian Struggle, 1920–1934.* London 1935

BRECHER, M. *Nehru, a Political Biography.* London 1959

COLLETT, S. D. *Letters of Ram Mohun Roy.* Calcutta 1962

DESAI, A. K. *Social Background of Indian Nationalism.* Bombay 1948

EDWARDES, M. *The Last Years of British India.* London 1963, paperback edn. London 1967

LAL BAHADUR *The Muslim League.* Agra 1954

MCCULLY, B. T. *English Education and the Origins of Indian Nationalism.* New York 1940

MAJUMDAR, B. B. *History of Political Thought in Bengal 1821–1884.* Calcutta 1934

MAJUMDAR, B. B. *Indian Political Associations and Reform of the Legislature, 1818–1917.* Calcutta 1965

MAJUMDAR, J. K. *Indian Speeches and Documents on British Rule 1821–1918.* London 1937

MEHROTRA, S. R. *India and the Commonwealth 1885–1929.* London 1965

MISRA, B. B. *The Indian Middle Classes.* London 1961

NEHRU, J. *An Autobiography.* London 1942

SINGH, IQBAL *Rammohun Roy.* Bombay 1961

SMITH, W. R. *Nationalism and Reform in India.* New Haven 1938

WOLPERT, S. A. *Tilak and Gokhale: Revolution and Reform in the Making of Modern India.* Berkeley 1962

# *Index*

Personal names are given in SMALL CAPITALS, except in the case of mythical or fictional characters, whose names appear in ordinary type. Foreign words, as well as titles of books, newspapers, and other publications, are printed in *italics*.